FROM PLURALISM TO EXTINCTION?

PERSPECTIVES AND CHALLENGES FOR CHRISTIANS IN THE MIDDLE EAST

MEDITERRANEAN POLITICS: 5

From Pluralism to Extinction?

Perspectives and Challenges for Christians in the Middle East

Edited by Sotiris Roussos

This edited volume was supported by the Hellenic Foundation for Research and Innovation (H.F.R.I.) under the 'First Call for H.F.R.I. Research Projects to support Faculty members and Researchers and the procurement of high-cost research equipment grant' (Project Number: 1422).

First published in 2023 by Transnational Press London in the United Kingdom, 13 Stamford Place, Sale, M33 3BT, UK.
www.tplondon.com

Transnational Press London® and the logo and its affiliated brands are registered trademarks.

Requests for permission to reproduce material from this work should be sent to: sales@tplondon.com

ISBN: 978-1-80135-224-6 (Paperback)
ISBN: 978-1-80135-225-3 (Digital)

Cover Design: Nihal Yazgan
Cover Photo by Fa7od on unsplash.com

Transnational Press London Ltd. is a company registered in England and Wales No. 8771684.

FROM PLURALISM TO EXTINCTION?

Perspectives and Challenges for Christians in The Middle East

Edited by

Sotiris Roussos

TRANSNATIONAL PRESS LONDON

2023

BOOKS IN MEDITERRANEAN POLITICS SERIES

Series Editor: Nikos Christofis

CONTENTS

NOTES ON CONTRIBUTORS

Zakia Aqra, Ph.D., Political Science and International Relations, University of the Peloponnese, Greece. She is also a Senior Editor at the Centre for Mediterranean, Middle East and Islamic Studies (CEMMIS). Her research focuses on foreign policy, armed non-state actors and religious pluralism in the Middle East. Researcher in the "Christianity and Religious Pluralism in the Modern Middle East: International Politics and Religion at the turn of the 20th and 21st century" Project (funded by the Hellenic Foundation for Research and Innovation).

Nikos Christofis, Associate Professor of Turkish and Middle Eastern history and politics at the Centre for Turkish Studies at Shaanxi Normal University; adjunct lecturer at the Hellenic Open University; and affiliate researcher in the Netherlands Institute at Athens. His work focuses on comparative historical analysis of Greece, Turkey, and Cyprus, and the Middle East.

Stavros Drakoularakos, Ph.D, Political Science and History, Post-Doctoral Researcher University of the Peloponnese, Editor-in-Chief at the Centre for Mediterranean, Middle East and Islamic Studies (CEMMIS). Researcher in the "Christianity and Religious Pluralism in the Modern Middle East: International Politics and Religion at the turn of the 20th and 21st century" Project (funded by the Hellenic Foundation for Research and Innovation).

Marina Eleftheriadou, adjunct lecturer at the University of the Peloponnese. Her research focuses on political violence and non-state armed actors, with an emphasis on the Middle East and North Africa (MENA) region. She is also a consulting editor at the Centre for Mediterranean, Middle East and Islamic Studies (CEMMIS) and has served as research associate at the Robert Schuman Centre for Advanced Studies at the European University Institute (EUI).

Anthony O'Mahony, Fellow and Tutor at Blackfriars Hall and Studium, University of Oxford. He was Reader in the History of Eastern Christianity, Heythrop College, University of London, between 1999-2018 and Director for the Centre for Eastern Christianity 2009–2018. In 2018 he was appointed Associate Fellow at School of Advanced Studies, University of London. He held the Sir Daniel & Countess Bernardine Murphy Donohue Chair in Eastern Catholic Theology in 2018/2019 at the Pontifical Oriental Institute, Rome.

Konstantinos Papastathis, Assistant Professor at the Department of Political Science of Aristotle University of Thessaloniki. Previously, he worked as a researcher at the Hebrew University of Jerusalem, the University of Luxembourg and Leiden University. His main scientific interests involve the fields of Politics and Religion, and Middle Eastern studies.

Charitini Petrodaskalaki, MA in History: Near and Middle East (SOAS, University of London), and coordinator at the Centre for Mediterranean, Middle East and Islamic Studies (CEMMIS). Researcher in the "Christianity and Religious Pluralism in the Modern Middle East: International Politics and Religion at the turn of the 20th and 21st century" Project (funded by the Hellenic Foundation for Research and Innovation).

Sotiris Roussos, Professor on International Relations and Religion in the Middle East at the Department of Political Science and International Relations of the University of the Peloponnese. He is the Head of the Centre for Mediterranean, Middle East and Islamic Studies (CEMMIS). Scientific Supervisor of the "Christianity and Religious Pluralism in the Modern Middle East: International Politics and Religion at the turn of the 20th and 21st century" Project (funded by the Hellenic Foundation for Research and Innovation).

Ilias Tasopoulos, Ph.D., University of the Peloponnese, Scholar of the Greek State Scholarships' Foundation, Senior editor at the Centre for Mediterranean, Middle East and Islamic Studies (CEMMIS). Researcher in the "Christianity and Religious Pluralism in the Modern Middle East: International Politics and Religion at the turn of the 20th and 21st century" Project (funded by the Hellenic Foundation for Research and Innovation).

Hratch Tchilingirian Associate Faculty member of the Faculty of Asian and Middle Eastern Studies, University of Oxford; Associate Professor of Armenian Studies (IMAS program), Institut National des Langues et Civilisations Orientales. He is the Director of Armenian Diaspora Survey, a 10-country, public opinion research project, funded by the Calouste Gulbenkian Foundation in Lisbon.

INTRODUCTION: THE "CANARY IN THE MINE" OR THE FATE OF CHRISTIANS IN THE MIDDLE EAST

Sotiris Roussos

The Middle East more often than not is perceived as a vast homogeneous sea of Islam with identical social organisation, hierarchies and relationships. While this view may be convenient for those who wish to promote religious conflict and erect cultural barbed wire, it is far from reality. Until two decades ago, the Middle East was an extraordinary mosaic of ethnicities and religions. As Emma Loosley puts it, "when events in the Middle East dominate world headlines and so much time and effort is spent trying to unravel the religious, ethnic, political, economic and social challenges of the region, one group is consistently absent from the debate about the future of the area. This is the native Christian population [...]".[1] Hence, a discussion on Christians in the Middle East could have a twofold purpose: first, to question main presuppositions and perceptions regarding Middle East societies and second, to cast new light on the living Christian communities in the region and reflect on their future role.

Christian communities in the Middle East were and still are organised around four groups of Churches. The first group is comprised of the Greek Orthodox Churches that follow the christological decisions of the Fourth Ecumenical Synod of Chalcedon and include the Patriarchates of Alexandria, Antioch, Constantinople and Jerusalem. Rome was separated from the Eastern Patriarchates due to the 'Great Schism' in 1054, which led to a formal break between western and eastern Churches due to interlocking theological issues and political antagonism between the Pope at Rome and the Emperor at Constantinople.

The second group includes those Churches originating from the historical theological battles in the 5th century and 6th centuries around the distinction between the divinity and the humanity of Christ. Those who followed the Christological teachings of Nestorius and the decisions of the Council of Ephesus, formed the Church of the East.[2] The controversy over the nature of Christ continued in the 6th century leading to the formation of

---

[1] Emma Loosley, "Peter, Paul and James of Jerusalem: The doctrinal and political evolution of the Eastern and Oriental Churches", in Anthony O'Mahony and Emma Loosley (eds.), *Eastern Christianity in the Modern Middle East*, London: Routledge, 2010, p. 1.

[2] Samuel Noble and Alexander Treiger (eds), *The Orthodox Church in the Arab World, 700–1700. An Anthology of Sources*, DeKalb, IL: Northern Illinois University Press, 2014, p. 8.

the group of Oriental Orthodox Churches: the Coptic Orthodox, the Armenian Apostolic, the Syrian Orthodox and the Ethiopian Church.

The Oriental Catholic Churches formed the third group. These Churches were established out of internal feuds and weaknesses and under European Catholic influence in the Ottoman period. To influence the Oriental Churches, Rome was to send missionaries in order to create a significant Catholic-leaning minority within these Churches, mostly by exploiting internal antagonisms, and then to secure the election of pro-Catholic bishops and create a new Patriarchate. This strategy was followed in the case of all Middle Eastern churches with the creation of the Chaldean Catholic, Syrian Catholic, Armenian Catholic and Greek Catholic Churches.[3]

The fourth group is that of the Evangelical and Anglican-Episcopal churches comprising, the Anglican and Episcopal Church (in Jerusalem and the Middle East) and various Protestant, Presbyterian and Lutheran Churches throughout the Middle East, who have emerged from Eastern Christian communities or converts from Islam to Christianity.

Notably, in 1914, approximately 20 per cent of the population in the Middle East and North Africa region was Christian, while, by 2019, Christians amounted to only 4 per cent, which would translate to merely 15 million people.[4] The genocide of Christians (Armenians, Greeks, Assyrians) by the Young Turks and Kemalist Turkey and the exodus of thousands of Christians from historic Palestine and Lebanon were powerful blows to religious pluralism and the historical character of the Middle East. These were compounded by the demographic decline and emigration of Christian populations in contrast to the rapid population growth of the Muslim element. The reasons for this decline must be sought in Christian communities' petty-bourgeois and urban character, which followed modern family models (parents and two children) and the particular educational, cultural and social links these communities maintained with Europe and America.

In the years after the Second World War, as Kenneth Cragg argued, Christians in the Middle East "were and still are adversely affected by their minority status, their ambivalent relations with the West, and the complexity

---

[3] John Flannery, "The Syrian Catholic Church: Martyrdom, Mission, Identity and Ecumenism in Modern History", in Anthony O'Mahony (ed.), *Christianity in the Middle East: Studies in Modern History, Theology and Politics*, London: Melisende, 2008, p. 146.

[4] Patrick Wintour, "Persecution of Christians 'coming close to genocide' in Middle East – report", *The Guardian*, 2 May 2019. Available at: https://www.theguardian.com/world/2019/may/02/persecution-driving-christians-out-of-middle-east-report.

of their inter-religious situation".[5] Christians, however, participated to a greater extent than their demographic distribution in all social emancipation movements in the Middle East. Many of them resorted to a survival strategy of secular nationalism or radical Marxist ideologies. The position of Christians as a minority in a large Muslim majority has pushed them (except for the Lebanese Maronites) into political initiatives that do not raise the banner of religion. In order to secure a position equal to that of Muslims, they raised the banner of common fatherland, national history and social revolution. They were pioneers in the Arab national liberation movements to throw off colonial and post-colonial hegemony. They were also co-founders of leftist movements supporting the international movements of the Third World, shaping landmark changes in Middle Eastern politics, such as the founding of the Ba'ath Party in Syria and radical Palestinian organisations of the 1960s and 1970s.

A major blow, however, was struck with the US invasion of Iraq and the collapse of the state in Syria. Seven hundred thousand Christians – about half of the Christian population of Iraq – fled the country after the American invasion, when the chaos created, and ethno-religious conflicts between Sunnis, Shia and Kurds left Christians at the mercy of violence and destruction. Similarly, Christians made up around 14 per cent of the Syrian population before the civil war, but now this figure has fallen to about 10 per cent. This means that the exodus of Christians is about twice as high as that of other ethno-religious groups, whose population share remains relatively stable.

Christians in both Iraq and Syria are easy targets and victims of the warring groups; the reasons for this are threefold. First, following an Ottoman tradition, they have based their security, religious freedom and development on their relationship with the state/establishment. Essentially, Christian religious leaders formed a consensus with the regime on political/social issues in exchange for religious freedom and social development of their communities. The existence of the Ba'athist regimes in Syria and Iraq and their semi-secular character facilitated this strategy, all the more so since Christians had participated in the theoretical and ideological formation of the movements of so-called Arab socialism and the Arab Left. Second, Christians in Syria and Iraq, unlike the Lebanese Maronites, did not have a tradition of armed organisations on a religious basis, such as the Druze or the Alevis. Third, very importantly, unlike the case in the 19th century, after World War II, Middle Eastern Christians have no international protection and allies neither among the major international powers nor

---

[5] Kenneth Cragg, *The Arab Christian. A History in the Middle East*, London: Mowbray, 1992, p. 235.

among regional powers. On the contrary, both Sunnis and Shia enjoy, especially since the Islamic revolution in Iran, the help and support of Saudi Arabia and Turkey for the former and Iran for the latter. Large numbers of Middle-Eastern migrants and exiles in the Americas, Europe and Australia have been, however, the basis of flourishing Eastern Churches' parishes and bishoprics overseas.

The threat concerns not only the populations but also monuments, especially holy places. Here too, several problems and questions arise. Firstly, is it possible to save monuments and sacred sites without saving the populations they refer to? In other words, will the monuments be "rescued" as a post-modern Disneyland for tourists and film sets? Secondly, who determines whether something is a monument or not? Are there criteria? And if so, who sets them? International organisations, the state – be it strong or failed – or the communities to which it refers? A monastery can be sacred to a community but not included in the relevant UNESCO list of monuments or not considered a monument by the state (the case of Turkey and Israel are typical).

International Relations and Political Science theories have, for analytical purposes, reduced Religion and particularly Churches to mere elements of civil society acting in accordance with rational choice theory. What stays out of scope in such definitions is the experience of communion with God, i.e., the spiritual life of the Christian communities.[6] The Orthodox spiritual renaissance in Lebanon in the 1950s, the Coptic renewal and revival in the 1980s and the role of the Maronite Church in the Catholic spiritual renewal initiated by the Vatican after the end of the civil war in 1991 were closely linked with the political and social developments of the communities and their respective countries. Most importantly, burning issues such as preserving the status quo in the Holy Places can be resolved neither on the basis of a fossilised form of national identity nor on the notion of a post-modern 'theme park' of multiple trajectories, particularities and subjectivities. The Churches ought to respond to the local-global dichotomy that has been raised primarily with regard to the Holy Places. In other words, are the Holy Places part of the universal heritage requiring international protection and control, or are they part of the national church configuration and thus belong to the local congregation?

The Arab uprisings of 2011 posed a new challenge for Christian communities in the Middle East. They shaped new strategies for survival and political participation in their societies. In Syria and Iraq, a significant

---

[6] Vendulka Kubálková, "Towards an International Political Theology", *Millennium-Journal of International Studies,* vol. 29, no. 3, 2000, pp. 682-683.

number of Christians abandoned co-optation by the state, choosing to form or join armed organisations. In other cases, particularly in Egypt in the first phase of the uprising, they sought and claimed a new citizenship identity consistent with the development of modern, democratic and socially just states. However, during the course of the Arab revolts, cross-sectarian alliances based on the protection of human and civil rights proved rather fragile and short-lived.

The Arab uprisings also led to a redefinition of relations between communities – especially the younger and socially active members – and the leadership of the Churches. Until then, the church leadership monopolised – with the exception of the Lebanese Maronites – the representation of communities vis-à-vis the state, discouraging political activism based on religious or ethno-religious identity (Copts, Assyrians). The collapse of the state and the imminent risk of ethnic cleansing caused severe cracks in the church's leadership monopoly of representation and elevated lay personalities and organisations to claimants of authority in the communities.

Although the West no longer uses the dangers faced by Christians to legitimise its interventions in the Middle East, the foreign policy of both the United States (US) and Russia is influenced by Christian organisations and institutions. In the US, a large part of evangelicals is represented by the organisations of the Christian Right, which lobby the decision-making mechanisms in Washington in favour of specific policies concerning Israel (Christian Zionism) and the Middle East in general. The intervention of the Russian Church was, on the other hand, perhaps the most vocal reaction against the danger of annihilation of Christians in the Middle East and gave an indirect political message of support. The Russian Church's announcements and actions, particularly in the case of Syria, were in line with Russian foreign policy in the region.

The last hundred years of Middle East Christianity's history have witnessed a profound series of crises. These have overtaken Middle Eastern Christianity in modern times. Displacement by war, genocide and interreligious conflict leading to loss, emigration and exile would seem to be the main experience of Christianity in the modern Middle East. Against this background of displacement, Christians have sought to resettle and build anew when allowed. They have been able to make a significant cultural, political and economic contribution to Middle Eastern society. Some observers have suggested that there is a 'Christian barometer', which provides the world with an accurate measurement of the political atmosphere in the Middle East.

This 'Christian barometer' shows us that as long as freedom and social development prevail in the Middle East and as long as the region is linked to international trends and global movements, the greater the likelihood they will continue to live in their ancient homelands. In the 19th century, workers in the mines would let a canary fly into the galleries to see if there were any poisonous gases. If the canary survived, then the gallery was safe. In turn, the safe existence of Christians in the Middle East is an irrefutable indicator that the poison of blind ethno-religious violence has been neutralised.

The sectarianisation of the civil strife during the 2011 Arab revolts has pitted the main contenders for power against each other, rendering future coexistence a very difficult yet still worthy goal. At the same time, sectarianism has also brought the smaller communities into a harrowing situation. The role of religious communities and leaders in a post-war, reconstruction era in Syria is vital, particularly in the field of community rehabilitation and reconciliation as well as the re-building of interreligious, interethnic balance.

The volume is an attempt to approach the Christian communities of the Middle East not through the lens of Islam nor their interaction between state and Islam but by examining the diverse Christian communities and their Churches in relation to the state, identity and politics. It comprises three main parts. The first is devoted to the life and history of the communities, their relationship with the state and the contribution of these communities to social and political developments. Hratch Tchilingirian's chapter connects the history of the Armenian community over the past centuries with the current problems and challenges as they face *imposed realities*. Importantly, he discusses the influence of relations with the state, social entrenchments and extremist political Islam on the present situation and prospects of Armenians in the Middle East. The chapter by Zakia Aqra, Stavros Drakoularakos and Charitini Petrodaskalaki examines the strategies of Copts and Maronites during the Arab uprisings through the lens of Ontological Security Theory (OST). Under the prism of OST, they study how the different standing of the communities in relation to the state exposed the contrasting abilities to react to dislocatory events. In the last chapter, Stavros Drakoularakos analyses changes in survival strategies and the development of militarisation options in the Christian communities of Syria and Iraq.

The second part of the volume includes two chapters on the relations between Christian communities and the state in the Middle East. Nikos Christofis describes and analyses the Turkish state's policies towards the Christian communities, especially during the Erdoğan period. The change in the identity of Turkishness and the emerging dominance of the Sunni Muslim identity element promoted by the Erdoğan regime created new challenges for Christian minorities. Konstantinos Papastathis's chapter studies how the Charter of the Greek Orthodox Patriarchate of Jerusalem regulates the relations between the Greek upper clergy, the Palestinian laity and the Jordanian state. He also touches upon how a revision of the Charter may change the relations within the Patriarchate that concern not only this ecclesiastical institution but also the Christian Holy Places and the regional and global consequences of a change in the status quo governing them.

The last part is devoted to the connection of the Christian communities in the Middle East to the foreign policies of US and Russia and to the world. Ilias Tasopoulos analyses how the relationship between the Russian Orthodox Church and the Russian state influences Russian policy towards Christians in the Middle East and Russian strategy in the region during the Arab uprisings. Marina Eleftheriadou examines the relationship between the American Christian Right and Christians in the Middle East. First, she touches upon Christian Right's policies for defending Christians from persecution and promoting conversion in the region. Second, she analyses the impact of Christian Right on US policy toward the Israeli state and the Arab-Israeli peace process. In the last chapter Anthony O'Mahony tackles the Political-Theological context for Christianity in the Middle East and its connection to the Holy See, the Diaspora Churches and World Christianity. He further addresses future challenges for the Christian communities in the region.

We would like to express our gratitude to Dr. Nikos Christofis for all his support and encouragement throughout the editing and publishing process of this volume.

The papers in this volume are the product of an international workshop on Christianity in the Middle Esat, held in Athens on 21 October 2022, to promote an academic discussion on Christianity and Religious Pluralism in the modern Middle East. The international workshop was conducted as part of the Research Project "Christianity and Religious Pluralism in the Modern Middle East: International Politics and Religion at the turn of the 20th and 21st century", which was supported by the Hellenic Foundation for Research and Innovation (H.F.R.I.) under the 'First Call for H.F.R.I. Research Projects to support Faculty members and Researchers and the procurement of high-cost research equipment grant' (Project Number: 1422).

Bibliography

Cragg, Kenneth, *The Arab Christian. A History in the Middle East*, London: Mowbray, 1992.

Kubálková, Vendulka, "Towards an International Political Theology", *Millennium - Journal of International Studies*, vol. 29, no. 3, 2000, pp. 675-704.

11

Wintour, Patrick, "Persecution of Christians coming close to genocide' in Middle East – report", *The Guardian*, 2 May 2019. Available at: https://www.theguardian.com/world/2019/may/02/persecution-driving-christians-out-of-middle-east-report.

Flannery, John, "The Syrian Catholic Church: Martyrdom, Mission, Identity and Ecumenism in Modern History", in Anthony O'Mahony (ed.), *Christianity in the Middle East: Studies in Modern History, Theology and Politics*, London: Melisende, 2008, pp. 143-165.

Noble, Samuel and Alexander Treiger (eds), *The Orthodox Church in the Arab World, 700–1700. An Anthology of Sources*. DeKalb, IL: Northern Illinois University Press, 2014.

Loosley, Emma, "Peter, Paul and James of Jerusalem: The doctrinal and political evolution of the Eastern and Oriental Churches", in Anthony O'Mahony and Emma Loosley (eds), *Eastern Christianity in the Modern Middle East*, London: Routledge, 2010, pp. 1-12.

ARMENIAN COMMUNITIES IN THE MIDDLE EAST: LOSING THE PAST IN THE FUTURE?

Hratch Tchilingirian

The Armenian presence in the Middle East dates back to ancient times, with the ancestral homeland of Western Armenia being located today in the eastern regions of the Republic of Turkey. While the Armenians are indigenous in some parts of the Middle East, in other parts, they have formed diaspora communities due to a variety of historical circumstances. "Since history has no secret pockets and private laws, things Armenian are also things Near Eastern", writes Seda Dadoyan, a leading scholar of the history of Armenian-Islamic relations. From the first century of the Christian era, there has been an Armenian presence in Jerusalem, when they came to Palestine as Roman legionnaires and administrators. There is a long and extensive history of "Armenian-Islamic *realpolitik* with Arabs, Turks, Persians, Kurds as well as heterodox Islam (such as Ismailism)", according to Dadoyan. Medieval Arab sources provide extensive accounts of Armenians in the Middle East. Indeed, "*Arminyah* and *al arman* were presented [in the Arab sources] as indigenous elements of the Near East and the narrative did not single them out from the regional texture", explains Dadoyan. Since the seventh century, Armenians "have been part of the Islamic world", and part of what is now the Middle East and its peoples.[1] In the late eighth century, heterodox Armenians allied with "the Muslims on the Abbasid frontiers lands". More significantly, medieval Armenian histories put the origin of all treaties regulating Islamic-Armenian relations in the Medinan period of Islam (622-632) and see them through a "so called 'Prophet's Oath to Armenians' (allegedly given to an Armenian delegation from Jerusalem to Medianh)".[2]

Today, Armenian communities are scattered in over ten countries in the Middle East, being mainly concentrated in Lebanon, Syria, Turkey, Iraq, Iran, Egypt, Israel/Palestine, Jordan, Kuwait, and the United Arab Emirates. In 1975, there were an estimated 625,000 Armenians in the Middle East.[3]

---

[1] Seta Dadoyan, *The Armenians in the Medieval Islamic World. Volume 1, The Arab Period in Arminyah, Seventh to Eleventh Centuries*, New Brunswick and London: Transaction Publishers, 2011, pp. 1, 60-61.

[2] Ibid, pp. 60-61, 150-151.

[3] Figures provided by the then Prelate of Lebanon, Archbishop Aram Keshishian (now Catholicos of Cilicia) based on various estimates; see Aram Keshishian, *The Christian Witness at the Crossroads in the Middle East*, Beirut: Middle East Council of Churches, 1981.

However, over the last five decades, given the wars, conflicts, revolutions and continued political and socio-economic turmoil in the region, the estimated combined figure declined to a little over 200,000 in 2022 (see *Table 1*). The Armenians may be considered to be a minority within the wide spectrum of confessional, religious and ethnic non-Muslim communities living in these respective countries.

In the 11th century, after the fall of the Bagratuni Kingdom, some 10,000 Armenians migrated to Egypt during the Fatimid period. In the early 17th century, Shah Abbas the Great forcibly resettled more than 300,000 Armenians from the Eastern and Western parts of Armenia in Persia, where the community still exists in New Julfa, Isfahan. In 1636, an Armenian priest in Isfahan established the first printing press in the Middle East.[4] Trade and commercial activities have also led to the wide dispersal of the Armenian communities. Between the 15th and 18th centuries, large numbers of Armenians lived on the important trade route that ran between Aleppo and Alexandretta.[5] Armenian craftsmen, especially jewellers, were well-known in Aleppo during the 19th century.[6] In the late 17th century, there were some 800 Armenian families in Basra, who had relocated there from various cities and towns in the Ottoman Empire, as well as from the Safavid territories. Armenian merchants came from New Julfa and the ancient Persian city of Hamadan. The first Armenian Church in Baghdad was built in 1640.[7] Armenians were also mostly involved in trade and craftsmanship.

In the early 19th century, a number of Armenians held significant commercial and political positions in both Egypt and Lebanon, and "distinguished themselves as statesmen and high officials".[8] Boghos Yusufian, an Armenian banker and businessman, who was an advisor to Muhammad Ali, the founder of modern Egypt.[9] Yusufian became head of bureau of commerce in 1819. Another prominent Armenian is Nubar

---

[4] The first book published in Isfahan was the *Psalter* in 1638. See Goriun Abp. Babyan, *"Khachatur Vardapet Gesaratsi himnatir N. J. Srp. Amenaprgich Vanki Dharani"* ["Khachatur Vardapet of Caesarea founder of the printing press of New Julfa's Holy Saviour Monastery"], *Hask*, no. 2-3, 2014, p. 160.

[5] For a discussion of Armenians in the Levant between 12th and 13th centuries, see Claude Mutafian, "Les princesses arméniennes et le Liban latin", in Aida Boudjikanian (ed.), *Armenians of Lebanon: from past princesses and refugees to present-day community*, Beirut and Belmost, MA: Haigazian University and Armenian Heritage Press, 2009, pp. 3-20; for a historian's perspective on modern times, see Avedis Krikor Sanjian, *The Armenian Communities in Syria under Ottoman Dominion*, Cambridge: Harvard University Press, 1965.

[6] Sanjian, *The Armenian Communities*, pp. 53-56.

[7] Seda Mouratyan, *Iraki Hay Hamaynkeh* [The Armenian community of Iraq], Yerevan: Baykar, 1997.

[8] Sanjian, *The Armenian Communities*, p. 157; Hovannisian, "The Ebb and Flow of the Armenian Minority in the Arab Middle East", Middle East Journal, vol. 28, no, 1, 1974, p. 22.

[9] Sona Zeitlian, *Armenians in Egypt. Contribution of Armenians to Medieval and Modern Egypt*, Los Angeles, CA: Hraztan Sarkis Zeitlian Publications, 2006, pp. 98ff.

Nubarian, who became the first Prime Minister of modern Egypt in 1876.[10] In the late 19th-early 20th century, the first and last governors of the autonomous province of Mount Lebanon were Catholic Armenians, Dawuid Pasha (1861-68) and Ohannes Pasha Kuyumjian (1912-15) respectively.[11] The Armenians of Lebanon "formed part of the socially most advanced sections" of society at the time. Many served in official and professional positions, such as the various branches of the Ottoman administration, the Ottoman Public Debt or the Tobacco *Régie*.[12]

Following the Hamidian massacres of 1894-96 in the Ottoman Empire, numerous Armenian refugees from Adana, Sis, Marash, Aintab, Urfa, Dikranagerd and other towns in what is now eastern Turkey came to Beirut and other parts of Lebanon. In 1896, Armenian orphans from Marash and Zeytoun were transferred to Beirut. These relocated Armenians gradually became assimilated into the Maronite community in Lebanon.[13] In the late 1920s a large number of orphanages and refugee camps in the Middle East, especially in Syria, Lebanon, Egypt, and Iraq housed thousands of Armenians, who survived the genocide in the Ottoman Empire at the beginning of the 20th century.[14] Another wave came when, in the late 1930s, the French Mandate in Syria ceded the province of Alexandretta to Turkey. Some 40,000 Armenians, from the region formerly known as Cilicia, were obliged to take refuge in Syria and Lebanon. The overwhelming majority of Armenians living in the Middle East today are third and fourth generation descendants of the genocide survivors.

At the beginning of the 21st century, the Armenian communities in the

---

[10] Ayman Zohry, "Armenians in Egypt", *International Union for the Scientific Study of Populations*, XXV IUSSP International Population Conference, Tours, France 18-23 July 2005.

[11] Hovannisian, "The Ebb and Flow", p. 29.

[12] Hilmar Kaiser, "The Armenians in Lebanon during the Armenian Genocide", in Aida Boudjikanian (ed.), *Armenians of Lebanon: from past princesses and refugees to present-day community*, Beirut and Belmost, MA: Haigazian University and Armenian Heritage Press, 2009, p. 35.

[13] Prior to World War I, Armenians in Syria and Lebanon numbered between 17,000 and 18,000. The communities in these countries swelled after the arrival and settlement of waves of refugees and survivors of the genocide in the opening decades of the twentieth century. Figures published in Soviet Armenia in 1925 give the Armenian population numbers as follows: Aleppo and its environs 90,000; Beirut 18,000; Damascus 8000; Iskenderun 8000; other parts of Lebanon 6000; Tripoli and Zgharta 5000; Beyli 6000; Patros 3000; Zahleh and nearby villages 2000; Saida & Sour 3000; Junieh 2500; Tagher 2500; see *Hayastani Kochnak*, 1925, p. 794, quoted in Ashot K. Abrahamian, *Hamarot Urvagits Hay Gaghtavayreri Batmutyan* (Brief Outline of the History of Armenian Colonies), vol. 2, Yerevan: Hayastan Publication, 1967, pp. 22-23.

[14] In the 1920s, there were 30,000 Armenians in Iraq, 25,000-28,000 in Egypt, some 150,000 in Syria (60,000 in Aleppo), 35,000-40,000 in Lebanon; see entries for relevant countries in *Hay Spiurk*: Hanragitaran (Armenian Diaspora Encyclopaedia), 2003. Hovannisian provides slightly different figures; he writes that "by 1925, well over 200,000 exiles had been received into the Arab lands under French or British mandate: 100,000 in Syria (augmented in 1938-39 when France ceded the sanjaq of Alexandretta to Turkey) 50,000 in the enlarged province of the Lebanon; 25,000 in Mesopotamian towns and refugee camps; 10,000 in Palestine and Transjordan, and 40,000 in Egypt", see Hovannisian, "The Ebb and Flow...", p. 20.

Middle East face a host of critical internal and external issues. Internally, questions of integration, assimilation, preservation and maintenance of community institutions are among the most hotly debated issues in Beirut, Aleppo, Cairo, Tehran and Istanbul. Externally, the existing security situation and ongoing conflicts, as well as the escalation of religious fundamentalism in recent years, and state-tolerated "othering" of minorities –i.e., discrimination sanctioned by constitutions based on the application of Sharia, whereby "non-Muslim minorities within an Islamic State do not enjoy rights equal to those of Muslim majority".[15] These processes are exacerbated by declining socio-economic conditions, which have caused mass migration of Christians in general and the Armenians in particular. As Catholicos Aram of the Cilician See has described the situation in the Middle East: "this region is now characterised by mutual tolerance and tension, mutual understanding and prejudice, rapprochement and polarisation".[16]

This chapter will briefly discuss some of the main institutional internal and external problems facing the Armenian communities in the contemporary Middle East – or what could be called the *imposed realities*. It will then draw some critical conclusions on how these processes affect identity construction and maintenance of a viable community life in what might be designated as the *uncertain future*.

Internal developments

Three main institutions play significant roles in defining and maintaining Armenian identity in the Diaspora and the Middle East in particular: the Armenian Apostolic Orthodox Church (hereafter termed the Armenian Church), schools and media, i.e., communications in the broader sense.

The Armenian Church

First, it is a historically, politically and sociologically significant fact that the three Hierarchical Sees of the Armenian Church are all located in the Middle East: the Catholicosate of Cilicia has been in Antelias, Lebanon, since 1930, but its roots go back to the 13th century Cilicia; the Patriarchate of Jerusalem which was established at the beginning of the 14th century; and the Patriarchate of Constantinople in Istanbul that was founded in the 15th century. The Patriarchate of the Armenian Catholic Church (otherwise known as the Armenian Rite) is based in Bzommar, Lebanon, as is one of the oldest Armenian Protestant church organisations – the Armenian

---

[15] Fatih Öztürk, *Ottoman and Turkish Law*, Bloomington: iUniverse LLC, 2014, pp. 5-6.

[16] Catholicos Aram I, "The Armenian Church in the Middle East: Some Facts and Perspectives", in Seta Dadoyan (ed.) *The Contribution of the Armenian Church to the Christian Witness in the Middle East*, Antelias, Lebanon: Armenian Catholicosate of Cilicia, 2001, p. 14.

Evangelical Union of Near East.

The Armenian Church belongs to the Orthodox family of churches, known as the Oriental Orthodox (or 'Non-Chalcedonian') Churches. Armenia adopted Christianity as a state religion in the early 4th century, following the conversion of King Trdat by St. Gregory the Illuminator.[17] From this integral link, the history of the Armenian Church has run parallel with the history of the Armenian people. Whether in times of political or social upheavals, or during invasions by foreign rulers, the Armenian Church has been at the forefront of national life. As Malachia Ormanian, a renowned church historian and Patriarch of Constantinople (1896–1908), puts it, the Armenian Church has been "the visible expression of the absent fatherland, the one that satisfies the noblest longings of the soul".[18] Since the demise of the last Armenian Kingdom in 1375, the Armenian Church has been a guarding religious, political, educational and cultural institution and has assumed a major role as the preserver of the Armenian religious-cultural heritage. Historically, the Armenian Church and clergy in Islamic states and societies, as Dadoyan explains, "were protected by law and gained political significance and economic prosperity".

Indeed, the church played the role of the "negotiator" in most of "the contacts and resulting agreements" in Islamic-Armenian relations.[19] In recent history, the national role and function assumed by the church were most evident in the Ottoman Empire (as part of the *Millet* system), the Russian Empire and later the Soviet Union. Indeed, arguably, a "republicanised" version of the Ottoman *Millet* system continues in the modern Middle East, especially as non-Muslim communities are recognized as "religious communities" (*tayifa* in Arabic, *cema'at* in Turkey). The late Jivan Tabibian, a political scientist and one of the rare, Lebanon-born ambassadors of the Republic of Armenia, provides a brief but expensive description of what being a *millet* in the Middle East implied for the Armenians:

> [It meant being] a community within the larger polity but apart, with self-administration, quasi-autonomous structures, socio-cultural in nature, with some form of legitimate representation, a sub-community, apart, in the large cauldron of the larger society, with a very pre-modern notion of the 'political.' The anchor of the

---

[17] For a history of the advent of Christianity in Armenia and the conversion of King Trdat by St. Gregory the Illuminator, see Malachia Ormanian, *The Church of Armenia: Her History, Doctrine, Rule, Discipline, Liturgy, Literature, and Existing condition*, 3rd edition, New York: St. Vartan Press, 1988, pp. 3-13.

[18] Ibid, p. 225. See also Archbishop Tiran Nersoyan, *Armenian Church Historical Studies*, New York: St Vartan Press, 1996, pp. 235-267.

[19] Dadoyan, *The Armenians in the Medieval Islamic World*, p. 9.

Armenian millet was the church, and the criterion of distinction was religion.[20]

Whereas constitutions in the Middle East give prominence to religion and religious institutions (unlike in Western democracies), churches or religious establishments provide essential spaces for group socialisation and interaction. For instance, the Armenian Church in the Middle East assumes the role of a significant identity marker and preserver of culture in the context of the dominant Islamic society. Besides religious duties, the Church administers schools and charities, as well as promoting cultural production. Moreover, the Armenian Church – and generally Christian churches in the Middle East – has state-recognised authority to issue marriage licences, hear and deliberate on divorce cases, as well as inheritance and other family dispute cases. In many instances, the Church is also the legal guardian and administrator of substantial community assets that have been bequeathed to the church over many decades, such as in Egypt, which includes trusts, real estate, agricultural lands and other income-generating properties.

One of the unique features of the Armenian Church is the involvement –by tradition and design– of laymen in running its affairs.[21] Unlike the Roman Catholic and the Orthodox Churches of the Byzantine tradition, lay people actively participate in the administrative, legislative and financial affairs of the Armenian Church. The laity elects almost all clerical leaders in the Armenian Church, including the Catholicos. Although this functional involvement of the laity has instilled a spirit of democracy, on the other hand, it has contributed to the politicisation of the Armenian Church by various Armenian political parties, especially during the Cold War era.

The three main and transnational political parties which have been active in the Middle East, or have affiliates are: (1) the Social Democratic Hunchakian Party which was founded in 1887, in Geneva and is the oldest political party; (2) the Armenian Revolutionary Federation (Dashnak) Party that was founded in 1889, in Tbilisi as a socialist party; and (3) the Ramkavar Democratic Liberal Party founded in 1921. During the Cold War, the Hunchakian and Ramkavar parties maintained a pro-Soviet Armenia stance, whereas the Dashnak party adopted a pro-American position. These differences of political orientation were sources of internal conflicts within the various communities, especially in Lebanon and Syria. Most notably, the internal political rivalries among the political parties developed into

---

[20] Jivan Tabibian, "The Risk of Democratization", *Armenian International Magazine*, vol. 10, no. 8 & 9, August-September 1999, p. 29.

[21] The Armenian Patriarchate of Jerusalem forms the exception, since the ordained members (monks) of the St. James Brotherhood elect the Patriarch and administer the affairs of the Patriarchate without any lay involvement.

consequential crises: first, in 1956, namely the administrative and jurisdictional schism in the Armenian Apostolic Orthodox Church –between the Catholicosate of All Armenians in Etchmiadzin, at the time in Soviet Armenia, and the Catholicosate of Cilicia in Lebanon– and, then, in 1958, the intra-Armenian political struggle –in the background of the controversial Lebanese elections the previous year– when the Dashnak Party supported the pro-American front of President Camille Chamoun (1952-1958) and the other Armenian parties sided with the Lebanese national opposition. The legacy of the Cold War on the diocesan jurisdictional level, which had started in the late 1950s between the two hierarchical Sees, remains unresolved.[22]

In the early 21st century, the life of the Armenian communities in the Middle East continues to be largely organised around the Armenian Church and its institutions. This is particularly so in countries where Islamic laws are dominant. Secular political, cultural and educational organisations are active in the life of the community, but the formal and legal status of the Armenian Church *vis-à-vis* the State gives prominence to the religious head of the community, as is evident in Turkey, Egypt, Lebanon, Iraq, Jordan, Kuwait, and Iran.

Nevertheless, as Sossie Kasbarian, a scholar of Middle East diasporas, observes, in recent years the role of community institutions and religious leaders are becoming increasingly "irrelevant" for the new generations. The socio-political lives of young people are not necessarily mediated through the traditional community institutions, at least in some countries in the Middle East. For instance, according to the Armenian Diaspora Survey conducted in 2019 in Lebanon, 76 per cent of Armenians in the 25-34 age group and 84 per cent of the 16–24-year-olds said they are not affiliated with any Armenian political party or movement.[23] "Young activists coalesce with fellow non-Armenian citizens around issues that unite them as Egyptians, Lebanese, and so on", writes Kasbarian. At least for the young people she interviewed, "the church and traditional institutions and narratives have done them a disservice in keeping them at a distance from the state and from active belonging, claiming rights and exercising agency as full and equal citizens".[24] Perhaps more than anywhere else, the new generation of

---

[22] For more on these developments, see Hratch Tchilingirian, "L'Eglise arménienne pendant la guerre froide: la crise Etchmiadzine-Antelias", NH Hebdo, 9 June 2016, pp. 6-9; Nicola Migliorino *(Re)constructing Armenia in Lebanon and Syria: Ethno-cultural Diversity and the State in the Aftermath of a Refugee Crisis*, Oxford: Berghahn, 2008, pp. 100-102.

[23] Hratch Tchilingirian (ed.), *Armenian Diaspora Public Opinion (1). Armenian Diaspora Survey 2019*. London: Armenian Institute, 2020, p. 89. Available at http://www.armeniandiasporasurvey.com/2019-survey.

[24] Sosie Kasbarian, "The Armenian Middle East. Boundaries, Pathways and Horizons", in Dalia Abdelhady, Ramy Aly (eds.), *Routledge Handbook on Middle Eastern Diasporas*, London: Routledge, 2023, p. 410.

Armenians in Turkey speak about "integration" into the wider society with equal rights and question as to why in the 21st century the Patriarch or the clergy should continue to represent the entire community. Even as the Armenian community is recognised as a religious community in Turkey, those who advocate integration demand "a civilian delegation, which should be formed within the Armenian society", to represent them.[25] Etyen Mahçupyan, a well-known intellectual and once advisor to former Prime Minister Ahmet Davutoğlu, calls this process the "civilianisation of the community". Mahçupyan believes, as others advocating integration do, that having a religious head of the community "takes the community farther away from being a democratic community".[26]

Armenian Schools

The Armenian Church and political parties have played pivotal roles in the development of Armenian education and spread of schools in the Middle East. These were essential community institutions that ensured the transmission and maintenance of the language and culture –the key aspects of Armenian identity. In Syria and Lebanon, during the 1930s and 1940s, "Armenian schools were present in virtually all cities and villages that had a sizeable Armenian presence".[27] In the 1980s, there were 38 Armenian day schools in Syria, with 24 being located in Aleppo and its environs. There were 60 schools in Lebanon. Prior to the start of the Civil War in Lebanon in 1975, some 21,000 students were enrolled in Armenian schools.[28] However, the current situation throughout the Middle East has led to a plummeting of the communities, with consequences for schools. In the last decade alone, schools in Lebanon, Egypt, Iraq, Iran, and Turkey have seen a drastic decline in enrolment numbers, as well as in the quality of teaching staff and available financial resources. Between 1991 and 2001, the number of Armenian schools in Lebanon fell from 45 to 33 and further down to 16 in 2022. The number of students has declined from about 12,000 in the 1990s to less than 5,000 in 2022 (see *Table 2*).[29] In Iran, the trend has been even more drastic. Before the Islamic Revolution, there were 17,000 students enrolled in Armenian schools, in 2022 the figure stands at less than 2,000. Similar trends are seen in Egypt and Syria. In Aleppo alone, the number of

[25] *Sunday's Zaman*, "Armenian youth complain elders imposing 'chosen trauma' on them", 7 November 2007. Available at: https://armenians-1915.blogspot.com/2007/10/2032-turkish-armenian-youth-complain.html.

[26] Hratch Tchilingirian, "The 'Other' Citizens: Armenians in Turkey between Isolation and (dis)Integration", *Journal of the Society for Armenian Studies*, vol. 25, 2016, p. 129.

[27] Migliorino, *(Re)constructing Armenia in Lebanon and Syria*, p. 71.

[28] See entries for Syria and Lebanon in *Hay Spiurk: Hanragitaran*, 2003.

[29] Op. cit. Migliorino, 2008, p. 202; see also, *Hay Spiurk: Hanragitaran*, 2003.

students has gone down by 75 per cent within a decade (2011-2022). In Jordan, the only Armenian school, which had 88 students in 2011, closed its doors for good in 2018.

Related to the perennial financial difficulties, there is lack of qualified teachers as schools are not able to pay the faculty decent salaries. Consequentially, as one school director in Lebanon worries, "many of the current teachers might abandon the profession completely".[30] Another former school principal in Istanbul laments that the community perceives the teaching profession in an Armenian school as "being idealistic, a sacrifice, without regard to financial conditions". In her experience, contemporary Armenian parents believe that beyond "the emotional and the personal" aspects, the use of the Armenian language "does not have any social-economic benefit".[31] Such attitudes deprive the schools of the vital support needed from parents, both moral and financial. Also, the educators in both countries point out the lack of appropriate textbooks for Armenian schools.[32] The late school principal Manuel Keshishian described the rapid decline of Armenian schools in once-dynamic Armenian community of Aleppo in more dramatic tone: "Our schools are on an unstoppable free fall".[33]

These problems are not just self-inflicted, but are the culmination of the gradual but debilitating effects of socio-economic and political conditions endured by the Armenian communities – and the resulting migration trend. The role of the state is no less insignificant. Catholicos Aram in Lebanon explains that, "due to restrictions imposed by many governments [in the Middle East] on the curriculum", courses related to religious education are becoming marginalised or ignored.[34] Armenian schools in the Middle East – in Syria, Egypt, Iraq, Iran and Turkey– the sole exception being Lebanon, are required to implement the state curriculum in its entirety. There are only a limited number of periods set aside for Armenian language and religion classes, all other teaching must be conducted in Arabic, Farsi or Turkish. Since the 1979 Revolution, the Iranian government, first completely banned minority language instructions, including Armenian in Armenian Schools, and then allowed only two hours per week (increased to five hours per week

---

[30] Personal correspondence on 20 December 2022.

[31] Personal correspondence on 18 December 2022.

[32] For similar problems in Armenian schools in Aleppo, see Manuel Keshishian, "Halebi Haygagan Varzharannere" (The Armenian Schools in Aleppo), *CivilNet*, 26 July 2022. Available at: www.civilnet.am/news/669250.

[33] Ibid.

[34] Catholicos Aram I, "The Armenian Church in the Middle East: Some Facts and Perspectives", in Seta Dadoyan (ed.) *The Contribution of the Armenian Church to the Christian Witness in the Middle East*, Antelias, Lebanon: Armenian Catholicosate of Cilicia, 2001, pp. 15-16.

in 1995). In 1984, in response to complaints by the Armenian community over the curriculum of the Armenian schools, Hashemi Rafsanjani, the Speaker of the Parliament at the time, admonished that "the Armenians can read their religious books in Armenian outside the state schools".[35] Some 17 Armenian schools were closed in Iran after the Revolution. In 2022, the number of schools in Iran stand at 11 in Tehran, with about 1400 students, and one in Isfahan with about 200 students. In the last decade, the communities in both cities have witnessed a decline of fifty percent in student numbers. In Syria, schools are permitted three additional periods for Armenian religion classes and four periods for instruction in the language of the religion per week.[36] Interestingly, the Syrian Constitution stipulates that the national teaching curriculum should "create an Arab, national, socialist generation with scientific training and one attached to its land, proud of its legacy, animated by a spirit of struggle for the realisation of the goals of the nation in unity, liberty, socialism".[37] The same constitution –as it had been the case in Turkey– imposes non-Armenian principals or vice-principals in Armenian schools.[38] These government-appointed officials serve as the "states' eyes". Referring to this overt state monitoring of minority schools in Turkey, the late Hrant Dink wrote:

> One of the vice-directors of the [Turkish] ministry of national education's Istanbul office –who was later convicted of corruption and bribe-taking– said the following to the 'vice-principals' he appointed [to the Armenian schools] whom the minority schools call 'Turkish vice-principals': 'You are our eyes and ears... You are to inform us of even the minutest mistakes that these people make'. He said this in the presence of the minority school principals, with total disregard for their dignity and common courtesy.[39]

The Media and cultural communication

In the past, when things looked bleak in the diaspora communities of the

---

[35] *Iran Times,* 22 June 1984, [. 2, quoted in Eliz Sanasarian, *Religious Minorities in Iran,* Cambridge: Cambridge University Press, 2000, p. 80; on the problems of education in Armenian and other minority schools in Iran, pp. 76-84.

[36] European Parliament, "The Current Situation of the Armenians in Lebanon, Turkey, Iran and the Soviet Union", Session Documents, Series A., Document A 2-33/97, Part A, B and C. Strasbourg, 15 April 1987.

[37] Migliorino, *(Re)constructing Armenia in Lebanon and Syria,* p. 163, quoting Chapter 4, Article 21 of the Syrian Constitution (1973).

[38] The practice goes back to the 1960s; the Armenian schools in Syria, as Hovanissian writes, "were brought under state control, initially through the aegis of inspector-informers and ultimately, in the fall term of 1967, through the imposition of discriminatory curricular re-visions and the appointment of principals responsible in no way to the Armenian school boards but solely to the ministry of education". Hovannisian, "The Ebb and Flow", p. 27.

[39] Hrant Dink, "Kinkel ve Valilik", *Agos,* 21 August 1998 (translated excerpts posted on groong.com).

West, they looked to the Middle East for hope. In Egypt, Syria and Lebanon, for instance, Armenians spoke, read and wrote Armenian guaranteeing the future of the language and the culture. Over the last few decades, there has been a dramatic decline in Armenian cultural production in the Middle East. Starting in the early decades of the 20th century, Cairo, Aleppo and Beirut were significant centres of literary and cultural production, hosting vibrant literary and intellectual activities for generations. Wide cultural production, that included Armenian theatre, music, and generally the arts, complemented the work of religious and educational institutions and in doing so reinforced the identity, language and ethnic traditions of the communities.[40] The bishop of the Armenian Church diocese of Damascus lamented the discontinuation of once vibrant Armenian dance ensemble and community choir because the community lacks young men.[41] Most young Armenian men in Syria have left the country to avoid the mandatory military service. Male citizens in Syria between the age of 18 and 42 are obliged to perform their military service. Since 2011, the 18 to 21 months period of the service has been extended at times for years by the government.

Armenian-language newspapers in the Middle East, that until recently were dominated by publications or official organs of Armenian political parties, have to deal with three major, perennial problems: a lack of readers, shortages of journalists and economic difficulties. The first is relatively new for the Middle East since there is a steady and alarming decline of Armenian language readers. Even in Lebanon, a country that was once considered the 'Mother of Diasporas', Arabic and English have become the preferred languages among the youth over Armenian. In 2010, UNESCO classified the Western Armenian dialect spoken in the Middle East (as well as in the Western diaspora) as a 'definitely endangered' language in its *Atlas of World Languages*.[42] Compounding this problem is a chronic shortage of journalists, writers and contributors who can write in Armenian. An editor at *Aztag* daily (est. in 1927) explained over two decades ago that his paper's "biggest problem is that there are not enough writers. We don't have intellectuals who

---

[40] For example, see Nora Salmanian, "La conribution des Arméniens libanais à la vie musicale et artistique au Liban de 1920 à nos jour", in Boudjikanian (ed.), *Armenians of Lebanon* and Roubina Artinian,"Armenian Choirs in Lebanon, 1930-1980. A bridge between the past and he present", in ibid. For Armenian artists, see Hratch Tchilingirian "Master of Grand Theater. Gerard Avedissian in the Cultural Landscape of Lebanon", *Armenian International Magazine*, vol. 10, no.6, June 1999, pp.46-48; Hratch Tchilingirian "Looking to the East. Chant Avedissian rediscovers and redefines Egyptian visual art", *Armenian International Magazine*, vol. 10, no. 8 & 9, August-September 1999, pp. 76-77, 79; Hratch Tchilingirian, "Witness of His Time. The Oppressed and the Rejected Find Dignity and Respect in Norikian", *Armenian International Magazine*, vol. 11, no. 3, March 2000, p. 62-64.

[41] Personal communication on 23 December 2022.

[42] UNESCO *Atlas of the World's Languages in Danger*. Available at: http://www.unesco.org/culture/languages-atlas.

23

are capable of writing, analysing and presenting local, regional and international issues in Armenian", adding that, "sadly, this pertains to all professions, not only to the media".[43] The situation in 2022 for the Armenian media in the Middle East is even more acute. Compounding the economic and administrative implications of the lack of readers and journalists is the fact that none of the newspapers are financially self-sufficient. They are largely financed and sustained as the organs of the established Armenian political parties or religious entities. Nevertheless, electronic media, the internet and social media have opened new sources of information and communications, especially among the youth. This phenomenal expansion of and access to means of communications has encouraged the use of English and Arabic as primary languages of communications –to the detriment of the Armenian mother tongue. Interestingly, a higher number of respondents of the 2019 Armenian Diaspora Survey in Lebanon completed the questionnaire in English (45 per cent) than in Armenian (42 per cent), and much less in Arabic (10 per cent) and French (3 per cent).[44] The open access to technologies have also weakened the traditional methods of communications of community institutions and their hold on information. Most significantly, the internet has opened a wider world to the youth beyond their parochial institutions and encouraged self-expression, broadcasting and publication. Armenian political parties, religious and community organisations have not caught up with the expensive development and rapid expansion of communications technologies. "In these conditions, the conservative, cautious, still unprofessional or semi-professional situation of the Armenian print media has created some distance between itself and the Armenian reader," notes Varoujan Tenbelian, the editor of the Beirut-based *Darperag21.net* online magazine.[45] In the early decades of the 21st century, publishing Armenian newspapers in the Middle East is no more than "a national obligation passed from one generation to another", as the publisher of *Chahagir* bi-weekly in Cairo (est. 1948) lamented.[46]

The Turkish-Armenian weekly newspaper *Agos*, founded by Hrant Dink and a group of intellectuals in Istanbul in 1996, is an exception to the aforementioned trends in publishing. With a readership in the thousands, *Agos* not only caters to the new generation of Armenians in Turkey who no

---

[43] Tchilingirian, "Crisis Without Borders", 1999.

[44] Tchilingirian (ed.), *Armenian Diaspora Public Opinion (1)*, p. 55.

[45] Varoujan Tenbelian, "Hay Dbakir Mamulin Daknabe" (The crisis of the Armenian print media), *Darperag21.net*, 6 June 2021. Available at: https://darperag21.net/հայ-տպագիր-մամուլին-տագնապը.

[46] Hratch Tchilingirian, "Crisis Without Borders. The Media in the Middle East", *Armenian International Magazine*, vol. 10, no. 7, July 1999, p. 37.

longer read Armenian but also attempts to shift the focus of the public discourse on Armenians and minorities from 'narrow' parochial issues to the larger issue of democratisation in Turkey. This arduous process saw its outspoken chief editor, Hrant Dink, dragged into Turkish courts and a vicious nationalist backlash. Dink was assassinated in January 2007.[47] Commentators and intellectuals contributing to *Agos* see themselves as agents of democracy and freedom in Turkey. Indeed, *Agos* is viewed in Turkey as a "newspaper promoting democracy, instead of just an Armenian newspaper ... 70-80 per cent of the paper [at kiosks] is bought by Muslim Turks".[48] Yet, given the internal complexities and multi-layered ideological and social stratifications in Turkey, it remains to be seen whether the herculean task of carrying out a Democratic Project in Turkey by members of a non-Muslim community will bear fruits in the long run, especially to ease the pressures on the collective life of the minorities.

In sum, as discussed in this section, the institutions that are critical to the preservation of Armenian identity, transmission of culture and cultural production –or in sociological parlance, the *plausibility structures* that provide belief and meanings to a group or individual– have steadily declined in the Middle East over the decades, more rapidly since the 2000s.

External Problems

The internal institutional changes and challenges discussed above take place against the larger background of external problems or *imposed realities*, as I call them. The periodic but persistent interstate and regional crises, long unresolved conflicts, ongoing wars and security operations, but most importantly, dire economic difficulties raise serious questions about the long-term viability and continuity of the Armenian communities in the Middle East.

The Middle East has witnessed numerous wars, political conflicts, inter- and intra-state devastating rivalries, and socio-political transformations in the last century. With the end of the Ottoman Empire in the early 20th century, the region was divided into French and British spheres of influence in the 1020s-1940s. Subsequent decades saw revolutions –Egypt 1952 and Lebanon 1958– and numerous coup d'états –Iran 1953, Syria 1963, Iraq 1964, 1968, and Turkey 1960, 1971, 1974, 1980, 1997. In more recent decades, the Civil War in Lebanon (1975-1990), the Islamic Revolution in

---

[47] See Hratch Tchilingirian, "Hrant Dink and Armenians in Turkey", The Open Democracy Quarterly, vol. 1, no. 2, 2007, pp. 117-124.

[48] David Barsamian, "An interview with Etyen Mahcupyan", Armenian Weekly On-line; vol. 73, no. 28, 14 July 2007.

Iran (1979), the wars in Iraq (1991, 2003), the failed popular uprisings against authoritarian or corrupt regimes (Egypt and Syria 2011, Lebanon 2019), and the brutal Islamic State in 2014 have had lasting and consequential impact on especially non-Muslim minorities in the Middle East.

Years of insecurity and continuing military and political conflicts in Iraq, Syria and Lebanon have caused major, perhaps irreversible, shifts in the Armenian communities in the entire region. Since the first decade of the 2000s alone, tens of thousands of Armenians have moved from one country to another in the Middle East, and many thousands have migrated to safer places outside the region. While the consequences of regional conflicts have affected all societies in the Middle East in general, the effects and impact on small non-Muslim communities have been more devastating, as the pool of their material and human resources are extremely limited. But the most crucial long-term problem that concerns these communities is the declining economic conditions. Economically, non-Muslim minorities were relatively successful as middle-class communities in their respective countries. Armenians have been active, for instance, in trade, manufacturing and craftsmanship. However, the downward economic spiral and the political, as well as security developments in the last few decades have resulted in increased unemployment, financial decline and loss of socio-economic status.

Socio-Economic factors

The Armenians who settled in the Arab Middle East after World War I, brought with them, as Hovanissian writes, "native skill[s] that had been refined through centuries of adversity" in the homeland. "Craftsmen and merchants pressed into the hearts of the bazaars and markets" and in certain places, such as Lebanon and Syria, created their own shopping districts.[49] In the 1950s-1960s the climb on the socio-economic ladder continued with well-educated and professionally trained second and third-generation Armenians. By the 1970s, the Armenians in the Middle East were predominantly middle class.

However, the disruption of labour markets in the last two decades of the 20th century, as a result of ongoing internal and regional conflicts, especially in Lebanon, Iraq, Israel/Palestine and Syria, has damaged the position of the middle classes particularly in these countries.[50] Traditional roles in industry have undergone changes, for instance the once Armenian dominated production of shoes in Lebanon "is in decline and increasingly taken over

---

[49] Hovannisian, "The Ebb and Flow", p. 20.

[50] Migliorino, 2008, pp. 198-199.

by Shi'a entrepreneurs".[51] In the past, Armenians also played a significant role in Lebanon's economy. Arthur Nazarian, a former cabinet minister and Member of Parliament in Lebanon, observed that before the civil war in the mid-1970s, "most of the factories in Lebanon used to be owned by Armenians, but that has changed since the war".[52] Hundreds of Armenian businessmen have emigrated or lost their assets in Lebanon since the mid-1970s. Indeed, in a 2019 survey, almost 6 in 10 Lebanese Armenians said it is "very likely/likely" that they would move "out of Lebanon in the coming 5 years".[53] Another example is Jerusalem, where "high rates of unemployment, particularly among the youth, and difficulty in securing adequate housing have all but emptied the city of its Christian community".[54] Likewise, tens of thousands of Armenians in war-torn Syria and Iraq have escaped to or migrated to the Republic of Armenia and other welcoming countries, such as Canada and Scandinavian countries. The economic decline and gradual loss of influence of the middle class has encouraged migration and weakened the overall presence of the Armenians in the Middle East. Indeed, the future remains uncertain, especially as the communities have to contend with the continuing brain drain and scarcity of financial resources caused by emigration.

The increasing migration over the last few decades has also had an impact on finding potential life-partners within the community. It has increased the rate of mixed-marriages, which is another contentious issue in the Middle East. In Lebanon, nearly half of the Armenian respondents in the same survey, considered mixed-marriages as one of the "biggest challenges to the strength of [the] Armenian community".[55] One school teacher in Lebanon notes, based on her experience, that this has also contributed to the decline of the number of speakers of the Armenian language.[56]

Islamic Militancy & State Policies

Catholicos Aram, the highest ranking Armenian religious leader in the Middle East, has spoken bluntly about the situation in the last few decades:

---

[51] Ibid., pp. 198-199.

[52] Hratch Tchilingirian, "Integration: The Point of No Return", *Armenian International Magazine*, vol. 10, no. 12, December 1999, pp. 46-48. In the early 1970s, as noted by Hovanissian "fully a fourth of the world-renowned gold bazaar of Beirut [was] Armenian-owned". Hovanissian, "The Ebb and Flow", p.30.

[53] Hratch Tchilingirian (ed.), *Armenian Diaspora Public Opinion (1)*. p. 142.

[54] Catholic Near East Welfare Association (CNEWA), One, September 2010, p. 27. Available at: http://www.cnewa.org/default.aspx?ID=201&pagetypeID=3&sitecode =HQ&pageno=1. The number of Christians in Palestine/Israel has gone down drastically: "from more than 10% of the Arab population in the first decades of the twentieth century to approximately 2.6%" in 2011; see Robson, Laura, 'Recent Perspectives on Christianity in the Modern Arab World", *History Compass*, vol. 9, no. 4. 2011, p. 313.

[55] Tchilingirian (ed.), *Armenian Diaspora Public Opinion (1)*, p. 87.

[56] Personal correspondence on 14 December 2022.

"Christianity presents a picture of small islands scattered in the huge ocean of Islam".[57] In recent years, senior clergymen and lay leaders in the Armenian community, as well as in other Christian communities, are gravely concerned about growing religious fundamentalism in the Middle East –especially since the rise of ISIS– and its effects on their personal and collective lives. Most leaders exercise care in their public statements, but privately are vocal, expressing hopelessness about future prospects. Targeted violence against Christians in Iraq, Egypt and Syria in the 2010s are but a few of the visible examples of such tensions.[58] A bomb explosion in front of the Armenian Catholic Diocese and Church in Baghdad, on 1 August 2004, wounded tens of Sunday worshippers, burned down part of the diocesan headquarters and caused major damage to the church building. In Turkey, random vandalism of Armenian churches, schools and cemeteries are common occurrences.[59]

While Islamic societies in the Middle East have been generally tolerant and respectful of their fellow Christians, the more vocal, religiously fervent segments of society tend to dominate the discourse on the non-Muslim communities in their midst. "Even if you have the majority who are moderate Muslims", said Egyptian lawyer Wagdi Halfa, "a minority of extremists can make a big impact on them and poison their minds".[60] Halfa made these remarks following an incident in the village of Sheik Fadl in southern Egypt, where a 15-year-old Christian schoolgirl was instructed to put on a headscarf or leave the school.[61] Coptic Christians in Egypt continue to be the target of deadly attacks and violence. The marginalisation of Christian communities in Arab societies and in Turkey has taken place gradually over the last five decades. A 2010 report prepared by the Cambridge Arab Media Project provides the wider context:

---

[57] Keshishian, *The Christian Witness*, p. 24; written when he was the Prelate of Armenian Church Diocese of Lebanon during the most intense period of the Lebanese civil war.

[58] See Steven Lee Myers, "More Christians Flee Iraq After New Violence", *The New York Times*, 12 December 2010 and Steven Lee Myers, "Al-Azhar condemns violence against Christians", Asia News, 3 March 2010; also, BBC News, "Syria crisis: Fierce battle in Christian town Maaloula", 11 September 2013 and Armenpress, "Aleppo's New Village Armenian neighbourhood is declared disaster zone", 5 June 2014.

[59] See, for example, *BirGün*, "Koronavirüsü bunlar bela etti' diyerek kiliseyi yakmaya çalıştı", 9 May 2022. Available at: https://www.birgun.net/haber/koronavirusu-bunlar-bela-etti-diyerek-kiliseyi-yakmaya-calisti-300256); *BIA News Desk*, "Istanbul Armenian Church Walls Vandalized", 25 February 2019. Available at: https://m.bianet.org/english/minorities/205815-istanbul-armenian-church-walls-vandalized; *Diken*, "Irkçılar 'iş başında': Ermeni lisesinin duvarına 'Azap Ermeni'ye yazdılar", 13 August 2016. Available at: https://www.diken.com.tr/irkcilar-basinda-ermeni-lisesinin-duvarina-azap-ermeniye-yazdilar/; *Cumhuriyet*, "Tarihi kilisede mangal partisi", 14 January 2021. Available at: https://www.cumhuriyet.com.tr/haber/tarihi-kilisede-mangal-partisi-1806020

[60] Maggie Michael, "Christians fear Islamist pressure in Egypt", Daily News Egypt, 9 October 2011. Available at: https://dailynewsegypt.com/2011/10/09/christians-fear-islamist-pressure-in-egypt/.

[61] Ibid.

Following independence from foreign occupation in the 1950s and 1960s in Arab countries, Christians had played a noticeable role in public life as politicians, senior public bureaucrats, intellectuals and professionals. Fifty years later, the situation had changed. As large numbers of Christians had migrated to the West, fewer remained to assume top positions in the state apparatuses. Islamic movements sweeping Arab countries had posed further challenges to them, especially concerning identity and citizenship rights. The use of Islamic terminology in media, social interactions, the public sphere, and political life in general had contributed to a sense of alienation among Christian communities.[62]

Christians in general and the Armenians in particular see the threats posed by certain groups in society towards non-Muslims, however marginal they may be, as a cause of significant concern and a serious factor endangering the long-term viability of their communities in the Middle East.

While it remains to be seen as to how the socio-political landscape in the Middle East will transition, in a 2019 study examining Muslim religiosity and democracy, scholars note that "uncertainty regarding Islam and attitudes toward democracy remains". They suggest,

> while we would expect that Muslim states made up of more pluralistic groupings may be more likely to produce or sustain democracy, such a result may depend on beliefs regarding the ability of democracy to produce religious public goods relative to its most likely political competitor.[63]

Even as in the last decade changes are taking place in the region, a five-country survey conducted between 2003 and 2006 by the Arab Barometer found that "56 per cent of respondents agreed that 'men of religion' should have influence over government decisions".[64] Another survey, which was held in 2003 and 2004, found that "half or more of four Arab publics" agreed that nothing but *Shari'a* law should be implemented by the government.[65] Indeed, after cross-tabulating "support for democracy" and "support for some kind of Islamic form of government", the "generic pattern" that

---

[62] "Christian Broadcasting in Arab Countries", Section 11, in *Religious Broadcasting in the Middle East Conference. Islamic, Christian and Jewish Channels: Programmes and Discourse*, University of Cambridge, April 2010, p. 58. Available at: http://www.cis.cam.ac.uk/wp-content/uploads/2016/01/Religious-Broadcasting-in-the-Middle-East.pdf.

[63] Sabri Ciftci, F. Michael Wuthrich and Ammar Shamaileh, "Islam, Religious Outlooks, and Support for Democracy", *Political Research Quarterly*, vol. 72, no, 2, 2019, p. 447.

[64] Larry Diamond, "Why are there no Arab democracies?", *Journal of Democracy*, vol. 21, no. 1, January 2010, p. 96.

[65] Ibid.

emerges from the study shows that "40 to 45 per cent of each public supports secular democracy while roughly the same proportion backs an Islamic form of democracy; meanwhile 5 to 10 per cent of the public supports secular authoritarianism and the same proportion supports Islamic authoritarianism".[66]

Compounding this socio-religious tension is the role of the state, along with its legal and political relationship with Christians and minorities in general. Virtually all the Arab states in the Middle East have constitutions where the principal source of law is *Shar'ia* law. Discrimination against religious or ethnic groups or minorities is built into these constitutions. As Rev. Robert Stern, the former president of Catholic Near East Welfare Association (CNEWA), has observed: "In almost all the countries of the Middle East where native or guest worker Christians exist, they are generally treated as second-class and are subjected to various forms of explicit or implicit discrimination".[67] Moreover, the existence of centralised, authoritarian regimes in the Middle East imposes restrictions on communal activities and autonomy and cultural diversity within the Armenian communities. Even the confessional arrangement that regulates public and political life in Lebanon, an exception in the Arab world, has enormous limitations and consequences.

With the exception of Lebanon and Syria, there are virtually no opportunities for political or civil appointments in high level state administration positions because of ethnic and religious origin.[68] Indeed, the treatment of Christian minorities in the Middle East, rather than promoting "integration" reinforces the idea of difference and "otherness", whereby members of minority groups lead a parallel ethnic or religious life in their respective societies. In this regard, the Armenian community in Turkey have to juggle constantly their national and state loyalties. As the former Patriarch explained, "Every Armenian in Turkey grows up with three elements in his personality: being a Turkish citizen, then his heritage as an Armenian, and then his faith as a Christian in a country which is overwhelmingly –99 per cent– Muslim".[69] In the United Arab Emirates, there are legal, social and cultural reasons for being in a constant state of "transition". By law, a

---

[66] Ibid.

[67] Robert L., "Perspectives: Caught in the Middle", *One* (CNEWA), September 2010. Available at: http://www.cnewa.org/default.aspx?ID=3495&pagetypeID=4&sitecode=HQ&pageno=1.

[68] Per the provisions of the 1989 Taif Accord, six of the Lebanese Parliament's 128 seats are reserved for Armenians, who represent about 9 percent of Lebanon's population; see Michael. Bluhm, "Outcome of Metn Polls May Hinge on Armenians", *The Daily Star*, 7 March 2009.

[69] Hratch Tchilingirian, "The People's Choice. Archbishop Mesrob Mutafyan Elected 84th Armenian Patriarchate of Turkey", *Armenian International Magazine*, vol. 9, no. 12, December 1998

foreigner cannot become a citizen of UAE. One Abu Dhabi Armenian explained the overriding uncertainty for Christians: "Whenever the government tells you to leave the country, you have to leave. The only thing that keeps people here is their jobs and businesses. If you lose your job, you have to leave the country, unless you find a new contract".[70] CNEWA reported that in Egypt discrimination against Christians is commonplace, especially in education and employment:

> The government places restrictions on the construction or repair of churches –restrictions that do not apply to mosques. A permit from the regional governor is required before a church may be renovated. Permits to build a church require Presidential approval, which often takes as long as ten years to obtain. Even with this go-ahead, security forces must investigate whether neighbouring Muslim communities object to the construction. If they do, the church may not be built.[71]

Concerned church leaders in Israel have pointed out to restrictions imposed by the Government, such as difficulties or denial of permits for the erection of housing, job creation programs and protection of the rights of Christians in the Holy Land. In 2018, the three Patriarchates (Greek, Armenian, Latin), who are the custodians of the Holy Places, took the dramatic step of closing the Holy Sepulchre church, one of Christianity's holiest sites, in protest against a new tax and a proposed Israeli legislation that would allow the government to confiscate land sold by the churches.[72] Similar draconian restrictions exist in Turkey, on renovation and construction of churches, and a host of administrative aspects of church community life.

Indeed, it seems that the biggest test of the tectonic changes sweeping the Middle East will be the treatment of minorities –whether confessional, religious or ethnic– and changes to their status. States and societies in the region have not dealt with the grievances and legitimate demands of minorities in any meaningful or effective way. The late Patriarch of the Coptic Orthodox Church, Pope Shenouda III was outspoken on such matters. Following a bomb attack on a church that killed 25 Copts in January 2011, he reiterated that "the Egyptian government has 'to start addressing Copts' problems', which he believe[d] lay at "the core of the religious

---

[70] Hratch Tchilingirian, "Instilling the Armenian Spirit. Armenian Education in a Transient Community", *Armenian International Magazine*, vol. 10, no. 7, July 1999, pp. 53-54.

[71] *One* (CNEWA), September 2010, p 11. Available at:

http://www.cnewa.org/default.aspx?ID=3484&pagetypeID=4&sitecode=HQ&pageno=4.

[72] Oliver Holmes, "Jerusalem's Holy Sepulchre church closed in tax protest", *The Guardian*, 25 February 2018. See also Ibid, p. 27.

animosities" in the country.[73]

Security, military conflicts and ISIS

Security concerns and on-going military conflicts in Syria, Iraq, Lebanon and Israel/Palestine –not to mention the Iran-Iraq war in the 1980s and the first Gulf War in the early 1990s– have also had significant implications and consequences for the Armenian communities in the Middle East. Thousands of Armenians, along with the citizens of Lebanon, Iraq and Iran, have been killed in the conflicts. A particularly poignant, but by no means isolated case, was the loss of more than 130 Armenian soldiers in the Iraqi army, hailing from the town of Zakho who died in the Iran-Iraq war. This was a significant number of men for a small community.[74] Hundreds of Armenian soldiers who had been conscripted into the Iranian army died on the other side of the border. As in the 1970s and 1980s, these conflicts caused a major exodus of long-established communities. In recent years, Christian communities have seen a slow wave of migration to the West with the consequence that, "generally, the churches historically rooted in the Middle East now have more of their faithful living in the Americas, Western Europe and Australia than in their homelands".[75]

The centuries-old Armenian community and the Patriarchate in the Holy Land face enormous challenges. Armenian interests in Jerusalem are not only religious, since the Patriarchate has vast assets and properties throughout the Holy Land. The 28-acre Armenian quarter in Jerusalem represents one-sixth of the Old City. The final status of Jerusalem, one of the most protracted and complex issue in the Middle East for more than 70 years, are very important and relevant to the Armenian community in Israel/Palestine. Additionally, the economic and political effects of the first and second Intifada and the still unresolved Israeli-Palestinian conflict have caused further migration and hardship within the Armenian community.[76]

By far, the biggest existential threat comes from jihadist groups. In June 2014, when the extremist Islamic State of Iraq and al-Sham (ISIS) –renamed Islamic State– entered Mosul, they rampaged, looted and burned government buildings, as well as churches and monasteries. The Armenian Church of Holy Etchmiadzin –which was bombed by terrorists in 2005 and was still under repairs– was bombed and burned, along with other Christian

---

[73] Amro Hassan, "Egyptian Christians' Christmas celebration clouded by New Year's Day bomb attack", *Los Angeles Times*, 7 January 2011, p. A3.

[74] Robert Fisk, *The Great War for Civilisation. The Conquest of the Middle East*, rev. edition, London & New York: Harper Perennial, 2006, p. 842.

[75] Stern, "Perspective", p. 41.

[76] Tchilingirian, "Dividing Jerusalem".

churches.[77] Virtually all communities (except Sunnis) from the Province of Nineve were expelled or had to flee to save their lives, including 250,000 Assyrian, Chaldean, Syriac, and Armenian Christians, 200,000 Yazidis, as well as Mandaeans, Shabaks and Turkomen.

The roots of the Armenians in Mosul, the oldest Armenian community in Iraq, go back to at least the 14th century.[78] In 2003, the community was made of 380 families, but by July 2014 no Armenians were left. Along with the other Christians of the region, the Armenians had escaped to various places in the Kurdish north, including Erbil, Dehok City and Zakho.[79] "It is through unspeakable suffering that we were able to come out of the cycle of death and annihilation", said Fr. Arakel Kasparian, the parish priest of Mosul, who had led some 65 remaining families of his congregation to Erbil. "The ruling mad people of ISIS are killing, beheading innocent Christians, Armenians, who refuse to obey their orders; [they are] exploding historical holy places", the pastor said about the horrors they witnessed.[80]

The conflict in Syria, which started as a protest movement in March 2011, turned into a sectarian war among government forces, insurgents and extremist groups. Hundreds of thousands of people have been killed and millions of Syrians have fled the country. A US State Department report had warned that "in Syria, as in much of the Middle East, the Christian presence is becoming a shadow of its former self".[81] Hundreds of thousands have fled the ongoing violence and daily threats to life. The Christian community in Homs, for instance, numbered about 160,000 before the conflict, but has been reduced to less than 1,000 Christians in the city, which had a population of 650,000 in 2004.

Armenian Churches were vandalised, trashed or burnt in Aleppo, Deir ez-Zour, Raqqa and Kessab (Kasab). The Genocide memorial Church in Deir ez-Zour (Der Zor), where tens of thousands of Armenians marched to

---

[77] "ISIS Expands Control, Begins Persecuting Christians in Mosul", *AINA News* (Assyrian International News Agency), 12 June 2014. Available at: http://www.aina.org/news/20140612011342.htm.

[78] A manuscript (homelitics) scribed in Mosul in 1352 by a priest Manuel is preserved in the library of the Mother See of Holy Ejmiatsin in Armenia. It attests to the existence of not only an Armenian community in Mosul, but a vibrant church and religious activity. See Vehuni Minasian, "Hayereh Musuli Mech" (Armenians in Mosul), *Aztag Daily* (Beirut), 28 July 2014. Available at: http://www.aztagdaily.com/archives/196613 .

[79] Sako Aroyan, "Musuli Hayutyan Daknabeh" (The Crisis of Armenians in Mosul), *Ararad Daily* (Beirut) 26 July 2014, p. 2.

[80] Hamo Moskofian, "Angitanank Irakahayeri Agherseh" (Should we ignore the plea of Armenians in Iraq?), *Norkhosq.net*, 3 August 2014. Available at: http://www.keghart.com/Moskofian-Mosul-Ankawa-Erbil.

[81] United States State Department, Bureau of Democracy, Human Rights and Labour, "International Religious Freedom Report for 2013". Available at: http://www.state.gov/j/drl/rls/irf/religious freedom/index.htm#wrapper.

their death during WWI, was heavily damaged.[82] Community schools, cultural and social centres have seen their share of destruction and damage. Like members of other minority communities, more than one hundred Armenians have been kidnapped in Syria and thousands have fled. In March 2014, the Armenian town of Kessab was overrun by jihadists, causing death, destruction and displacement of some 2,500 Armenians, many of who found shelter in the Armenian Church in the nearby city of Latakia. Most of the blame was placed on Turkey for allowing the jihadists to attack Kessab, which is situated near the Syrian-Turkish border. According to reports, "Turks winked as Reyhanli [town near the Syrian border] and other Turkish towns became way stations for moving foreign fighters and arms across the border".[83] For Kessab Armenians, the "Turkish hand" in the takeover of their town by jihadists was a reminder of the Genocide and continued Turkish hostility towards the Armenians. "All of us perfectly remember the history of Kessab, which was unfortunately full of hellish realities of deportations in the last 100 years", said the President of the Republic of Armenia at the time.[84] Kessab was recaptured by the Syrian military in June and many Armenians returned to their homes.

The genocidal brutality of jihadists against their scores of "enemies" have posed direct existential threat to millions of people. Fawaz Gerges explains that unlike the borderless, transnational al Qaeda movement of Osama bin Laden, "which has never been able to find a social base", the Islamic State and similar groups like the Jabhat (Front) al-Nusra in Syria are "like a social epidemic, feeding on sectarian tensions and the social and ideological faultlines in Arab societies". Indeed, "the phenomenon of the Islamic State", Gerges suggests, "is a manifestation of the weakening and dismantling of the Arab state as we know it".[85] The imposition of strict Sunni Islamic law in towns, villages and territories captured by ISIS and other groups, such as the al-Qaeda-affiliated al-Nusra in Syria, pose serious existential danger to

---

[82] Beyond the physical church building, the Primate of the Diocese of Damascus, Bishop Armash Nalbandian, was concerned about the "destruction of the memory" of the Armenian Genocide from these lands that had been the "open graveyard" of thousands of Armenians; see Robert Fisk, "Nearly a century after the Armenian genocide, these people are still being slaughtered in Syria", *The Independent*, 1 December 2013. Available at: http://www.independent.co.uk/voices/comment/nearly-a-century-after-the-armenian-genocide-these-people-are-still-being-slaughtered-in-syria-8975976.html.

[83] Anthony Faiola and Souad Mekhennet, "In Turkey, a late crackdown on Islamist fighters", *The Washington Post*, 12 August 2014. Available at: http://www.washingtonpost.com/world/how-turkey-became-the-shopping-mall-for-the-islamic-state/2014/08/12/5eff70bf-a38a-4334-9aa9-ae3fc1714c4b_story.html.

[84] *Panorama*, "Serzh Sargsyan makes press statement on Kessab in The Hague", 25 March 2014. Available at: http://www.panorama.am/en/politics/2014/03/25/president-kessab-statement.

[85] Samia Makhoul, "Islamic State carves jihadist hub in heart of Middle East", *Reuters*, 12 August 2014. Available at: http://www.reuters.com/article/2014/08/12/us-iraq-security-mideast-insight-idUSKBN0GC1FB20140812.

Christians in particular and non-Sunni communities in general. Such drastic changes have resulted in ongoing religious persecution, ethnic cleansing, population transfers and genocide in the fullest definition of the term.[86]

The larger context of Muslim-Christian Relations

The future of Armenians and other Christian communities in the Middle East looks bleak in the larger context of the developments since early 2000 in the region and in the extremely challenging prospects of the coming years. The expectation that the "Arab Spring" would usher the "remaking" of the Middle East, has turned into "a dark winter for most Arabs", as Peter Schwartz puts it, and a "large-scale slaughter", especially in Syria and Iraq.[87] The growing anti-Shi'a Sunni extremism, on one hand, and Shi'a groups, such as the Lebanese Hezbollah movement's anti-Takfiri political and military discourse,[88] on the other, add to the long-term concerns.

Open discrimination and growing intolerance of Christians in Islamist-dominated parts of the Middle East are serious future risks. The socio-political danger and existential threat come from multiple sources. A few examples would suffice to draw attention to such socio-political and systemic problems. Even as the Grand Mufti of Saudi Arabia, Sheikh Abdul Aziz bin Abdullah, condemned the Islamic State and al-Qaeda militants as "enemy number one of Islam" and "not in any way part of the faith",[89] in August 2014, some two years earlier this highest religious law official in Saudi Arabia and the head of the Supreme Council of Islamic Scholars said that "all churches in the Arabian Peninsula must be destroyed".[90] Speaking in

---

[86] See, for instance, Jean Aziz, "Syria's Christians Threatened by Ideology, Geography", *Al Monitor*, 23 April 2013. Available at: http://www.al-monitor.com/pulse/originals/2013/04/syria-christians-threatened-ideology-geography.html.

[87] *The Independent*, "Peter Schwartz responds to Brian Eno's open letter on Israel-Gaza crisis", /l August 2014. Available at: http://www.independent.co.uk/voices/comment/peter-schwartz-responds-to-brian-enos-open-letter-on-israelgaza-crisis-9643922.html).

[88] The term *takfiri*, from *kafir* (unbeliever/infidel), is used in this context to denote Muslims (Sunnis) who accuse other Muslims (the Shia) of apostasy and are subject to excommunication. The Sunni-Shi'a tension is exemplified by counter accusations and condemnations among, especially, religious leaders. For instance, in June 2013, the Qatar-based prominent Egyptian Islamic scholar, Sheikh Yusuf al-Qaradawi, condemned Hezbollah's role in Syria since 2011 in support of the Assad regime. This was in sharp contrast to al-Qaradawi's praise of Hezbollah's resistance of Israeli incursion into Lebanon in July 2006 and the month-long Hezbollah-Israel war. Andrew McGregor, "Muslim Brothers' Spiritual Leader Yusuf Al-Qaradawi Condemns Hezbollah", *Terrorism Monitor* (The Jamestown Foundation), vol. 11, no. 12, 2014. Available at: http://www.jamestown.org/regions/middleeast/single/?tx_ttnews%5Btt_news %5D=41020&tx_ttnews%5BbackPid%5D=676&cHash=11a70be15173e5c55c1a6cc5daf3a9b4#.U_8zAvl dWSr.

[89] "'ISIS is enemy No. 1 of Islam,' says Saudi grand mufti", *Al Arabiya News*, 19 August 2014. Available at: http://english.alarabiya.net/en/News/middle-east/2014/08/19/Saudi-mufti-ISIS-is-enemy-No-1-of-Islam-.html.

[90] *Russia Today* (RT), "Destroy all churches in the Arabian Peninsula – Saudi Grand Mufti", 16 March 2014. Available at: http://rt.com/news/peninsula-saudi-grand-mufti-701/; also posted with comments on *The Muslim Times*, 16 March 2012. See also http://www.themuslimtimes.org/2012/03/countries/

March 2012, the Grand Mufti cited a story that at his deathbed Prophet Mohammed had declared: "There are not to be two religions in the [Arabian] Peninsula".[91] He was asked at a conference by a Kuwaiti NGO, called the Society of the Revival of Islamic Heritage, to clarify what Islamic law says about an MP's recent proposal to Parliament calling on "a ban on the construction of new churches" in Kuwait.[92] Christians as far as in Egypt, Lebanon, Jordan and other parts of the Middle East were deeply concerned with the gravity of such statements. Another example is the new Constitution of Iraq, where Christians have a quota of 5 seats in the 325-member Parliament, but have virtually no political influence. Similarly, in the 290-member Iranian Parliament, the *Majlis*, five seats are reserved for recognised religious minorities: Armenians (2), Assyrians (1), Jews (1), Zoroastrians (1). Nevertheless, discrimination and various forms of repression take place even in states where Christian minorities are ostensibly "protected" by the constitution, such as in Iran and Turkey.[93] In the *2011 Annual Report*, the United States Commission on International Religious Freedom notes that Iraq's smallest religious minorities, including Christians, Yazidis and Sabean Mandeans (followers of John the Baptist),

> suffer from targeted violence, threats, and intimidation, against which the government does not provide effective protection. Perpetrators are rarely identified, investigated, or punished, creating a climate of impunity. The smallest minorities also experience a pattern of official discrimination, marginalisation, and neglect, particularly in areas of northern Iraq over which the Iraqi government and the Kurdistan Regional Government (KRG) dispute control.[94]

Hundreds of Christians had fled to northern Iraq amid increasing acts of violence against Christians, especially following the siege of Our Lady of Salvation Church in Baghdad that killed 51 worshippers and two priests in October 2010. ISIS (called the Islamic State of Iraq at the time) claimed responsibility for the siege and vowed that they would kill Christians "wherever they can reach them". This existential threat has resulted in disproportionate emigration of Christians from Iraq. The United Nations

---

saudi-arabia/destroy-all-churches-in-the-arabian-peninsula-saudi-grand-mufti-not-islam.

[91] Ibid.

[92] Ibid.

[93] Cf. *Annual Report of the United States Commission on International Religious Freedom,* May 2011, pp. 11, 29, 30, 79, 317. Available at: http://www.uscirf.gov/sites/default/files/resources/book%20with%20cover %20for%20web.pdf.

[94] Ibid, p. 88. Available at: http://www.uscirf.gov/sites/default/files/resources/book%20with%20 cover%20for%20web.pdf.

High Commissioner for Refugees reported that Christians and other targeted minorities "account for 20 per cent of the Iraqis who have gone abroad, while they were only 3 per cent of the country's prewar population".[95] The number of Christians in Iraq was estimated at 800,000-1.4 million before 2003, however, ten years later only a few hundred thousand are left in the country.[96]

Commenting on the fate of the Christians in Mosul and referring to centuries of Christian-Muslim relations, Lebanon's Minister of Labour and a member of the Christian Kataeb Party, Sejaan Azzi, was blunt: "We are not embarrassed to raise [our] voice and publicly say: We have tried all forms of common life, common state, region and village; what have we gained from all these experiences since 1400 years [when Islam was established]?". The Minister was expressing the view increasingly shared by other Christian leaders when he said: "What they couldn't get in the era of conquests, they are trying to get it in the era of revolutions".[97]

Conclusion

In the aftermath of WWI and the genocide in the Ottoman Empire, the surviving Armenians succeeded in rebuilding communities, churches, schools, cultural infrastructure and institutions largely in Syria, Lebanon, Egypt, Iraq and other smaller communities in the Middle East. This was possible due to the fact that the mandated Arab states had granted them certain religious and civil rights similar to the *millet* system in the Ottoman Empire and the determination of the survivors and their generations to reconstruct the lost Armenian communal life in dispersed countries. For more than a century, the Armenians have invested billions of dollars in money, labour and community efforts to establish and perpetuate their culture, language, and traditions in the Middle East.

Starting in the 1970s, waves of Armenians in the Middle East have migrated –mostly to North America, Europe and Australia– largely due to the Civil War in Lebanon, the Islamic Revolution in Iran, the wars in Iraq

---

[95] Myers, "More Christians Flee Iraq". Indeed, the displacement and exodus of Christians have been ongoing and increasing after regular violent incidents targeting non-Moslem communities. Some 12,000 Christians left, for instance, when 14 Christians were killed in October 2008. In February 2010, another targeted killing of 10 Christians resulted in over 4,000 Christians fleeing to the Kurdish-controlled north of the country or to Syria.

[96] *Annual Report of the United States Commission*, p. 89.

[97] *The Daily Star*, "Syriac Orthodox bishop: Muslims enemies of Christ", 20 July 2014. Available at: http://www.dailystar.com.lb/News/Lebanon-News/2014/Jul-30/265488-syriac-orthodox-bishop-muslims-enemies-of-christ.ashx?utm_source=Magnet&utm_medium=Recommended%20Articles%20widget&utm_campaign=Magnet%20tools#axzz3BhQczXJV.

and the continuing economic hardships. If the trend of exodus continues, it could mean the socio-cultural demise of one of the most ancient Christian communities in the region.

Less visible are the roles of the state, society, and the religious establishment in the long-term viable presence of Armenian and generally Christian communities in the Middle East. The burden of being the "other" –a member of a minority Christian group in the Middle East– is heavy. The "othering" plays out on different levels: (a) there is what I would call "soft othering" by the *state*, vis a vis laws, restrictions and in many cases, discrimination against non-Muslim groups; (b) by the social boundaries intentionally or unintentionally set by the larger *society* in Muslim-majority countries in the Middle East; and (c) the "hard othering" by the *Islamist* segments in society that portrays non-Muslims as "infidels", thus by definition second-class citizens.

Fifty years ago, historian Richard Hovannisian observed that the Armenians and other non-Muslim communities in the Middle East "are confronted with factors so adverse that their future may at best be regarded as precarious".[98] Today, the situation is not only precarious but also extremely critical. The realities currently facing the Armenians in the Middle East, and Christians in general, paint an uncertain future –as the ongoing conflicts could continue for many years to come. As the subtitle of this chapter notes, what is at stake is the loss in the future of a rich religious and cultural heritage rooted in the past –in the Middle East.

---

[98] Hovannisian, "The Ebb and Flow", p. 32.

Table 1. Estimates of Armenian Population in the Middle East*

	1975[1]	% of total Christian population	1985[2]	2003[3]	2008[4]	2014[5]	2020[5]
Iran	200,000	87.5	202,000	80,000	75,000	70,000	55,000
Lebanon	175,000	17.5	176,000	75,000	70,000	65,000	50,000
Syria	150,000	26.8	136,500	70,000	70,000	55,000	35,000
Turkey	60,000	43.0	89,000	80,000	75,000	65,000	50,000
Egypt	10,000	0.5	12,000	6,000	6,000	6,000	4,000
Iraq	20,000	3.4	16,000	10,000	8,000[6]	7,000	5,000
Israel & Palestine	2,500	3.5	5,000	3,000	1,500	1,500	1,500
Kuwait	2,000	76.0	3,000	5,000	4,000	4,000	3,000
Jordan	2,000	1.9	4,000	3,000	4,000	4,000	3,000
UAE	1,000		1,500	2,000	5,000	5,000	5,000
TOTAL	**622,500**		**645,000**	**334,000**	**318,500**	**282,000**	**211,500**

* Precise numbers of Armenians in the Middle East –and in the Diaspora for that matter– are virtually non-existent as there are no official census figures nor methodologically accurate statistics. The figures presented here are based on estimates given by various church representatives and publications over the last few decades.

1. Figures provided by the Prelate of Lebanon; Archbishop Aram Keshishian (now Catholicos of Cilicia) based on various estimates (see Keshishian 1981). Other sources provide different estimates; Courbage and Philippe put Armenian Orthodox and Catholics in Syria at 136,000 and Lebanon at 214,000 in 1995. Youssef Courbage and Philippe Fargues, *Christians and Jews Under Islam*, London: I.B. Taurus, 1997, p. 209.

2. Except estimates for Egypt, Kuwait and UAE, the figures are from a special issue of *Al Montada* (*The Forum*), Middle East Council of Churches, No. 116-117, April-June 1985, p. 25.

3. As provided in entries for respective communities in the *Hay Spiurk: Hanragitaran* (*Armenian Diaspora Encyclopaedia*), Yerevan: Armenian Encyclopaedia Publication, 2003.

4. Estimates from news sources and per the figures provided by the Archbishops of the Armenian Churches in Iraq and Kuwait. Interviews 25 & 27 September 2008.

5. Estimates gathered from various church representatives and community members.

6. Does not include the number of Armenians who have fled Iraq in recent years, primarily to Jordan and Syria. In 2008, the Diocese of Iraq reported the number of the Armenian community at 17,000. *Nor Gyank* (Los Angeles) 6 August 2008.

Table 2. Armenian Schools in the Middle East [1]

COUNTRY	CITY	2010-2011 School Year		2021-2022[2] School Year	
		SCHOOLS	STUDENTS	SCHOOLS	STUDENTS
Lebanon	Beirut	23	6400[3]	13	4911[3]
	Tripoli	1		1	
	Anjar	3		2	
Syria	Aleppo	12	6393	7	1561[7]
	Kamishli	1	700	1	250[8]
	Kessab	2	350	2	200
	Damascus	3	490	3	150[9]
	Latakia	1	200	1	80
	Raqqa	3	300	n/a	
Turkey	Istanbul	16	2965	16	2828
Iran	Tehran	14	2800	14[4]	1600
	New Julfa	5	400[5]	1	200
	Shahinshaher	1	200[5]	n/a	
	Tabriz	1	100[5]	n/a	
Kuwait	Kuwait	1	400	1	320
Egypt	Cairo	2	250[6]	1	160
	Alexandria	1	35	n/a	
Iraq	Baghdad	1	220	1	33
Israel/Palestine	Jerusalem	1	110	1	176[10]
Jordan	Amman	1	88	(closed)	
		93	**22,401**	**65**	**12,539**

1. Sources: Hovsep Nalbandian, "Haygagan Amenorya Tbrotsneru Iravijageh Spuirki Daradzkin" [The Status of Armenian Day Schools in the Diaspora], Nor Haratch (Paris) 12 May 2011; interview with former Primate of dioceses of Isfahan and Kuwait, Archbishop Goriun Babyan, 30 September 2011; "Meeting with Primate of the Diocese of Iraq, Archbishop Avak Assadourian", *Nor Gyank*, 36 August 2008; Armenian Patriarchate of Jerusalem, Liturgical Calendar, 2011.

2. I am grateful to a number of people who checked or verified the numbers with local school contacts; many thanks to Varoujan Tenbelian and Ara Vassilian for the numbers in Lebanon; Setrag Hovsepian for Egypt, Iraq, Kuwait; Arusyak Monnet for Istanbul; Marie Matian for Iran; and Anush Nakkashian for Jerusalem. For Aleppo, see Manuel Keshishian, "Halebi Haygagan Varzharannere" (The Armenian Schools in Aleppo), *CivilNet*, 26 July 2022. Available at: www.civilnet.am/news/669250.

3. Total number in all of Lebanon.

4. Three are Kindergarten.

5. Estimates provided by former Primate of Isfahan, Archbishop Goriun Babyan, 30 September 2011.

6. Estimate.

7. Includes unspecified percent of non-Armenian students. For instance, in one Armenian school, there were four non-Armenian students among the 28 who succeeded in their Baccalaureate II examinations; in another school, 6 out of 9 successful Baccalaureates were non-Armenians, see op. cit. Keshishian, "Halebi" 2022.

8. Estimates for Kamishli, Kessab, Damascus, Latakia, Raqqa provided by Bishop Armash Nalbandian, Primate of the Diocese of Damascus. Personal communication on 23 December 2022.

9. Number of Armenian students among the 500 or so students in Armenian schools in Damascus.

10. Fifteen percent of the students are non-Armenian.

Bibliography

Abrahamian, Ashot K., *Hamarot Urvagits Hay Gaghtavayreri Batmutyan* [Brief Outline of the History of Armenian Colonies], vol. 2, Yerevan: Hayastan Publication, 1967.

Aram I, Catholicos, "The Armenian Church in the Middle East: Some Facts and Perspectives", in Seta Dadoyan (ed.) *The Contribution of the Armenian Church to the Christian Witness in the Middle East,* Antelias, Lebanon: Armenian Catholicosate of Cilicia, 2001.

Armenpress, "Aleppo's New Village Armenian Neighbourhood is Declared Disaster Zone', 5 June 2014. Available at: http://armenpress.am/eng/news/764601/aleppo%E2%80%99s-new-village-armenian-neighborhood-is-declared-disaster-zone.html.

Artinian, Roubina, "Armenian Choirs in Lebanon, 1930-1980. A Bridge Between the Past and the Present", in Aïda Boudjikanian (ed.), *Armenians of Lebanon: From Past Princesses and Refugees to Present-Day Community*, Beirut: Haigazian University; Belmont, MA: Armenian Heritage Press, 2009, pp. 133-151.

Azarya, Victor, *The Armenian Quarter of Jerusalem: Urban Life Behind Monastery Walls*, Berkeley; London: University of California Press, 1984.

Barsamian, David, "An Interview with Etyen Mahcupyan", *Armenian Weekly On-line*, vol. 73, no. 28, 14 July 2007.

BBC, "Syria crisis: Fierce battle in Christian town Maaloula", 11 September 2013. Available at: http://www.bbc.co.uk/news/world-middle-east-24057202.

Berberyan, Bercuhi, "I know that Suitcase!", Agos, 16 November 2007.

Bluhm, Michael, "Outcome of Metn Polls May Hinge on Armenians", *The Daily Star*, 7 March 2009.

Boudjikanian, Aïda, (ed.), *Armenians of Lebanon: From Past Princesses and Refugees to Present-Day Community*, Beirut: Haigazian University; Belmont, MA: Armenian Heritage Press, 2009.

Catholic Near East Welfare Association (CNEWA), "Christians in the Middle East", Special Edition of ONE, (New York) September 2010. Available at: http://www.cnewa.org/

default.aspx?ID=201&pagetypeID=3&sitecode =HQ&pageno=1.

"Christian Broadcasting in Arab Countries", Section 11, in *Religious Broadcasting in the Middle East Conference. Islamic, Christian and Jewish Channels: Programmes and Discourse.* Organised by Cambridge Arab Media Project (CAMP) and in association with the HRH Prince Alwaleed Bin Talal Centre of Islamic Studies, 30-31 January 2010, University of Cambridge, April 2010. Available at: http://www.cis.cam.ac.uk/wp-content/uploads/2016/01/Religious-Broadcasting-in-the-Middle-East.pdf.

Dadoyan, Seta, *The Armenians in the Medieval Islamic World. vol. 1, The Arab Period in Armnyah, Seventh to Eleventh Centuries,* New Brunswick and London: Transaction Publishers, 2011.

Diamond, Larry, "Why Are There No Arab Democracies?", *Journal of Democracy*, vol. 21, no. 1, January 2010, pp. 93-104.

Dink, Hrant, "Kinkel ve Valilik", *Agos*, 21 August 1998.

Ertan, Özlem, "Foundations in search of justice", Agos, 16 November 2007.

Fisk, Robert, *The Great War for Civilisation. The Conquest of The Middle East,* rev. ed., London & New York: Harper Perennial, 2006.

Hay Spiurk: Hanragitaran (Armenian Diaspora Encyclopaedia, Yerevan: Armenian Encyclopaedia Publication, 2003.

Hovannisian, Richard G., "The Ebb and Flow of the Armenian Minority in the Arab Middle East", *Middle East Journal,* vol. 28, no. 1, 1974, pp. 19-32.

Jamal, Amaney and Tessler, Mark, "The Democracy Barometers: Attitudes in the Arab World", *Journal of Democracy,* vol. 19, no. 1, 2008, pp. 97–110.

Kaiser, Hilmar, "The Armenians in Lebanon during the Armenian Genocide", in Aïda Boudjikanian (ed.), *Armenians of Lebanon: From Past Princesses and Refugees to Present-Day Community,* Beirut: Haigazian University; Belmont, MA: Armenian Heritage Press, 2009, pp. 31-56.

Kasbarian, Sossie, "The Armenian Middle East. Boundaries, pathways and horizons", in Abdelhady Dalia and Ramy Aly (eds.), *Routledge Handbook on Middle Eastern Diasporas,* Routledge, 2023.

Keshishian, Aram, *The Christian Witness at the Crossroads in the Middle East,* Beirut: Middle East Council of Churches, 1981.

Keshishian, Manuel, "Halebi Haygagan Varzharannere" (The Armenian Schools in Aleppo), *CivilNet,* 26 July 2022. Available at: www.civilnet.am/news/669250.

Michael, Maggie, "Christians Fear Islamist Pressure in Egypt", *Daily News Egypt,* 9 October. 2011. Available at: https://dailynewsegypt.com/2011/10/09/christians-fear-islamist-pressure-in-egypt/.

Migliorino, Nicola, *(Re)constructing Armenia in Lebanon and Syria: Ethno-Cultural Diversity and the State in the Aftermath of a Refugee Crisis,* Oxford: Berghahn, 2008.

Mouratyan, Seda, *Iraki Hay Hamaynkeh* [The Armenian Community of Iraq], Yerevan: Baykar, 1997.

Mutafian, Claude, "Les princesses Arméniennes et Le Liban Latin", in Aïda Boudjikanian (ed.) *Armenians of Lebanon: From Past Princesses and Refugees to Present-Day Community,* Beirut: Haigazian University; Belmont, MA: Armenian Heritage Press, 2009, pp. 3-30.

Myers, Steven Lee, "More Christians Flee Iraq After New Violence", *The New York Times,* 12 December 2010. Available at: http://www.nytimes.com/2010/12/13/world/middleeast/13iraq.html.

_____, "Al-Azhar Condemns Violence against Christians", Asia News, 3 March 2010. Available at: http://www.asianews.it/news-en/Cairo,-Al-Azhar-condemns-violence-against-Christians-20996.html.

Nalbandian, Hovsep, "Haygagan Amenorya Tbrotsneru Iravijageh Spuirki Daradzkin" [The Status of Armenian Day Schools in the Diaspora], *Nor Haratch* (Paris), 12 May 2011.

Nersoyan, Archbishop Tiran, *Armenian Church Historical Studies,* New York: St. Vartan Press, 1996.

Ormanian, Malachia, *The Church of Armenia,* New York: St. Vartan Press, 1988.

Öztürk, Fatih, *Ottoman and Turkish Law,* Bloomington: iUniverse LLC, 2014.

Robson, Laura, "Recent Perspectives on Christianity in the Modern Arab World", *History Compass,* vol. 9, no. 4. 2011, pp. 312–325.

Sanasarian, Eliz, *Religious Minorities in Iran,* Cambridge University Press, 2000.

Sanjian, Ara, "The Armenian Minority Experience in the Modern Arab World", *Bulletin of the Royal Institute for Inter-Faith Studies* (Amman, Jordan), vol. 3, no. 1, 2001, pp. 149-179.

Salmanian, Nora, "La Contribution des Arméniens Libanais à la Vie Musicale et Artistique au Liban de 1920 à Nos Jours*",* in Aïda Boudjikanian (ed.), *Armenians of Lebanon: From Past Princesses and Refugees to Present-Day Community,* Beirut: Haigazian Universitzy; Belmont, MA: Armenian Heritage Press, 2009, pp. 153-172.

Sanjian, Avedis Krikor, *The Armenian Communities in Syria under Ottoman Dominion,* Cambridge: Harvard University Press, 1965.

Stern, Robert L., "Perspectives: Caught in the Middle", *One* (Catholic New East Welfare Agency (CNEWA), September 2010. Available at: http://www.cnewa.org/default.aspx?ID=3495&pagetypeID=4&sitecode=HQ&pageno=1.

Tabibian, Jivan, "The Risk of Democratization", *Armenian International Magazine,* vol. 10, no. 8 & 9, August-September 1999, pp. 28-31. Available at: https://issuu.com/armenian internationalmagazine/docs/aug_sep1999.

Tchilingirian, Hratch, "The People's Choice. Archbishop Mesrob Mutafyan Elected 84th Armenian Patriarchate of Turkey", *Armenian International Magazine,* vol. 9, no. 12, December 1998, p. 36. Available at: http://oxbridgepartners.com/hratch/index.php/publications/articles/77-the-people-s-choice.

_____, "Master of Grand Theater. Gerard Avedissian in the Cultural Landscape of Lebanon", *Armenian International Magazine,* vol. 10, no. 6, June 1999, pp. 46-48. Available at: http://issuu.com/armenianinternationalmagazine/docs/june1999.

_____ "Crisis Without Borders. The Media in the Middle East", *Armenian International Magazine,* vol. 10, no. 7, July 1999, pp. 37-39. Available at: http://issuu.com/armenian internationalmagazine/docs/july1999.

_____ "Instilling the Armenian Spirit. Armenian Education in a Transient Community", *Armenian International Magazine,* vol. 10, no. 7, July 1999, pp. 53-54. Available at: http://issuu.com/armenianinternationalmagazine/docs/july1999.

_____, "Looking to the East. Chant Avedissian Rediscovers and Redefines Egyptian Visual Art", *Armenian International Magazine,* vol. 10, no. 8 & 9, August-September 1999, pp. 76-79. Available at: http://issuu.com/armenianinternationalmagazine/docs/aug_sep 1999.

_____, "Integration: The Point of No Return", *Armenian International Magazine,* vol. 10, no. 12, December 1999, pp. 46-48. Available at: http://issuu.com/armenian internationalmagazine/docs/december1999.

_____, "Witness of His Time. The Oppressed and the Rejected Find Dignity and Respect in Norikian", *Armenian International Magazine,* vol. 11, no. 3, March 2000, pp. 62-64. Available at: http://issuu.com/armenianinternationalmagazine/docs/march2000.

_____, "Dividing Jerusalem. Armenians on the Line of Confrontation", *Armenian International Magazine,* vol. 11, no. 10, October 2000, pp. 40-44. Available at: http://issuu.com/armenianinternationalmagazine/docs/october2000?e=9063215/4419 897.

_____, "Recognition or Reconciliation? Turkish-Armenian Relations Need Untangling", *Aztag Daily* (Special Edition), 24 April 2006. Available at: http://www.oxbridgepartners.com/hratch/images/pdf/Tchilingirian_Hratch_Recognit ion_or_Reconciliation_2005.pdf.

_____, "Hrant Dink and Armenians in Turkey", in *Turkey: Writers, Politics and Free Speech. In Memoriam, Hrant Dink (1954-2007). The open Democracy Quarterly,* vol. 1, no. 2, 2007, pp. 117-124. Available at: http://www.opendemocracy.net/democracy-turkey/dink_armenian_4378.jsp.

_____, "L'Eglise Arménienne Pendant la Guerre Froide: la Crise Etchmiadzine-

Antelias", NH Hebdo, 9 June 2016. Available at: https://oxbridgepartners.com/hratch/images/Publications/NorHaratch_Tchilingirian_Hratch_Hebdo_265_9juin2016.pdf.

_____, "The 'Other' Citizens: Armenians in Turkey between Isolation and (Dis)Integration", *Journal of the Society for Armenian Studies*, vol. 25, 2016, pp. 123-155.

Treviño, Joshua, "Turks and Tolerance. Putting Islamist Victory in Turkey in Context", *National Review* (on-line edition), 27 July 2007.

UNESCO Atlas of the World's Languages in Danger, 2010. Available at: https://unesdoc.unesco.org/ark:/48223/pf0000187026.

USCIRF (United States Commission on International Religious Freedom) Annual Report 2011. Available   at: http://www.uscirf.gov/sites/default/files/resources/book%20with%20cover%20for%20web.pdf.

Vick, Karl, "In Turkey, a Deep Suspicion of Missionaries. Priest's Killing Shows Complex Ties of Islam to Nationalism in Officially Secular State", *The Washington Post*, 9 April 2006, p. A21. Available at: http://www.washingtonpost.com/wp-dyn/content/article/2006/04/08/AR2006040801278_pf.html.

Zeitlian, Sona, *Armenians in Egypt. Contribution of Armenians to Medieval and Modern Egypt,* Los Angeles, CA: HSZ Publications, 2006.

Zohry, Ayman, "Armenians in Egypt", *International Union for the Scientific Study of Populations*, XXV IUSSP International Population Conference, Tours, France 18-23 July 2005. Available at: https://www.academia.edu/1300264/Armenians_in_Egypt.

ONTOLOGICAL SECURITY THEORY: CHRISTIAN 'EXISTENTIAL ANXIETY' IN EGYPT AND LEBANON

Zakia Aqra, Stavros Drakoularakos & Charitini Petrodaskalaki

Introduction

Christian communities in the Middle East have drawn a great deal of attention, given their precarious status amidst the violent wind that came along with the Arab uprisings that swept the region in the post-2011 era. Even though there is no doubt that they were all affected, each Christian community has its own context within the nation-state it belongs to and, by extension, the angst of the post-2011 dynamics has different implications for each one. In order to better understand these implications, this paper will employ Ontological Security Theory (OST), which provides conceptual tools with which state identity and foundational narratives are cultivated vis-à-vis the Christian community in Egypt and Lebanon. The dialectic relation between state and religious communities allows us to explore in-depth how Christian communities are impacted by political and/or societal changes as well as the extent to which they may drive or inhibit particular state identity formation in times of crisis.

OST introduces the concept of dislocatory events as developments that trigger existential anxiety and ontological insecurity for both the state and society. In turn, the state proceeds through various attempts to decrease the anxiety level and restore security, which may include or exclude some components of society. In the cases of Egyptian and Lebanese Christians, the dislocatory events, which unfold and affect differently the respective communities, occur in different acts. For the former, the Egyptian uprising in 2011 triggered two acts of dislocatory events: the brief stay of the Muslim Brotherhood (MB) in power and the al-Sisi 2013 coup. For the Lebanese Maronite community, the first act of dislocatory event was the 1975 Lebanese civil war, and the second was the grave implications of the Syrian crisis on Lebanon and its Christian community since 2011. These dislocatory events indicate the peak of anxiety of the communities and a narrative crisis of their respective states. What shall be examined here is the state and/or the community's response to restore ontological security. In essence, examining two Christian communities that have relatively different standings in their respective societies—the Egyptian Copts hold the status of a minority, while the Maronites and Lebanese Christians had a dominant role in the state—within the framework of OST will provide a deeper understanding of Christian communities' angst from different angles.

For the Egyptian Copts, while their religious affiliation distinguished them from the image of the Sunni Muslim Egyptian citizen, the Coptic Church's relationship with the state often accentuated their status as a religious minority to the detriment of the sought-out secular Egyptian identity. Meanwhile, the organic relation between the Lebanese state and its Christian community, mainly the Maronites, positioned the latter on a different status from other Christians in the region. With Maronites always perceiving themselves as creators and natural leaders of Lebanon, they were often forced to renegotiate and compromise their Christian state identity, particularly in the post-civil war era. However, the growing Muslim communities within the country after 2011 further challenged the Lebanese confessional system of governance based on the equal representation of Christians and Muslims, leading to a constant state of insecurity not only for the Maronites but also for other Lebanese Christians. OST will trace the common denominators in the trajectory of the two communities and explore their different reactions to critical events that compromised their survival.

To this end, the first section will present conceptual tools of OST, which will be applied throughout the analysis of the case studies. The second section will examine the shifting priorities and interests of the Copts with regard to the concept of Egyptian national identity before and after the Arab uprisings, as well as the relationship of the Coptic Church with its followers and the state. The final section will focus on the Maronites and their status within Lebanese society before and after the civil war and the rise of Christian nationalism at the outset of the Arab uprisings.

Through the lens of Ontological Security Theory

Ontological security was coined by Laing within the field of psychology and was later transferred by Giddens to the sociological context in an effort to determine the relationship between an individual, his perceived identity, and the impact that his surroundings have on his psychological equilibrium.[1] Ontological security refers to a sense of calm and satisfaction that a person is imbued with in relation to his environment and his future prospects. In direct contrast, ontological insecurity refers to the state of worry and instability that a person feels when confronted with changes in his environment or disillusionment regarding his role and identity in society, as well as his future. Mitzen and Kinnvall transposed OST to the field of

---

[1] Anthony Giddens, *Modernity and Self-Identity, Polity, Self and Society in the Late Modern Age,* Cambridge: Cambridge University Press, 1991.

International Relations (IR) and the state-centric global order. The aim was to highlight the ways with which state entities also have a sense of self and identity that go through similar motions when confronted with either changes to the environment or identity challenges, resulting in the need for corrective measures for sustaining their (auto)biographical continuity. All states strive to define a sense of self through state identity formation. The latter is ensured by a foundational narrative based on historical, traditional, cultural or religious factors. Nonetheless, the foundational narrative is prone to reconfiguration according to the needs of the period and the fluctuations in a society's dynamics. While the state's self is singular, its identity can go through different articulations in line with societal evolution and statehood itself.[2]

OST provides the conceptual tools and framework in order to decipher state biographical narrative origins, articulate the reasons behind policy changes or the promotion of security measures, and even locate the engines behind societal discourse, as well as determine the catalysts that lead to identity development or restructuring.

According to IR and OST, the state is considered the provider and caretaker of ontological security within its territory. Ontological security can be achieved through the promotion and repetition of behavioural routines, predictability, as well as through providing an environment deemed safe and secure for the state's citizens.[3] Essentially, the state is the gatekeeper of continuity, the provider of order and security and the repository of society's identity tenets.[4] Defending memory emerges as another vital task of the state regarding the societal collective shared identity, or, in layperson's terms, the glue that holds society together. This sense of unity is crucial in establishing a common narrative that the majority of society can rally behind. In times of crisis, available or underused narrative tropes are often employed in order to bring about a sense of continuity. The animosity of a state's population towards another neighbouring state is a typical example of such a narrative trope.[5]

---

[2] Christopher S Browning and Pertti Joenniemi, "Ontological Security, Self-Articulation and the Securitization of Identity", *Cooperation and Conflict*, vol. 52, no. 1, 2017, p. 2; Catarina Kinnvall and Jennifer Mitzen, "Anxiety, Fear, and Ontological Security in World Politics: Thinking with and Beyond Giddens", *International Theory*, vol. 12, 2020, p. 248.

[3] Ilse Helbrecht et al., "Ontological Security, Globalization and the Geographical Imagination", in Angela Million (ed), *Spatial Transformations. The Effect of Mediatization, Mobility and Social Dislocation on the Re-Figuration of Spaces*, London: Routledge, 2021, p. 8.

[4] Umut Can Adisonmez and Recep Onursal, "Governing Anxiety, Trauma and Crisis: The Political Discourse on Ontological (In)Security after the July 15 Coup Attempt in Turkey", *Middle East Critique*, vol. 29, no. 3, 2020, pp. 294-295.

[5] Dovile Budryte, Erica Almeida Resende, and Douglas Becker, "'Defending Memory': Exploring the Relationship between Mnemonical in/Security and Crisis in Global Politics", *Interdisciplinary Political*

By the same token, this narrative trope may also be exercised within the state by bringing forward an 'us versus them' mentality, which divides society in favour of the majority. This particular mentality is rooted in the concept of the 'other', which originates from it being a foreign element, either inserting itself into society, or aiming to destabilise it. The definition of the 'other' is often kept vague and is utilised to unite the majority of society against a perceived 'shared threat'.[6] Its purpose is multifaceted as it brings together a large part of society, while alienating the remaining minorities from the state narrative. Cupac articulates anxiety dilemma as 'a situation in which a social order that provides one group of people with a sense of ontological security is a perceived source of anxiety for the other group and vice versa'.[7] Essentially, the state focuses on the needs of the main majority to the detriment of the rest.

This usually occurs in times of crisis, which OST defines as dislocatory events. The latter are considered developments that trigger seismic effects on a society's calm and stability. Although dislocatory events bring a sense of angst and call for state initiatives aiming at ontological security restoration, they are also able to rejuvenate discourse for state identity. Moreover, dislocatory events can be catalysts from which state identity is placed under the microscope and reshaped according to the needs of each era.

Regarding identity continuity, Ejdus introduces ontic spaces as comprised of the material environment, either man or nature-made which act as concrete reminders of society's identity.[8] Since ontic spaces are usually preserved throughout time, they are able to represent a society's longevity and influence beyond the lifespan of a few generations. As such, ontic spaces define identity through projection and introjection, acting as the cultural link between different generations of society. For instance, the Eiffel Tower is one of the most recognisable monuments of France, and often acts as a rallying symbol in times when the French society's unity is required. However, ontic spaces are also at times used for identity reconstruction. The reappropriation or repurposing of a monument can alter its symbolism, which can then be redirected via the tenets of a refocused biographical narrative.[9] The establishment of new cultural monuments, such as the grand

---

Studies, vol. 6, no. 1, 2020, pp. 6-7; Jelena Subotić, "Narrative, Ontological Security, and Foreign Policy Change", *Foreign Policy Analysis,* vol. 12, no. 4. 2016, pp. 613-624.

[6] Adisonmez and Onursal, "Governing Anxiety, Trauma and Crisis", pp. 299-300.

[7] Jelena Cupać, "The Anxiety Dilemma: Locating the Western Balkans in the Age of Anxiety", *Journal of Regional Security,* vol. 15, no. 1, 2020, p. 3.

[8] Filip Ejdus, "'Not a Heap of Stones': Material Environments and Ontological Security in International Relations", *Cambridge Review of International Affairs,* vol. 30, no. 1, 2017, p. 2.

[9] Ejdus, pp. 4-6; Helbrecht et al., "Ontological Security, Globalization and the Geographical Imagination", pp. 6-7.

openings of new Coptic Christian churches in Egypt, reinforces the role of the Egyptian Copts as an integral part of the country's cultural mosaic and history. Similarly, ontic space hosts a competition between communities in Lebanon that cement their presence in the public space, such as the adjacent Saint George's Church and the Blue Mosque in Beirut.

In addition, defending mnemonic identity becomes the primary purpose of the state and informs policy directives based on securitisation. In the name of defending memory and history, state initiatives may circumvent basic human rights and other societal acquis to ensure state identity viability. State survival—as the main priority—becomes a means to an end, trumping any and all other societal alternatives and simplifying state identity as one flag, one nation, and one religion. In this vein, nationalist and religious identities come to the forefront, effectively decreasing security for those excluded from state identity. When the state fails to bring a sense of stability and confidence and society feels that its wellbeing and future are being jeopardised, then corrective measures need to be taken in order to rectify this predicament. As such, these corrective actions often fall under but not restricted to three categories: either the state doubles down on its foundational narrative through the implementation of tough security measures, aiming to ensure the previously established status quo; or the state diverts the identity narrative in order to create a divide in society, essentially promoting polarisation; or, finally, the state opens up its foundational narrative to discourse in order to incorporate the new factors emphasised or born out of the dislocatory events.

The case studies that follow will be analysed within the OST framework under different prisms. In the case of the Egyptian Copts, OST is applied initially on the Egyptian state in which its anxiety, triggered by the uprising of 2011, leads to ontological insecurity and emotional anxiety vis-à-vis the Egyptian state narrative and the status of the Copts. Whereas in the Lebanese case, OST will be applied first on the Maronites as they dominated the Lebanese political scene up until the 1990s, and then the Lebanese Christians *in toto* as they still maintain a high level of representation, power and involvement in the state.

The Egyptian Copts

Prior to the Arab uprisings

The Copts consider themselves to be indigenous people of Egypt dating back to the early first centuries. The word Copt originates from the Greek word for Egypt (Aigyptos), then translated in Arabic into Qibt and finally

Copt in English.[10] Their numbers have slowly dwindled throughout the times, with the majority of the Egyptian population adhering to the Sunni Muslim faith. Nowadays, the Egyptian Copts are estimated to be between five and fifteen percent of the almost a hundred million population of Egypt, although no official population census has been conducted for the past few decades. In addition, in fear of discriminatory practices, many Copts conceal their religious faith, declaring themselves as agnostics or, in some cases, as Muslims. Egyptian Copts share many similarities with Egyptian Muslims. They account for the same history, speak the same language, and share the same right to independence from the British during the early twentieth century. The sole characteristic which distinguishes them from Egyptian Muslims is their religious faith.[11]

Ever since the second half of the twentieth century, a debate had been slowly raging regarding the status of the Copts within Egyptian society. The two arguments shape the following conundrum: either the Copts are citizens with equal secular and religious rights as their Muslim brethren or they are a religious minority in a Muslim-majority country, defined by a neo-millet system. The equal citizenship argument found its footing in the early twentieth century and during the establishment of the modern Egyptian state in 1919-22. Against British colonialism, both Copts and Muslims declared their will and resolved for an independent Egypt. During this period, religious differences were set aside in favour of a secular Egyptian nation-state that would promote the rights and interests of all Egyptian citizens. This initiative eventually led the way for creating a pluralistic political society that grew until the 1950s under Nasser's regime. The needs of the latter's regime dictated the atrophy of the pluralistic Egyptian political party system and primordially focused on the Arab characteristics of the Egyptian citizen. As a result, renewed emphasis was placed on the relationship between the state and the Coptic Orthodox Church, which slowly devolved into delegating the representation of both the religious rights and interests of the Coptic community to the Coptic Orthodox Pope.[12]

---

[10] JD Pennington, "The Copts in Modern Egypt", *Middle Eastern Studies,* vol. 18, no. 2, 1982, p. 158.

[11] Paul Rowe, "The Church and the Street: Copts and Interest Representation from Mubarak to Sisi", *Religion, State & Society,* vol. 48, no. 5, 2020, pp. 344-345; Ana-Maria Gajdo, "Copts and Power in Egypt, before and after the Arab Spring", in Giuseppe Motta (ed), *Dynamics and Policies of Prejudice from the Eighteenth to the Twenty-First Century,* Newcastle upon Tyne: Cambridge Scholars Publishing, 2018, 203-207; Mark Purcell, "A Place for the Copts: Imagined Territory and Spatial Conflict in Egypt", *Ecumene,* vol. 5, no. 4, 1998, p. 434; Mai Mogib, "Copts in Egypt and Their Demands: Between Inclusion and Exclusion", *Contemporary Arab Affairs,* vol. 5, no. 4, 2012, p. 536.

[12] Paul Sedra, "Copts and the Millet Partnership: The Intra-Communal Dynamics Behind Egyptian Sectarianism", *Journal of Law & Religion,* vol. 29, 2014, p. 492; Mariz Tadros, "Vicissitudes in the Entente between the Coptic Orthodox Church and the State in Egypt (1952-2007)", *International Journal of Middle East Studies,* vol. 41, no. 2, 2009, pp. 282-283.

However, the subsequent Sadat regime focused on the Sunni Muslim identity of the Egyptian people to the detriment of the relationship with the Coptic Church. It is of note that this generated tense relations with Pope Shenouda—in addition to the latter's disapproval of the Camp David Accords in 1978—that eventually led to his forced exile. Following his return from exile and support of Mubarak's regime, the role of the Coptic Orthodox Church was strengthened once again as the chief representative of Coptic rights. During the growth of Coptic civil society in the 1990s, the argument in favour of the Coptic minority status stemmed from the belief that the longevity of the state-church relationship had led to an impasse with regard to equal citizenship rights due to the state's Muslim identity, and that there needed to be a different – and previously forbidden – discourse concerning Coptic interests through the minority identity lens. In other words, the discourse potentially shifted from Egyptian unity to Coptic persecution. The nascent Coptic civil society movement argued for a potential Egyptian society guided by secular lay values rather than religious interests and priorities.[13]

There are three main examples typically cited when attempting to show an Egyptian national identity, which encompasses citizens from both Muslim and Coptic walks of life: the first is found during the 1919-22 Egyptian revolution when Copts and Muslims demanded an independent State; the second is located in Pope Shenouda's public and negative reaction to the normalisation of ties with Israel after 1978 in unison with the rest of the Egyptian population; and, the third is set during the Arab uprisings when Copts and Muslims demonstrated together and protected each other during prayer times against the regime's attempts to disperse them. The latter remains the most recent and most publicised instance and speaks to the argument for an Egyptian national identity rooted in the idea of shared history, language, and territory rather than one founded on religious hues.[14]

The Arab uprisings and the Muslim Brotherhood era

The Mubarak decades, from the 1980s to the early 2010s, established a close relationship and understanding between the Egyptian President and

---

[13] Paul Rowe, "Christian-Muslim Relations in Egypt in the Wake of the Arab Spring", *Digest of Middle East Studies,* vol. 22, no. 2, 2013, pp. 262-263; Saba Mahmood, "Religious Freedom, the Minority Question, and Geopolitics in the Middle East", *Comparative Studies in Society and History,* vol. 54, no. 2, 2012, pp. 437-438; Randall P. Henderson, "The Egyptian Coptic Christians: The Conflict between Identity and Equality", *Islam and Christian–Muslim Relations,* vol. 16, no. 2, 2005, p. 164.

[14] Ibrahim, "Beyond the Cross and the Crescent: Plural Identities and the Copts in Contemporary Egypt", pp. 2589-91; Mahmood, "Religious Freedom, the Minority Question, and Geopolitics in the Middle East", pp. 434-435; Jason Brownlee, "Violence against Copts in Egypt", *Carnegie Endowment for International Peace,* 2013, p. 13.

the Coptic Orthodox Pope, but, at the same time, the distancing of Coptic civil society from the Coptic Orthodox Church. While Muslims and Copts demonstrated together during the Egyptian uprising, the Coptic Orthodox Church was initially called for its followers to refrain from participating. The reason behind this lack of endorsement stemmed from the fear that the special relationship between the state and the church would be downgraded following the uprisings, or that the neo-millet system established after 1914, when Egypt became a British protectorate, would cease to exist.[15] Essentially, the previous Ottoman millet system remained de facto in effect. Nonetheless, due to the large participation of Copts, the Coptic Orthodox Church would eventually end up shifting its rhetoric and tacitly supporting the demonstrators.[16]

In essence, the 2011 Arab Spring uprisings, at least regarding the Copts, were a social and political vehicle for reversing a decades-long predicament that was exacerbated by a privileged relationship between the Coptic Orthodox Church and the state. The inability to freely and openly practice their religion, societal marginalisation, and discriminatory practices were the main grievances related to the Coptic community. Moreover, the church-state relationship was also perceived as promoting special treatment for the Copts to the detriment of the Muslim-majority population. While unfounded in practice, this perception further complicated matters, leading to sectarian incidents in central areas; such as, the Minya and Sinai regions, and in large cities; such as, Alexandria and Cairo. Church-building was ruled by legislation inspired by Ottoman times, making the process of obtaining the necessary permits a difficult and frequently unachievable task. The problems related to church-building led to houses of worship being built illegally and hidden from plain sight. Nevertheless, this was often followed by the resentment of the local Muslim population, which perceived the presence of illegal churches as an affront to their way of life and frequently resulted in sectarian conflict. Furthermore, another commonly highlighted issue was related to the kidnappings of Coptic girls and their forced conversion and marriage within the Muslim faith. It is of note that Coptic men and women often sport a tattoo of a religious cross on their wrist, making them easy targets both for discrimination as well as for sectarian attacks. More often than not, sectarian strife was dealt with through informal reconciliatory sessions rather than via police and judicial intervention. This resulted in the

---

[15] Maurits H Van den Boogert, "Millets: Past and Present", in Anne Sofie Roald and Ahn Nga Longva (eds.), *Religious Minorities in the Middle East: Domination, Self-Empowerment, Accommodation*, Leiden & Boston: Brill, 2012, pp. 39-40.

[16] Magdi Guirguis, "The Copts and the Egyptian Revolution: Various Attitudes and Dreams", *Social Research: An International Quarterly*, vol. 79, no. 2, 2012, pp. 511-514; Mogib, "Copts in Egypt and Their Demands: Between Inclusion and Exclusion", p. 547.

sessions' decisions favouring the aggressors and leading to the Coptic population's exile from the locality.[17]

Additionally, sports, television, cinema, society and the military were areas where discrimination was commonly in effect due to the religious aspect of the Coptic Egyptian citizen. Another issue within the day-to-day life of the Coptic community was the rise of blasphemy lawsuits regarding the mention of the prophets as presented in the Quran. These lawsuits had essentially hindered the Copts' ability to express themselves freely concerning their faith, as well as to promote their religious culture and history within the confines of society. With many cases resulting in severe sentences, blasphemy prosecutions were supposed to act as a buffer against religious emancipation and were the product of the belief that there were actors within Egyptian society that strove for the conversion of Muslims to the Christian faith. While this belief was not unfounded due to the presence of western-funded evangelical proselytising missions throughout the Middle East, it included the Coptic community within this narrative and severely limited their freedom of expression. In fact, while Christians could convert to the Muslim faith, the opposite was not available or recognised option by Egyptian law.[18]

The failings in state protection, coupled with the divisive church-state relationship and its ramifications within the rest of the population, played an essential factor in the active participation of Copts in the 2011 uprisings. The Arab Spring shone further light on Coptic civil society, in particular, the Maspero Youth Organization (MYO), which was formed following the killing of 28 Copts in October 2011 that were protesting in front of the national television building in the Maspero district of Cairo.[19] While President Mubarak was no longer in power, the Supreme Council of Armed Forces was transitionally governing the country and preparing for the next elections. The military intervention that violently repressed the protests

---

[17] Saba Mahmood, "Sectarian Conflict and Family Law in Contemporary Egypt", *American Ethnologist*, vol. 39, no. 1, 2012, pp. 54-55; Brownlee, "Violence against Copts in Egypt", pp. 4-5, 20; Hyun Jeong Ha, "Emotions of the Weak: Violence and Ethnic Boundaries among Coptic Christians in Egypt", *Ethnic and Racial Studies*, vol. 40, no. 1, 2017, p. 135.

[18] Nada Shaker, "Meet Egypt's Christian Soccer Team", *Al-Monitor*, 9 February 2021. Available at: https://www.al-monitor.com/originals/2021/02/egypt-je-suis-soccer-team-christians-rejection-sports.html; David Zeidan, "The Copts—Equal, Protected or Persecuted? The Impact of Islamization on Muslim-Christian Relations in Modern Egypt", *Islam and Christian-Muslim Relations*, vol. 10, no. 1, 1999, pp. 57-58; Mahmoud Salem, "Blasphemy in New and Old Egypt", *Middle East Institute*, 12 June 2013. Available at: https://www.mei.edu/publications/blasphemy-new-and-old-egypt; Johannes Makar, "Persecution Lurks for Converts from Islam in Egypt", *Open Democracy*, 6 August 2015. Available at: https://www.opendemocracy.net/en/north-africa-west-asia/persecution-lurks-for-converts-from-islam-in-egypt/.

[19] Paul Sedra, "Reconstituting the Coptic Community Amidst Revolution", *Middle East Report*, no. 265, 2012, p. 35.

underlined the systemic issues related to the Copts and was viewed as a concrete example of sectarianism in Egyptian society. The public outcry against the Maspero incident provided necessary visibility for Coptic civil society, which in turn formed the Coptic Consultative Council, independent from the Coptic Orthodox Church, throughout 2013, aiming at representing the religious, political and civil rights of their community.[20]

The Egyptian uprisings were the result of a state of ontological insecurity and emotional anxiety with regard to the Egyptian state narrative of the Mubarak era as well as the need of the Egyptian mosaic for identity inclusion. Moreover, while Coptic civil society could play an important part in this conversation, it was the Sunni Muslim majority of the Egyptian population which would decide what an Egyptian identity should entail.

With the MB winning the 2012 elections, Muslim-Coptic relations entered a new era. While the Morsi government made promises regarding the peaceful coexistence between the two religious communities and the President himself appointed members from the Coptic community in an advisory capacity, sectarian incidents as well as blasphemy prosecutions, were on the rise. The newly elected government moved forward with constitutional reforms and an increasing reliance on legislation inspired by Shar'ia law. Moreover, while government officials condemned incidents against Copts, the measures taken against their repetition were unsuccessful. The above demonstrated a willingness from the state to distance itself from the previously established status quo of the past decades and forge ahead with the re-definition of a different Egyptian identity that did not include non-Muslim communities. A symbolic example of the latter was President Morsi's non-attendance to the inauguration ceremony of newly elected Pope Tawadros, who succeeded Pope Shenouda after his passing.[21] With the Copts no longer being considered part of Egyptian identity, they would be designated as a religious minority at best.[22]

The collective shared identity of the majority of the Egyptian population can be found in its history as well as in the Sunni Muslim religion as formulated by state narratives. As dislocatory events go, the Egyptian uprisings led to a state of angst with regard to the future of the country, its people and their identity. As a result, and in order to break with the past, the

---

[20] Ibrahim, "Beyond the Cross and the Crescent: Plural Identities and the Copts in Contemporary Egypt", p. 2593; Emman El-Badawy, "Nationalism and Institutionalized Sectarianism in Egypt", *The Muslim World*, vol. 106, 2016, p. 164; Caroline Barbary, "Une Autre Jeunesse 'Copte' De La Révolution En Égypte", *Revue Tiers Monde*, no. 226/227, 2016, pp. 134-136

[21] Rowe, "Christian-Muslim Relations in Egypt in the Wake of the Arab Spring", p. 271.

[22] Ibid, pp. 243-245; Gajdo, "Copts and Power in Egypt, before and after the Arab Spring", p. 213; Ha, "Emotions of the Weak: Violence and Ethnic Boundaries among Coptic Christians in Egypt", p. 146.

mnemonic identity and shared religion of the majority would be vital to establishing unity and ensuring state longevity. Hence, it would be easier to guarantee Egyptian unity by promoting the characteristics of the many rather than accepting the needs of the few. In this regard, the Coptic community found itself at a disadvantage, being relegated to the outsider status when talking about Egyptian identity. The identity continuity of the Egyptian Sunni Muslim majority would take precedence over the mnemonic identity of the entire Egyptian population and aim to re-establish the new state's ontological security tenets. In other words, the Arab uprisings and the advent of the MB government essentially acted as a dislocatory event for the Coptic community since it sent ripples to the previously established status quo, both regarding the position of the Coptic Orthodox Church and concerning the activism of the nascent Coptic civil society. For the former, the dislocatory event meant that the special relationship that it enjoyed in its dealings with the state was downgraded, while, for the latter, the rise of Political Islam as a predominant force in Egyptian politics would potentially minimise the impact of civil society for a secular democratic Egypt. The existential anxiety of the Coptic community, which came to the forefront following the rise of the MB party, created a situation where Copts feared that they would no longer be considered part of Egyptian society and identity. This led to a refocused and closer relationship between the Coptic Church and the Egyptian regime, similar to the Shenouda era. Fundamentally, while in classic OST the remedy to existential anxiety is usually found in securitisation, the Coptic Church re-enforced its status as a political player and as a mediator with the state. The concept of survival would be tied to the dealings of the Coptic Orthodox Church rather than in the civil society discourse that had gained traction in previous years.[23]

The military coup and the al-Sisi era

The 2013 military coup that overthrew the elected Morsi-led government was immediately and publicly supported by the head of the Coptic Orthodox Church, Pope Tawadros. He was joined by the Grand Imam of al-Azhar, providing further religious support and legitimacy to the new military regime. The self-appointed President al-Sisi allegedly aimed at restoring Egypt's secular political status quo, moving forward with institutional reforms intended to minimise religious radicalism and toning down sectarian strife. In a sense, while the MB government saw the Muslim Egyptian identity as a bridge with the Ottoman past and Middle Eastern countries, the al-Sisi

---

[23] Bosmat Yefet, "Defending the Egyptian Nation: National Unity and Muslim Attitudes toward the Coptic Minority", *Middle Eastern Studies*, vol. 55, no. 4, 2019, pp. 644-645; Elizabeth Iskander Monier, "The Arab Spring and Coptic–Muslim Relations: From Mubarak to the Muslim Brotherhood", *European Yearbook of Minority Issues Online*, vol. 11, no. 1, 2014, pp. 177-178.

regime saw the rebranding of Egyptian identity as a threefold opportunity: for strengthening its future electoral base, capitalising on the Coptic diaspora and re-energising ties with western and non-Muslim countries. The foundational narratives of both governments were diametrically opposed, both stemming from different but intricately connected dislocatory events. Where the foundational narrative of the MB government was rooted in democratic reform and in adherence to Islamic values, the foundational narrative of the al-Sisi government would be based on religious reform, secularism and on the return to traditional relationships both within the country and the wider region.[24]

The 2013 coup, as viewed through the lens of OST, acted as a second dislocatory event, since it restored the pre-Spring identity narrative. While the first dislocatory event effectively removed the Coptic community from the Egyptian citizen conversation, the second one reintroduced the concept of Egyptian citizenship as non-restrictive to non-Muslims. However, the post-2013 identity narrative bridged the current regime with the previous Mubarak one, both course-correcting the results of the Egyptian uprisings and negating the impact of Egyptian civil society laymen in relation to economic, political, and societal reforms. By rejecting the results of the 2012 elections, the new regime exacerbated the rift within society. Meanwhile, MB followers considered Copts to have betrayed the values of the Arab uprisings due to the vocal support of the Coptic Orthodox Church for the al-Sisi government,fueling to instances of sectarian strife in the months following the regime change. To complicate matters further, the relationship of the Coptic Church with the pre-MB governments led to the Copts being considered as their porte-parole and to be against the tenets and demands of the Egyptian uprising. With their religious attribute acting as a distinguishing element, it was easy for a rhetoric of an 'us versus them' to develop and escalate. while the Coptic community strove for inclusion in the Egyptian foundational narrative, the rising sectarian incidents presented a radicalised rhetoric averse to their inclusion. In this particular instance, the 'other' is not part of the strict religious Sunni identity and personifies the enemy.[25]

In an attempt to promote the concept of religious pluralism within the country, the al-Sisi government moved forward with promises of restoring destroyed or unusable houses of worship for the Coptic Orthodox Church.

---

[24] Paola Pizzo, "The 'Coptic Question'in Post-Revolutionary Egypt: Citizenship, Democracy, Religion", *Ethnic and Racial Studies*, vol. 38, no. 14, 2015, pp. 2605-2606; Brownlee, "Violence against Copts in Egypt", p. 19; Khalil Al-Anani, "All the Dictator's Sheikhs", *Foreign Policy,* 20 July 2020. Available at: https://foreignpolicy.com/2020/07/20/all-the-dictators-sheikhs/

[25] Rowe, "Democracy and Disillusionment: Copts and the Arab Spring", p. 247; El-Badawy, "Nationalism and Institutionalized Sectarianism in Egypt", pp. 162-163.

In addition, projects such as the megachurch of the Cathedral of the Nativity of Christ near the new administrative capital were pushed to the forefront. Thus, due to their symbolic nature, church restorations and church-building could be categorised as ontic spaces through the OST lens. Their presence and exposure both to the public and abroad underlined the al-Sisi government's willingness to promote religious coexistence as a concept of state identity and political system rooted in Egyptian history. This identity notion was further promoted by church-building legislature and the increased security presence in events such as the inauguration of the Cathedral of the Nativity of Christ. In other words, churches – as ontic spaces – essentially reaffirmed the long-standing presence of the Coptic community in Egyptian history and symbolised the community's continued coexistence within Egyptian society. In contrast, the almost defunct Jewish Egyptian community saw its synagogues closed or in ruins, as the lacklustre attendance could not justify their continued presence.[26]

The al-Sisi government's 'religious revolution' and societal reform declarations , which would provide a sense of security for the Copts, were considered half-measures as they were hindered by the rise of sectarian strife and public instances of violence against Copts. On the one hand, President al-Sisi seemed to aim to accommodate the Coptic Orthodox Church and to cultivate his relationship with the Pope through initiatives such as the reform of the church-building law, the more significant presence of police personnel and security measures in Coptic religious celebrations and his yearly attendance of Christmas mass. On the other hand, and with an eye to the Sunni-majority society, the President attempted to balance his recognition of the Coptic community with the sporadic implementation of the Coptic-centric reforms. This balancing act, while providing perhaps a better *modus vivendi* for the Copts in cities such as Alexandria and Cairo, nonetheless exacerbated a tense situation in Egyptian society. By recognising Pope Tawadros as the official representative for all Coptic affairs, the aspirations of Coptic civil society for a more secular relationship were undercut as they brought back the arguments of the Coptic religious minority to the Ottoman millet system and the second-class citizenship to the forefront.[27]

---

[26] Rania Rabeaa Elabd, "Will Egypt's Copts Get to Build More Churches?", *Al-Monitor*, 9 June 2016. Available at: https://www.al-monitor.com/originals/2016/06/egypt-construction-churches-draft-law-copts-mosques.html; Rasha Mahmood, "What Reopening the Eliyahu Hanavi Synagogue Means for Egypt", *Al-Monitor*, 20 January 2020. Available at: https://www.al-monitor.com/originals/2020/01/egypt-opens-eliyahu-hanavi-synagogue.html.

[27] Rowe, "Democracy and Disillusionment: Copts and the Arab Spring", pp. 248-249; *World Watch Monitor*, "Church Construction Slows under Egypt's New Church-Building Law", 21 December 2018. Available at: https://www.worldwatchmonitor.org/2018/12/church-construction-slows-under-egypts-new-church-building-law/; *Arab News*, "Egypt's El-Sisi Attends Christmas Mass Amid Tight Security", 6 January 2018. Available at: https://www.arabnews.com/node/1220396/middle-east; Candace Lukasik,

Nevertheless, the problems related to forced marriages, kidnappings, sectarian strife and societal discrimination were in effect during the post-Arab spring era, mainly originating from the political priorities of the 1970s Sadat era; the issues were symptoms of an older disease. The inconsistencies stemmed from the Egyptian national identity conversation, which seesawed from being inclusive or non-inclusive of the Coptic community. At the same time, the Islamic State's presence following the ramifications of the Syrian civil war further complicated matters, evident in radical rhetoric and the persecution of Copts mainly in the Sinai region, as well as during religious celebrations in Cairo and Alexandria. The argument for the inclusiveness of the Coptic community within the Egyptian national identity remains at a crossroads both despite and as a consequence of the two dislocatory events that occurred during the 2011-13 period. With Coptic civil society joining the societal demands of the Arab uprisings, it was subsequently sidelined both during the Morsi and al-Sisi eras. The former focused on the religious reform promises, which informed his electoral success, while the latter highlighted the religious identity of the Copts by reinstating the state's close relationship with the head of the Coptic Orthodox Church. Hence, in both instances, religious characteristics were emphasised to the detriment of the demands of civil society regarding secular citizenship. In other words, religious hues undercut the secular identity narrative formation during the Arab uprisings.

Lebanese Christians

Identity Framing: Lebanese or Maronite state?

Contrary to the Egyptian Copts, Maronites once constituted the majority in Lebanon, allowing them to dictate Lebanese state identity. This began to materialise around Mount Lebanon in the late nineteenth century with the creation of the *Mutasarrifiya*, an autonomous Maronite political entity created through French intervention. A small group of Maronites, however, conceived a future Lebanese entity, which would include other communities with a distinct western face and orientation, propagating the idea of *Grand Liban* with Maronites at its helm. Therefore, in order to formulate the Lebanese state identity, the exclusivist Christian – Maronite identity had to cater to other religious communities. More specifically, the Lebanese Christian state identity was mainly based on two pillars: the notion of Mount refuge and ancient Phoenician ancestry. By combining elements of Maronite

---

"Copts, Church, and State: Egypt's Christians Frustrated with Lack of Protection", *Tahrir Institute for Middle East Policy*, 15 February 2019. Available at: https://timep.org/commentary/analysis/copts-church-and-state-egypts-christians-frustrated-with-lack-of-protection/.

ecclesiastical historiography with orientalist and colonial discourses, the Lebanese state was able to create a continuity and longevity of the national identity without any significant input from the other non-Maronite communities.[28]

The concept of mount refuge stands as the most crucial foundational narrative of the Lebanese state that Maronites propagate. As Makdisi notes, "nineteenth-century Mount Lebanon became the location of a host of competing armies and ideologies".[29] The narrative heavily relied on Maronite Church historiography and imaginary, and was also prominent in orientalist and colonial discourse; Lammens, a prominent Jesuit priest and orientalist historian popularised the idea of the *Asile du Liban*, whose main narrative is that various minorities escaped persecution, seeking refuge to the mountain where religions were practiced freely, unlike other places in Syria, thus able to resist assimilation.[30] This narrative transformed Mount Lebanon, a natural geographical location, as an ontic space, a concrete reminder of society's identity, defined through projection and introjection. The mountain as a locus becomes the historical bastion and the heart of the Lebanese identity, and a constant reminder of its past, revoking images and narrative tropes of refuge and freedom as well as a homeland. Even in the more secular interpretations of the Lebanese imaginary, such as Corm's book of poetry, *la montagne inspiree*, the message is explicitly taken from Christian theology and highlights Christian moments in Lebanese history.[31] This foundational narrative, instead of building up a collective identity, juxtaposes the communities of Mount Lebanon with the Sunni Muslim minority, emphasising the notion of 'us versus them'.

The second origin narrative traces the lineage of modern Lebanon in ancient Phoenicia, showcasing the continuity and pertinence of the Lebanese nation with the land.[32] This theory initially surfaced among groups diverging from ecclesiastical historiography, aiming at justifying a separate Lebanese entity with a distinct history, disputing the idea that Lebanon was a French artificial construct at the Maronites' service.[33] The Phoenician idea appealed

---

[28] Candice Raymond, "Vie, Mort Et Résurrection De l'histoire Du Liban, Ou Les Vicissitudes Du Phénix", *Revue Tiers Monde*, vol. 216, no. 4, 2013, p. 72.

[29] Ussama Makdisi, *The Culture of Sectarianism*, Berkeley: University of California Press, 2000, p. 11.

[30] Mouannes Mohamad Hojairi, "Church Historians And Maronite Communal Consciousness: Agency And Creativity In Writing The History Of Mount Lebanon", New York: Columbia University Press, 2011, p. 232.

[31] Asher Kaufman, "'Tell Us Our History': Charles Corm, Mount Lebanon and Lebanese Nationalism", *Middle Eastern Studies*, vol. 40, no. 3, 2004, pp. 1-28.

[32] Asher Kaufman, "Phoenicianism: The Formation of an Identity in Lebanon in 1920", *Middle Eastern Studies*, vol. 37, no. 1, 2001, p. 173.

[33] Raymond, "Vie, Mort Et Résurrection De l'histoire Du Liban, Ou Les Vicissitudes Du Phénix", p. 75.

to the Maronites because it created various narrative tropes that applied to the modern view of the state; it presented the Lebanese as entrepreneurs, bridging East with West. The combination of Phoenician myth, Christian faith and western orientation provided an appropriate justification for a non-Arab nation, as there was clear evidence of a civilisation distinct from the Arabs. The Maronites' systematic attempts to separate Lebanon from its environs or to adopt any facet of Arab identity aimed to preserve their ontological security. However, this clearly separated them from the rest of the Lebanese nation; all those who identified as Arabs are marginalised from this narrative.[34]

Since the exclusivist Christian narratives were meant to justify the existence of a different, non-Arab entity around Mount Lebanon, they were partly or entirely rejected by non-Maronite communities as inconsistent with their history, identity or presumed homeland.[35] As a result, existential anxiety was borne out of the absence of a unifying historical myth and the lack of an inclusive collective shared identity. The Maronites' privileged position in state affairs was rooted in the demographic distribution of the day and in the fact that other communities were not active nor willing to participate in Lebanese politics.[36] Sunni Muslims were the primary advocates of Arab nationalism, rejecting the division of Greater Syria; Shi'a Muslims were also directed towards unity with Greater Syria, claiming stronger affinity with the areas in Southern Syria and Northern Palestine than those in the newly established state.[37] Similarly, a substantial number of Orthodox and Greek Catholics also rejected the French mandate and wished for unification with Syria.[38] As for the Druzes, the *Grand Liban* formula further solidified their peripheral role in politics.[39] When these communities endorsed the idea of an independent Lebanon, between 1920 and 1943, the Christian, or at least the non-Muslim nature of Lebanon, was a reality, as most government institutions were already developed and controlled by Christians. With the National Pact of 1943, Maronite dominance was institutionalised in

---

[34] Kamal S. Salibi, "The Lebanese Identity", *Journal of Contemporary History*, vol. 6, no. 1, 1971, pp. 78-79, 84; Yusri Hazran, "Between Authenticity and Alienation: The Druzes and Lebanon's History", *Bulletin of the School of Oriental and African Studies*, vol. 72, no. 3, 2009, pp. 468-470

[35] Raymond, "Vie, Mort Et Résurrection De l'histoire Du Liban, Ou Les Vicissitudes Du Phénix", pp. 78-79

[36] Kail C. Ellis, "Greater Lebanon: The Problems of Integrating a Religiously and Ethnically Diverse Population", *Journal of South Asian and Middle Eastern Studies,* vol. 42, no. 4, 2019, pp. 3, 5.

[37] Rami Siklawi, "The Social and Political Identities of the Shi'i Community in Lebanon", *Arab Studies Quarterly*, vol. 36, no. 4, 2014, p. 283.

[38] Fawwaz Traboulsi, *A History of Modern Lebanon*, 2nd edition, London: Pluto Press, 2012, p. 81.

[39] Yusri Hazran, "Between Authenticity and Alienation: The Druzes and Lebanon's History", pp. 459–487.

exchange for political and socio-cultural promises for the Muslims.[40] Notably, during the negotiations, the Maronites did not support their claims of predominance on their demographic strength as much as on fear of absorption and oppression, arguing that among Arab countries, only in Lebanon did Christians have a voice in national political affairs.[41] For them, survival was only possible in a state controlled by them, securing long-term protection measures for their community. Maronite political supremacy was secured by the exceptional power bestowed on the president of the republic, who was agreed to be a Christian.[42] Thus, the National Pact missed the mark and could not locate a genuinely national base.[43]

Consequently, the Maronite position was particularly vulnerable in front of the gradually increasing participation of other groups in Lebanese politics, demographic changes and international developments. The fact that the overall Christian population was gradually losing the majority created existential anxiety in the Maronite political elite, fearing for their dominant position in the Lebanese state. Wanting to keep the state's political structure at all costs, they avoided having a census that would measure religious affiliation.[44] According to Hagopian, 'contemporary Maronitism, in response to demographic and ideological challenges to its hegemony, sought to emulate the Jewish state by creating a Christian majority and Christian-dominated state in present-day Lebanon using the same ideological strategy as Zionism, but it failed.'[45]

In fact, the Maronites were in a consistent state of anxiety as they were unable to counter the narratives of other communities successfully. In order not to trigger domestic upheavals, Lebanon abstained from taking a stance on foreign policy matters where Christians and Muslims disagreed. However, the union between Egypt and Syria under the United Arab Republic in 1958 created panic among the Maronite circles. Nasserism appealed to many Lebanese as an alternative version of Arab nationalism that did not rely on Islam, viewing it as an opportunity to decrease both the pro-western

---

[40] Such promises include the adoption of an Arab face of the state, thus becoming one of the Arab League's founding members in 1944.

[41] Edward E. Azar and Robert F. Haddad, "Lebanon: An Anomalous Conflict?", *Third World Quarterly*, vol. 8, no. 4, 1986, p. 1346.

[42] Traboulsi, *A History of Modern Lebanon*, pp. 107-110.

[43] Ussama Makdisi, "Reconstructing the Nation-State: The Modernity of Sectarianism in Lebanon", *Middle East Report*, no. 200, 1996, p. 25.

[44] The last official census was conducted in 1932. Muhammad A. Faour, "Religion, Demography, and Politics in Lebanon", *Middle Eastern Studies*, vol. 43, no. 6, 2007, pp. 909-921; Arnon Soffer, "Lebanon – Where Demography Is the Core of Politics and Life", *Middle Eastern Studies*, vol. 22, no. 2, 1986, p. 197.

[45] Elaine C. Hagopian, "Maronite Hegemony to Maronite Militancy: The Creation and Disintegration of Lebanon", *Third World Quarterly*, vol. 11, no. 4, 1989, p. 101.

orientation of Lebanon[46] and the Christian hegemony.[47] These regional developments kept fueling the 'us versus them' narrative as the state tried to defend itself from this perceived threat, thus alienating a large section of society and ultimately resulting in the brief 1958 civil war. Even though the Maronites managed to preserve their role in the political landscape, it deeply shook society's calm and stability while exacerbating the Maronites' ontological insecurity. Subsequent events, such as the military coup in 1961- fueled by Christian phobias about Greater Syria and Muslim hostility-[48] and the 1967 war, continued to feed the Maronites' anxiety.[49] Consequently, this led to the 1975 civil war, which constituted the first act of dislocatory event for the Maronite community.

Civil war and Taif Accords: The Maronite anxiety spillover to other Christians

What was fundamentally different in the period leading to the 1975 civil war in contrast to previous conflicts was that the 'other'—identified by the Maronites as Muslims—did not simply seek more parliamentary representation; instead, they questioned the very basis of Maronite hegemony in Lebanese politics. The Lebanese National Movement (LNM), led initially by a coalition of leftist and secular forces and Muslim political groups, demanded greater participation of the non-Christian forces in the system.[50] In addition, the dissatisfaction of many Christians with their leadership further exacerbated the sense of threat among the community, especially after the Cairo Agreement of 1969, in which the Maronite President, Charles Helou, allowed Palestine Liberation Organization (PLO) to establish its headquarters on Lebanese territory, which prompted the proliferation of militias. For the Maronites, their leadership had failed to protect them and Lebanon from "Muslim" radicalisation, causing unprecedented anxiety among Christians. In response, the Lebanese Front (LF) was established, an emblem of Lebanese Christian nationalism at the

---

[46] Already identified as 'the merchant republic', Lebanon developed a significant economy under the lead of primarily the Maronite elite. During Sham'un's presidency, Lebanon adopted a clear pro-Western attitude, given its close cooperation with the West, which would secure national integrity, especially against Arab Nationalism. Traboulsi, *A History of Modern Lebanon*, pp. 110-128; Kamal S. Salibi, "Lebanon under Fuad Chehab 1958-1964", *Middle Eastern Studies*, vol. 2, no. 3, 1966, pp. 211–226.

[47] Omri Nir. "The Shi'ites during the 1958 Lebanese Crisis", *Middle Eastern Studies*, vol. 40, no. 6, 2004, pp. 109-129; David Ignatius, "How to Rebuild Lebanon", *Foreign Affairs*, vol. 61, no. 5, 1983, pp. 1140–1156.

[48] Traboulsi, *A History of Modern Lebanon*, p. 140.

[49] Walid Khalidi, "Lebanon: Yesterday and Tomorrow", *Middle East Journal*, vol. 43, no. 4, 1989, pp. 375–387.

[50] Joseph Bahout, "The Unraveling of Lebanon's Taif: Agreement Limits of Sect-Based Power Sharing", *Carnegie Endowment for International Peace*, pp. 9, 24.

time and predominantly a Maronite militia, which viewed itself as a revivalist of the phalangist movement.[51] Initially, it coordinated between various political Christian parties to counter LNM' efforts 'to Arabise Lebanon completely' in 'an attempt to appropriate or to dissolve the specificity of the Christian presence'.[52] LF became the defender of Maronite mnemonic identity, eventually enabling the mobilisation and armament of many dissatisfied Christians and Maronite hardliners among the political elite around the idea of safeguarding the identity of the 'Christian Maronite homeland, [...] against the centuries of onslaught by Muslim invaders', creating a 'Maronite counter elite' that defined the re-emergence of Lebanese Christian nationalism.[53] Despite its multilayered dynamics, the civil war was interpreted as 'us versus them', the former being the Christians – mainly Maronites-and the latter the Muslims.

The civil war was a dislocatory event that rejuvenated the discourse on state identity. The Taif Accords in 1990 sealed the end of the civil war , which pertained to the *de jure* end of Maronite hegemony as the Christian-Muslim representation would be equal in all state positions. However, considering the demographic reality of Christians comprising one-third of Lebanon, their community's position remained privileged, in many ways preserving its interests.[54] In the eyes of the Maronites, it was an unfavourable outcome; they accepted this compromise due to the post-Cold War era's uncertainty and the intra-Christian rift that weakened the Christians' position towards the end of the civil war.[55] The Taif Accords' main byproduct, however, was the reinforcement of Syria's presence in almost all of Lebanon's vital sectors, which set the pace of the political dynamics for over a decade.

This created a new dynamic amongst the Lebanese in the post-Taif era. The pro and anti-Syrian rift briefly replaced the classic Christian-Muslim divide[56] and, by extension, sidelined the Christian community from the

---

[51] Lewis W. Snider, "The Lebanese Forces: Their Origins and Role in Lebanon's Politics", *Middle East Journal*, vol. 38, no. 1, 1984, pp. 14-15.

[52] Ghassan Hage, "Nationalist Anxiety or the Fear of Losing Your Other", *The Australian Journal of Anthropology*, vol. 7, no. 2, 1996, p. 122.

[53] Elizabeth Crighton and Martha Abele Mac Iver, "The Evolution of Protracted Ethnic Conflict: Group Dominance and Political Underdevelopment in Northern Ireland and Lebanon", *Comparative Politics*, vol. 23, no. 2, 1991, p. 136.

[54] Muadth Malley, "The Lebanese Civil War and the Taif Accord Conflict and Compromise Engendered by Institutionalized Sectarianism", *The History Teacher*, vol. 52, no. 1, 2018, pp. 124-125.

[55] Notably, approximately 670,000 Christians were displaced during the civil war, four times more than Muslims; Anthony O'Mahony, "Christianity in the Wider Levant Region: Modern History and Contemporary Contexts", in Kail C. Ellis (ed.), *Secular Nationalism and Citizenship in Muslim Countries: Arab Christians in the Levant*, Cham: Springer, 2018, p. 79.

[56] As'ad Abukhalil, "The New Sectarian Wars of Lebanon", in Nubar Hovsepian (ed.), *The War on Lebanon:*

political scene. Already in 2002, this angst was translated into a competition for ontic spaces. The Sunni Prime Minister Hariri funded the reconstruction of a small mosque next to the nineteenth-century Maronite cathedral, the Mohammad Al-Amin Mosque—also known as the Hariri Mosque. Upon completion, the mosque's minarets surpassed the cathedral's campanile by sixty-five meters. In protest, the Church was quick to add another sixty-five meters on the campanile, exposing that the Christians continued to be wary of the Muslim expansionist tendencies.[57] Despite the Churches efforts to rival it, to this day, the Mohammad Al-Amin Mosque is one of the most dominant features of the capital's skyline.

The Sunni-Shia rift was further fueled after the withdrawal of Syrian troops from Lebanon in 2005. The Christian community's anxiety was growing proportionally with the growing power of Muslim communities – be it the Shia community via Hizbullah's arsenal, the most potent military power in Lebanon, or the Sunni community via Hariri's financial network-fueled the Christians' fear and anxiety. Even though some Maronite Christians, such as the Free Patriotic Movement (FPM) and some prominent Greek Orthodox Christians, supported good relations with Hizbullah, other Christians—(including LF Party, Kataeb Party and the Independent Movement)—remained apprehensive of Hizbullah since they viewed Shia Islamists as yet another 'Muslim' threat to Lebanon and their community. Notwithstanding, survival anxiety had become a central element within the Christian community *in toto*, not only the Maronites.

Christian identity after Arab Spring

The Christian community in Lebanon experienced a new wave of anxiety at the onset of the Syrian crisis in 2011. The large influx of mainly Sunni Syrian refugees and the infiltration of Syrian Salafi-Jihadist groups such as ISIS, and Jabhat al-Nusra, amongst others, into Lebanon triggered extraordinary anxiety vis-à-vis their demographic disadvantage and concerns posed to non-Sunnis. In fact, this peaked in early August 2014 as the Syrian sectarian violence spilled over into Lebanon. The security threat prompted the Christians in the areas of Bekaa Valley and Mount Lebanon to form defence forces. Even though the anxiety vis-à-vis the 'Salafi threat' was quelled after the 2016 defeat of ISIS, the all-growing number of Sunni Syrian refugees in Lebanon caused an unprecedented demographic discrepancy between Muslims and Christians. While religious Christian leaders tend to pose the refugee crisis as a national concern, there is a clear element of

---

A Reader, Northhampton: Olive Branch Press, 2008, p. 360.

[57] Ward Vloeberghs, "The Genesis of a Mosque: Negotiating Sacred Space in Downtown Beirut", *EUI RSCAS Mediterranean Programme Series*, no. 17, 2008, pp. 17-18.

sectarian hue. In fact, Maronite Patriarch al-Rai emphasises on the political challenge posed by the refugees. In mid-2021, he explained that the foundation of Lebanon is based on the 50/50 (Christian-Muslim) power-sharing system; thus,the additional 2 million Muslim refugees (which include 1.5 million Syrians and half a million Palestinians) among the 4 million Lebanese are to the detriment of the Christian community.[58]

The argument of Patriarch al-Rai has been cultivated for over a decade among Lebanese Christians beyond the Maronites. Originally, there was some distinction between Maronites and other Christian denominations, such as Greek Orthodox, MelkiteCatholics, Protestants, Assyrian to name a few, as the latter Christians tended to identify with Arabism.[59] As Ellis notes, '[f]or Christians, Lebanon was essentially a Maronite national home or a Christian refuge'.[60] In OST terms, the Syrian crisis ramifications constituted the second dislocatory event which was a catalyst to unite the Christians across the board against the 'Muslim' threat. According to Hage, Lebanese Christian nationalism, an anxiety-driven movement, initially emerged among the Maronite community, which peaked during the Lebanese 1975 civil war.[61] While other Christian denominations—particularly Greek Orthodox, the second largest Christian community—opposed the Maronite discourse and hegemony at the time, Lebanese Christian nationalism started to appeal to various Christians in the post-Syrian crisis era.

At the heart of this perception, threat lays the demographic balance, which is challenged by the 'Muslim/Arab other' and constitutes the basis of existential anxiety of the Christian community and unifies them.[62] The discourse depicted the 'other', the antagonist and agent of anxiety, as a Muslim/Arab regardless of nationality (be it Lebanese, Palestinian or Syrian), political ideology or orientation (be it secular or religious). The politics of Christian nationalism aim at maintaining a Christian-dominated Lebanese state, a solid confessional identity among the Christian Lebanese, and a high degree of Christian community autonomy. Contrary to the past, secular Christian groups who had opposed the Maronite hegemony and favoured a secular Lebanon shifted towards 'confessionalism as an indispensable

---

[58] FACE, "The Future of Christians in Lebanon and the Region", 2021. Available at: https://facecharity.org/future-of-christianity-in-lebanon/

[59] Hagopian, "Maronite Hegemony to Maronite Militancy: The Creation and Disintegration of Lebanon", p. 103.

[60] Ellis, "Greater Lebanon: The Problems of Integrating a Religiously and Ethnically Diverse Population", p. 6.

[61] Hage, "Nationalist Anxiety or the Fear of Losing Your Other".

62 The increase birthrates of Muslims and Christian emigration caused the Christian population to drop from thirty to nineteen percent during the 1940s and 2000s, respectively, see *Table 1* in Faour, "Religion, Demography, and Politics in Lebanon", p. 912.

institution for the protection of Christian rights and power'; such an example is FPM.[63] One of the main differences between this trend of Lebanese Christian nationalism and the previous one substantiated by LF is that the non-Maronite communities revoke the ideological underpinnings of 'Phoenicianism'.[64] Nevertheless, the constituencies of FPM, LF and other Christian parties share the view that Christians' rights are being marginalised, which prompted their leaders to form a joint Christian block for the first time in 2018.

The alarming situation has triggered the Lebanese Christians to become involved in a process of securitisation since 2011, which has, first, taken the form of preserving the Christians and 'their' land and, second, it is indulged by the political elite, the civil-society and religious institutions. The notion of Christian land put forth by the majority of the community is that Lebanese territory 'is naturally divided into ancestral [and sacred] confessional homelands'.[65] In the eyes of the Christians, who own approximately half of Lebanon's territory due to selling land to non-Christians, the loss of land signals the retreat from 'the glorious days' when Christians once owned eight thousand square kilometers of land (around seventy percent).[66] The initiatives to take measures to re-claim the Christian land ownership are mainly being taken on an institutional level by Christian-dominated municipalities, such as Beirut, Jezzine or Qbayet, who have the ability to authorise land sales.[67] In fact, not only do they refuse to authorise land sells but they proceed in shaming the Christians that managed to do so.[68] In addition, these efforts have been supported by active civil-society organisations; such as, 'Lebanese Land-Our Land Movement' or 'Ardi', who assist municipalities in purchasing 'Muslim land' and 'create administrative obstacles' for Muslims seeking to purchase Christian land.[69]

---

[63] Maximilian Felsch, "Christian Political Activism in Lebanon: A Revival of Religious Nationalism in Times of Arab Upheavals", *Studies in Ethnicity and Nationalism*, vol. 18, no. 1, 2018, p. 8.

[64] A poll in January 2010 indicated that most Christians favored political confessionalism, seventy-five per cent of Lebanese Muslims favored its abolition; Gulay Turkmen-Dervisoglu, "Lebanon: Parody of a Nation? A Closer Look at Lebanese Confessionalism", *The Yale Review of International Studies*, 2012. Available at: http://yris.yira.org/essays/316.

[65] Felsch, "Christian Political Activism in Lebanon: A Revival of Religious Nationalism in Times of Arab Upheavals", pp. 7-8.

[66] Venetia Rainey, "Lebanon's Refugee Influx Alarms Christians", *Al-Jazeera*, 11 May 2014. Available at: https://www.aljazeera.com/news/2014/5/11/lebanons-refugee-influx-alarms-christians.

[67] Samya Kullab and Rayane Abou Jaoude, "Christian Land Issue Raises Decades-Old Anxieties", *Daily Star*, 15 February 2014. Available at: http://www.dailystar.com.lb/ArticlePrint.aspx?id=247440&mode=print.

[68] Akhbar al-Yawm News Agency, "Kobayat People Refuse That the Sale of Land in the Town Goes Unnoticed", 16 September 2012. Available at: https://www.al-akhbar.com/Politics/57530.

[69] Maximilian Felsch, "The Rise of Christian Nationalism in Lebanon", in Maximilian Felsch and Martin Wählisch (eds.), *Lebanon the Arab Uprisings: In the Eye of the Hurricane*, London: Routledge, 2016, p. 74;

These NGOs' campaign to raise awareness regarding the 'Muslim' threat is supported by the Maronite Patriarch. In fact, religious institutions had already embraced such practices; for instance, the Maronite Social Fund, founded by the Maronite Patriarchy in 1987, purchases land in Christian-majority areas exclusively for the Church. In 2014, the Syriac Catholic community also established a real-estate agency with the same mandate. According to Felsch, the Maronite Foundation, created in 2006 by the Church, was the policy's 'main initiator' policy, whose mandate was to incentivise Christian Lebanese expatriates' return.[70] Given the Christian community's sense of insecurity, its political leadership has rallied behind Lebanese Christian nationalism both on a level of discourse and praxis around the issue of Christian land. Christian politicians purchased property in contested areas such as Jezzine, including the property of the Jihadist-Salafist leader in Lebanon, right before the 2013 parliamentary elections.[71] The Christian elite further channelled its efforts within the legal system by putting forth the 'Orthodox Gathering's Proposal',[72] which aimed to reform the electoral law to rectify Christian parliamentary underrepresentation. Each citizen would vote for candidates from their own confession, guaranteeing Christian MPs to prioritise exclusively Christian interests. Even though the Orthodox Proposal *per se* was rejected by non-Christian parties, in 2017, some of its provisions were accepted; such as rearranging electoral districts along sectarian lines, thus rendering them more homogeneous and allowing Lebanese expatriates to vote in embassies, giving the Christian diaspora a voice within Lebanon.[73]

Even though the Lebanese Christian nationalism of the twenty-first century differs gravely from the Maronite nationalism in the twentieth, it may be argued that it is always reinvigorated by an environment of insecurity entrenched in the us/other dichotomy. By the same token, the sense of anxiety has catalysed a securitisation process, which enabled the community to seek a return to the previous status quo in order to retrieve their lost ontological security. On a rhetorical level, the mnemonic identity of

---

Felsch, "Christian Political Activism in Lebanon: A Revival of Religious Nationalism in Times of Arab Upheavals", pp. 9-10.

[70] Felsch, "Christian Political Activism in Lebanon: A Revival of Religious Nationalism in Times of Arab Upheavals", p. 13.

[71] Felsch, "The Rise of Christian Nationalism in Lebanon", p. 75; Mohammed Zaatari, "Assir Sells Real Estate to Political Rivals", *The Daily Star*, 23 January 2013. Available at: https://www.dailystar.com.lb/News/Politics/2013/Jan-23/203423-assir-sells-real-estate-to-political-rivals.ashx.

[72] Qifa Nabki, "Orthodox Gathering Proposal", 2011. Available at: https://qifanabki.files.wordpress.com/2011/12/orthodox-gathering-proposal.pdf

[73] Eli Hajj, "March 14 Coalition Threatened By Draft Lebanese Electoral Law Read", *Al-Monitor*, 22 February 2013. Available at: https://www.al-monitor.com/originals/2013/02/orthodox-law-threatens-march-14.html.

Lebanese Christian nationalism, to some extent, has been displaced from a Maronite connection with Phoenicianism to a more Christian-encompassing identity. In turn, this displacement has redirected how Christians seek to secure their existence in the country. In this sense, the Christians' goal is not to pursue a hegemonic role in the state but to reform the confessional power-sharing system in a way that would favour and protect Christian rights. Since Lebanon's independence, all its communities have experienced an anxiety dilemma within a zero-sum game. The Christians' historic relation to the state, however, has rendered them more vulnerable in adapting to changes, which are continuously perceived as an existential threat to their mnemonic identity. Even though Christians still hold key state positions, especially compared to the demographic reality, their anxiety is yet to be appeased.

Conclusion

This paper examined the tenets of ontological security theory pertaining to Christian religious communities in Lebanon and Egypt. First, the authors elaborated on the theatrical framework of ontological security. Second, we thoroughly examined Egyptian Copts' status within society vis-à-vis secular or religious state identity and the relationship of the Coptic Church with the state itself. Lastly, we articulated the rise and fall of Maronite hegemony in the Lebanese state identity and how it was re-invented under the banner of Christian nationalism by expanding to other Christian denominations through the lens of the 'other'.

Under the prism of OST, the different standing of the communities in relation to the state exposed the contrasting abilities to react to their ontological insecurity. On the one hand, the Egyptian Copts endured two acts of dislocatory events during which the state – both under Morsi and al-Sisi, relegated them to religious minority status. The al-Sisi measures to rectify societal anxiety endured by all Egyptians echoed the Mubarak era's narrative and policy, negating the efforts and demands of civil society with regard to secular citizenship by reinstating the state's close relationship with the head of the Coptic Orthodox Church. Thus, the Copts' concept of survival is susceptible to the Coptic Orthodox Church—State relations rather than civil society. On the other hand, the corrective measures of the Lebanese Maronites in 1975 and the Christian nationalists today in response to the dislocatory events aim at implementing measures to ensure the previously established status quo rather than reconstruct the state discourse on the equal citizenship narrative. The Maronite efforts in the twentieth century were futile as they failed to preserve their state hegemony since they had to concede to equal authority with the Muslims. The Taif Accords re-established the sectarian power-sharing system, with the promise of abolishing it eventually and moving on to a secular Lebanese state. In the post-2011 era, the Lebanese Christian community seeks to reinforce sectarian power-sharing as it is perceived as the only way to safeguard the Christians' existence. In both instances, the majority of the Maronites invoked Christian nationalism as a narrative to guide the corrective measures, counter the challenges posed to their status within the Lebanese state and restore the Christian community's ontological security.

Despite the common insecurity regarding their survival, the ontic space dynamics exposed the different sorts of agony that the two communities endured. For the Egyptian Copts, Church restorations and church-building under al-Sisi reflected merely a state effort to promote religious coexistence as opposed to equal citizenship. While in Lebanon, the ontic space has become a theatre of *bras de fer* between which religious identity will dominate the state. Yet, in both cases, we see the trend of religious coexistence is the antidote for the Christian community's anxiety. Even though in the case of the Copts, the community is attempting to re-establish their ontological security by advocating for a secular Egyptian society in which they may belong as equal citizens, the Lebanese Christians are pursuing policies that reinforce the confessional system. This difference occurs mainly to the different trajectories of their mnemonic memory; while Egypt had cultivated a narrative of equal citizenship, Lebanon was constructed on the basis of a religious-based state identity, while many central elements of the Lebanese identity continue to rely on the Christian imaginary. It remains to be seen whether both states' foundational narratives will manage to incorporate religious differences through the promotion of secularism or if religious affiliation will prove to be the main element determining the state identities in flux.

Bibliography

Abukhalil, As'ad, "The New Sectarian Wars of Lebanon", in Nubar Hovsepian (ed), *The War on Lebanon: A Reader*, Northampton: Olive Branch Press, 2008.

Adisonmez, Umut Can and Onursal, Recep, "Governing Anxiety, Trauma and Crisis: The Political Discourse on Ontological (in)Security after the July 15 Coup Attempt in Turkey", *Middle East Critique*, vol. 29, no. 3, 2020, pp. 291-306.

Akhbar al-Yawm News Agency, "Kobayat People Refuse That the Sale of Land in the Town Goes Unnoticed", (2012), https://www.al-akhbar.com/Politics/57530.

Al-Anani, Khalil, "All the Dictator's Sheikhs", *Foreign Policy*, 20 July 2020. Available at: https://foreignpolicy.com/2020/07/20/all-the-dictators-sheikhs/.

Arab News, "Egypt's El-Sisi Attends Christmas Mass Amid Tight Security", 6 January 2018. Available at: https://www.arabnews.com/node/1220396/middle-east.

Azar, Edward E and Haddad, Robert F, "Lebanon: An Anomalous Conflict?", *Third World Quarterly*, vol. 8, no. 4, 1986, pp. 1337-1350.

Bahout, Joseph, "The Unraveling of Lebanon's Taif: Agreement Limits of Sect-Based Power Sharing", *Carnegie Endowment for International Peace*, 2016, pp.1-26.

Barbary, Caroline, "Une Autre Jeunesse 'Copte' De La Révolution En Égypte", *Revue Tiers Monde*, vol. 226/227, 2016, pp. 123-145.

Browning, Christopher S and Joenniemi, Pertti, "Ontological Security, Self-Articulation and the Securitization of Identity", *Cooperation and Conflict*, vol. 52, no. 1, 2017, pp. 31-47.

Brownlee, Jason, "Violence against Copts in Egypt", *Carnegie Endowment for International Peace*, 2013, pp. 1-28.

Budryte, Dovile Resende, Erica Almeida and Becker, Douglas, "'Defending Memory': Exploring the Relationship between Mnemonical in/Security and Crisis in Global Politics", *Interdisciplinary Political Studies*, vol. 6, no. 1, 2020, pp. 5-19.

Crighton, Elizabeth and Mac Iver, Martha Abele, "The Evolution of Protracted Ethnic Conflict: Group Dominance and Political Underdevelopment in Northern Ireland and Lebanon", *Comparative Politics*, vol. 23, no. 2, 1991, pp. 127-142.

Cupać, Jelena, "The Anxiety Dilemma: Locating the Western Balkans in the Age of Anxiety", *Journal of Regional Security*, vol. 15, no. 1, 2020, pp. 7-38.

Ejdus, Filip, "Not a Heap of Stones': Material Environments and Ontological Security in International Relations", *Cambridge Review of International Affairs*, vol. 30, no. 1, 2017, pp. 23-43.

El-Badawy, Emman, "Nationalism and Institutionalized Sectarianism in Egypt", *The Muslim World*, vol. 106, 2016, pp. 155-168.

Elabd, Rania Rabeaa, "Will Egypt's Copts Get to Build More Churches?", *Al-Monitor*, 9 June 2016. Available at: https://www.al-monitor.com/originals/2016/06/egypt-construction -churches-draft-law-copts-mosques.html.

Ellis, Kail C, "Greater Lebanon: The Problems of Integrating a Religiously and Ethnically Diverse Population", *Journal of South Asian and Middle Eastern Studies*, vol. 42, no. 4, 2019, pp. 1-16.

FACE, "The Future of Christians in Lebanon and the Region", 2021. Available at: https://facecharity.org/future-of-christianity-in-lebanon/.

Faour, Muhammad A, "Religion, Demography, and Politics in Lebanon", *Middle Eastern Studies*, vol. 43, no. 6, 2007, pp. 909-921.

Felsch, Maximilian, "Christian Political Activism in Lebanon: A Revival of Religious Nationalism in Times of Arab Upheavals", *Studies in Ethnicity and Nationalism*, vol. 18, no. 1, 2018, pp. 19-37.

Felsch, Maximilian, "The Rise of Christian Nationalism in Lebanon", in Maximilian Felsch, Martin Wählisch (eds.), *Lebanon the Arab Uprisings: In the Eye of the Hurricane*, London: Routledge, 2016, pp. 70-86.

Gajdo, Ana-Maria, "Copts and Power in Egypt, before and after the Arab Spring", in Giuseppe Motta (ed.), *Dynamics and Policies of Prejudice from the Eighteenth to the Twenty-First Century*, Cambridge: Cambridge Scholars Publishing, 2018, pp. 203-216.

Giddens, Anthony, Modernity and Self-Identity, Polity, Self and Society in the Late Modern Age, Cambridge: Cambridge University Press, 1991.

Guirguis, Magdi, "The Copts and the Egyptian Revolution: Various Attitudes and Dreams", Social Research: An International Quarterly, vol. 79, no. 2, 2012, pp. 511-530.

Ha, Hyun Jeong, "Emotions of the Weak: Violence and Ethnic Boundaries among Coptic Christians in Egypt", Ethnic and racial studies, vol. 40, no. 1, 2017, pp. 133-151.

Hage, Ghassan, "Nationalist Anxiety or the Fear of Losing Your Other", The Australian Journal of Anthropology, vol. 7, no. 2, 1996, pp. 121-140.

Hagopian, Elaine C, "Maronite Hegemony to Maronite Militancy: The Creation and Disintegration of Lebanon", Third World Quarterly, vol. 11, no. 4, 1989, pp. 101-117.

Hajj, Eli, "March 14 Coalition Threatened By Draft Lebanese Electoral Law Read", Al-Monitor, 22 February 2013. Available at: https://www.al-monitor.com/originals/ 2013/02/orthodox-law-threatens-march-14.html

Hazran, Yusri, "Between Authenticity and Alienation: The Druzes and Lebanon's History", *Bulletin of the School of Oriental and African Studies, University of London*, vol. 72, no. 3, 2009, pp. 459-487.

Helbrecht, Ilse et al., "Ontological Security, Globalization and the Geographical Imagination", in Angela Million (ed.), *Spatial Transformations. The Effect of Mediatization, Mobility and Social Dislocation on the Re-Figuration of Spaces*, London: Routledge, 2021, pp. 243-257.

Henderson, Randall P, "The Egyptian Coptic Christians: The Conflict between Identity and Equality", *Islam and Christian–Muslim Relations*, vol. 16, no. 2, 2005, pp. 155-166.

Hojairi, Mouannes Mohamad, *Church Historians And Maronite Communal Consciousness: Agency And Creativity In Writing The History Of Mount Lebanon*, New York: Columbia University Press, 2011.

Ibrahim, Vivian, "Beyond the Cross and the Crescent: Plural Identities and the Copts in Contemporary Egypt", *Ethnic and Racial Studies*, vol. 38, no. 14, 2015, pp. 2584-2597.

Ignatius, David, "How to Rebuild Lebanon", *Foreign Affairs*, vol. 61, no. 5, 1983.

Johannes, Makar, "Persecution Lurks for Converts from Islam in Egypt", *Open Democracy*, 6 August 2015. Available at: https://www.opendemocracy.net/en/north-africa-west-asia/persecution-lurks-for-converts-from-islam-in-egypt/.

Kaufman, Asher, "Phoenicianism: The Formation of an Identity in Lebanon in 1920", *Middle Eastern Studies*, vol. 37, no. 1, 2001, p. 173-194.

Kaufman, Asher, "'Tell Us Our History': Charles Corm, Mount Lebanon and Lebanese Nationalism", *Middle Eastern Studies*, vol. 40, no. 3, 2004, pp. 1-28.

Khalidi, Walid, "Lebanon: Yesterday and Tomorrow", *Middle East Journal*, vol. 43, no. 4, 1989, pp. 375-387.

Kinnvall, Catarina and Mitzen, Jennifer, "Anxiety, Fear, and Ontological Security in World Politics: Thinking with and Beyond Giddens", *International Theory*, vol. 12, 2020, pp. 240-256.

Kullab, Samya and Abou Jaoude, Rayane, "Christian and Issue Raises Decades-Old Anxieties", *Daily Star*, 15 February 2014. Available at: http://www.dailystar.com.lb/ArticlePrint.aspx?id=247440&mode=print

Lukasik, Candace, "Copts, Church, and State: Egypt's Christians Frustrated with Lack of Protection", *Tahrir Institute for Middle East Policy*, 15 February 2019. Available at: https://timep.org/commentary/analysis/copts-church-and-state-egypts-christians-frustrated-with-lack-of-protection/.

Mahmood, Rasha, "What Reopening the Eliyahu Hanavi Synagogue Means for Egypt", *Al-Monitor*, 20 January 2020. Available at: https://www.al-monitor.com/originals/2020/01/egypt-opens-eliyahu-hanavi-synagogue.html.

Mahmood, Saba, "Religious Freedom, the Minority Question, and Geopolitics in the Middle East", *Comparative Studies in Society and History*, vol. 54, no. 2, 2012, pp. 418-446.

Mahmood, Saba, "Sectarian Conflict and Family Law in Contemporary Egypt", *American Ethnologist*, vol. 39, no. 1, 201, pp. 54-62.

Makdisi, Ussama, "Reconstructing the Nation-State: The Modernity of Sectarianism in Lebanon", *Middle East Report*, no. 200, 1996.

Makdisi, Ussama, *The Culture of Sectarianism*, Berkeley: University of California Press, 2000.

Malley, Muadth, "The Lebanese Civil War and the Taif Accord: Conflict and Compromise Engendered by Institutionalized Sectarianism", *The History Teacher*, vol. 52, no. 1, 2018, pp. 121-159.

Mogib, Mai, "Copts in Egypt and Their Demands: Between Inclusion and Exclusion", *Contemporary Arab Affairs*, vol. 5, no. 4, 2012, pp. 535-555.

Monier, Elizabeth Iskander, "The Arab Spring and Coptic–Muslim Relations: From Mubarak to the Muslim Brotherhood", *European Yearbook of Minority Issues Online*, vol. 11, no. 1, 2014, pp. 167-186.

Nir, Omri, "The Shi'ites during the 1958 Lebanese Crisis", *Middle Eastern Studies*, vol. 40, no. 6, 2004, pp. 109-129.

O'Mahony, Anthony, "Christianity in the Wider Levant Region: Modern History and Contemporary Contexts", in Kail C Ellis (ed.), *Secular Nationalism and Citizenship in Muslim Countries*, Springer, 2018, pp. 61-88.

Pennington, JD, "The Copts in Modern Egypt", *Middle Eastern Studies*, vol. 18, no. 2, 1982, pp. 158-179.

Pizzo, Paola, "The 'Coptic Question' in Post-Revolutionary Egypt: Citizenship, Democracy, Religion", *Ethnic and Racial Studies*, vol. 38, no. 14, 2015, pp. 2598-2613.

Purcell, Mark, "A Place for the Copts: Imagined Territory and Spatial Conflict in Egypt", *Ecumene*, vol. 5, no. 4, 1998, pp. 432-451.

Qifa Nabki, "Orthodox Gathering Proposal", 2011. Available at: https://qifanabki.files.wordpress.com/2011/12/orthodox-gathering-proposal.pdf.

Rainey, Venetia, "Lebanon's Refugee Influx Alarms Christians", *Al-Jazeera*, 5 November 2014. Available at: https://www.aljazeera.com/news/2014/5/11/lebanons-refugee-influx-alarms-christians.

Raymond, Candice, "Vie, Mort Et Résurrection De l'histoire Du Liban, Ou Les Vicissitudes Du Phénix", *Revue Tiers Monde*, vol. 216, no. 4, 2013, pp. 71-87.

Rowe, Paul, "Christian-Muslim Relations in Egypt in the Wake of the Arab Spring", *Digest of Middle East Studies*, vol. 22, no. 2, 2013, pp. 262-275.

Rowe, Paul, "Democracy and Disillusionment: Copts and the Arab Spring", *Sociology of Islam*, vol. 2, 2014, pp. 236-251.

Rowe, Paul, "The Church and the Street: Copts and Interest Representation from Mubarak to Sisi", *Religion, State & Society*, vol. 48, no. 5, 2020, pp. 343-360.

Salem, Mahmoud, "Blasphemy in New and Old Egypt", *Middle East Institute,* 12 June 2013. Available at: https://www.mei.edu/publications/blasphemy-new-and-old-egypt.

Salibi, Kamal S, "The Lebanese Identity", *Journal of Contemporary History*, vol. 6, no. 1, 1971, pp. 76-86.

Salibi, Kamal S, "Lebanon under Fuad Chehab 1958-1964", *Middle Eastern Studies*, vol. 2, no. 3, 1966, pp. 211-226.

Sedra, Paul, "Copts and the Millet Partnership: The Intra-Communal Dynamics Behind Egyptian Sectarianism", *JL & Religion*, vol. 29, 2014, pp. 491-509.

Sedra, Paul, "Reconstituting the Coptic Community Amidst Revolution", *Middle East Report,* no. 265, 2012.

Shaker, Nada, "Meet Egypt's Christian Soccer Team", *Al-Monitor,* 9 February 2021. Available at: https://www.al-monitor.com/originals/2021/02/egypt-je-suis-soccer-team-christians-rejection-sports.html.

Siklawi, Rami, "The Social and Political Identities of the Shi'i Community in Lebanon", *Arab Studies Quarterly,* vol. 36, no. 4, 2014, pp. 278-291.

Snider, Lewis W, "The Lebanese Forces: Their Origins and Role in Lebanon's Politics", *Middle East Journal*, vol. 38, no. 1, 1984, pp. 1-33.

Soffer, Arnon, "Lebanon - Where Demography Is the Core of Politics and Life", *Middle Eastern Studies,* vol. 22, no. 2, 1986, pp. 197-205.

Subotić, Jelena, "Narrative, Ontological Security, and Foreign Policy Change", *Foreign Policy Analysis*, vol. 12, no. 4, 2016, pp. 610-627.

Tadros, Mariz, "Vicissitudes in the Entente between the Coptic Orthodox Church and the State in Egypt (1952-2007)", *International Journal of Middle East Studies*, vol. 41, no. 2, 2009, pp. 269-287.

Traboulsi, Fawwaz, *A History of Modern Lebanon*, Pluto Press, 2012.

Turkmen-Dervisoglu, Gulay, "Lebanon: Parody of a Nation? A Closer Look at Lebanese Confessionalism", *The Yale Review of International Studies*, 2012, pp. 61-72.

Van den Boogert, Maurits H, "Millets: Past and Present", in Anne Sofie Roald and Ahn Nga Longva (eds), *Religious Minorities in the Middle East: Domination, Self-Empowerment, Accommodation,* Leiden & Boston: Brill, 2012, pp. 27-45.

Vloeberghs, Ward, "The Genesis of a Mosque: Negotiating Sacred Space in Downtown Beirut", *EUI RSCAS Mediterranean Programme Series*, no. 17, 2008, pp. 1-27.

World Watch Monitor, "Church Construction Slows under Egypt's New Church-Building Law", 21 December 2018. Available at: https://www.worldwatchmonitor.org/2018/12/church-construction-slows-under-egypts-new-church-building-law/

Yefet, Bosmat, "Defending the Egyptian Nation: National Unity and Muslim Attitudes toward the Coptic Minority", *Middle Eastern Studies*, vol. 55, no. 4, 2019, pp. 638-654.

Zaatari, Mohammed, "Assir Sells Real Estate to Political Rivals", *Daily Star*, 23 January 2013. Available at: https://www.dailystar.com.lb/News/Politics/2013/Jan-23/203423-assir-sells-real-estate-to-political-rivals.ashx

Zeidan, David, "The Copts—Equal, Protected or Persecuted? The Impact of Islamization on Muslim-Christian Relations in Modern Egypt", *Islam and Christian-Muslim Relations*, vol. 10, no. 1, 1999, pp. 53-67.

MIDDLE EASTERN CHRISTIANITY IN SYRIA AND IRAQ: AT THE EPICENTRE OF THE RISE OF THE ISLAMIC STATE

Stavros Drakoularakos

Introduction

The slogan "property of the Islamic State" was found graffitied on walls of houses, buildings and farms wherever and whenever Daesh forces successfully captured a city or village in Iraq and Syria.[1] The exodus of Christians from those regions during the decade of the 2010s, and especially throughout the times of the rise and fall of the Islamic State, is estimated to amount to approximately at least one million people. The factors behind the mass exodus are chiefly located in the atrocities committed by Islamic State fighters, in addition to the wider ramifications of the various and ongoing infighting in the Syrian and Iraqi states, ever since the 2010 Arab uprisings and the 2003 Gulf war, respectively. Both Syria and Iraq host a large part of Middle Eastern Christianity followers and have been subject to numerous studies with regard to the co-optation policies between Church and state during the previous decades. However, the impact of the state-building and identity homogenisation processes of the Islamic State on the Christian communities themselves have been mainly confined within the larger examination of international and regional geopolitical antagonisms, the Sunni-Shia sectarian tensions, Kurdish state-building and irredentism, or the impact and aftermath of the Arab uprisings. Instead, this chapter opts for a focused lens on the Christian communities' life shifts and limited options, both during the rise and initial establishment of the Islamic State, as well as following its eventual collapse.

The rise and initial successes of Daesh in the theatres of war of Syria and Iraq during the 2013-2014 period greatly impacted the Christian communities residing in both countries. On the one hand, the clash between Daesh and other forces created an unsafe environment for non-Sunni Muslims, while the seizing of large cities such as Homs, Raqqa and Mosul left Christians unprotected and to their own devices. On the other hand, the state-building process of Daesh, coupled with the heritage destruction

---

[1] *France24*, "Iraq fighters take 'victory selfies' at Tal Afar citadel", 28 August 2017. Available at: https://www.france24.com/en/20170828-iraq-fighters-take-victory-selfies-tal-afar-citadel.

strategy and its proliferation via social media, attempted to erase the Christian cultural linkage with its historical regions in Iraq and Syria. Moreover, Christians were considered to represent the Christian West and both the people and their heritage markers were identified by jihadist fighters as public and symbolic targets. With the Islamic State moving forward with the foundation of a religious state identity and narrative in its conquered territories, Christians were faced with both an ultimatum and an impasse: to leave immediately with the clothes on their back; to become second-class subjects and go into dhimmi contracts under the Islamic Caliphate; or to meet the sword. The policies enacted by the Islamic State engineered varying but disproportionate results. A considerable percentage of Iraqi Christians left the country en masse to neighbouring Middle Eastern countries and Europe, leaving in their stead a couple hundred thousand fellow practitioners that became internally displaced people to the north of the country in and near the Iraqi Kurdistan region in the hope of a safer environment. In contrast, the majority of Syrian Christians residing in the southwestern parts of the country, under Assad's rule, were mostly left untouched by the wider ramifications of the civil war and Islamic State operations. Nonetheless, the Assyrians that stayed behind in north and eastern Syria felt the brunt of the conflict while remaining sandwiched between different antagonisms.

The chapter proceeds as follows. The first section presents the main tenets of the co-optation relationships of the Christian Church communities with the Syrian and Iraqi regimes prior to the Arab uprisings and the advent of the Islamic State. The second section examines the state-building process of Daesh with regard to the significance of cultural heritage destruction at its core. The third section focuses on the Christian dilemma within the Islamic State entity and the ensuing external and internal displacement as a direct result of the Islamic State's successes and established policies. The final section sheds light on the modus vivendi and prospects of the Iraqi and Syrian Christians in their respective homes in the aftermath of the Islamic State.

The co-optation policy as the longstanding Christian modus operandi

Middle Eastern Christianity is predominantly categorised into four distinct Church branches: first, the Greek Orthodox Churches, namely the Eastern Patriarchates of Alexandria, Antioch, Jerusalem and Constantinople, following the 1054 Great Schism between Rome and Constantinople; second, the Church of the East – resulting from theological differences during the fifth and sixth centuries regarding the divine and human nature of Christ – which later on split further into the Syriac Orthodox Church, the Coptic Orthodox Church, the Armenian Apostolic Church and the Ethiopian Church, as the Oriental Orthodox Churches; third, the Maronite, Chaldean Catholic, Syriac Catholic, Armenian Catholic, Melkite Greek Catholic, and Coptic Catholic Churches, as the Eastern Catholic Churches which were created during the times of the Ottoman Empire following internal disagreements; and fourth, the Lutheran, Reformed, Episcopal and Anabaptist Protestant Evangelical Churches, established from American and British missionary initiatives during the nineteenth century found in regions ranging from the Fertile Crescent to Mesopotamia.[2]

With estimates varying greatly, Christians constitute approximatively fifteen million people in the Middle Eastern region and account for roughly four percent of its population. The largest Christian group resides in Egypt, at ten percent of the population and is projected to amount to around ten million people. What is more, although smaller in numbers, Lebanon holds the largest Christian percentage at thirty percent of its population. Christians currently constitute around ten percent of the Syrian population and less than one percent of the Iraqi one at two million and 200,000 people, respectively. These numbers however are estimates at best due to the lack of a recent official census, the various crises, the mass population exodus and regional displacement during the previous decades.[3]

The traditional and longstanding strategy of Christians in Egypt, Syria and Iraq was based on co-optation with regimes promoting secular nationalism. The latter emphasized shared history, traditions and language instead of religion as the main identity and citizenship tenets. The co-optation strategy was more successful in Egypt and Syria, rather than in Iraq. Nonetheless, the co-optation policy seemed – at least at its inception – to integrate well with the Baathist regimes of Syria and Iraq, under Assad and Hussein, respectively.[4] Although religion would not be an integral part of state identity, the various Christian denominations and their religious rights would be respected and protected, all the while Christian leaders would serve as representatives of the Christian population guaranteeing the communities'

---

[2] Elizabeth Monier, "The Chaldean patriarch and the discourse of 'inclusive citizenship': restructuring the political representation of Christians in Iraq since 2003", *Religion, State & Society*, vol. 48, no. 5, 2020, p. 363-365; Georges Fahmi, "The Future of Syrian Christians after the Arab Spring", *Robert Shuman Centre for Advanced Studies*, 2018, pp. 5-6; Fiona McCallum, "Christian Political Participation in the Arab World", *Islam and Christian-Muslim Relations*, vol. 23, no. 1, 2012, pp. 4-5.

[3] United States Commission on International Religious Freedom, *Annual Report 2021*. Available at: https://www.uscirf.gov/sites/default/files/2021-04/2021%20Annual%20Report.pdf

[4] Mark Farha and Salma Mousa, "Secular Autocracy vs. Sectarian Democracy? Weighing Reasons for Christian Support for Regime Transition in Syria and Egypt", *Mediterranean Politics*, vol. 20, no. 2, 2015, p. 182.

loyalty to the regime. Additionally, Christians would see their interests, societal inclusion and accession to higher echelons safeguarded and promoted due to this particular relationship with the state.[5]

Under the Assad regimes, Christian celebrations, holidays, places of worship and cemeteries were recognised, subject to state protection and even occasional aid. As a direct result, Syrian Christians effectively became part of both the Alawi interest network and the state narrative that any Sunni-led alternative to the Assad regimes would be detrimental to Syrian and Christian prerogatives.[6] The majority of Syrian Christians mainly resided in large business and residential urban centers such as Damascus, Homs, and Aleppo in the southwestern and northwestern parts of the country, in contrast to the Sunni Muslim population, who were located in more rural areas.[7] Assyrian Christians, however, – who had resisted the Baathist Arabisation project in keeping with their particular ethnic and religious identity – resided in eastern Syria and had shied away from a clear pro-regime stance.

Whereas the decades-spanning co-optation policy in Syria had seemingly borne fruit for at least the majority of Christians, the Iraqi Chaldean and Assyrian denominations did not share the same fate. The once Assyrian Christian historical regions of the Nineveh plains and Mosul in northern Iraq were emptied of the Christians that were being forced to external emigration or internal displacement and resettlement to Baghdad and southern Iraq following the clashes between Iraqi forces and Kurdish paramilitary irredentist groups, as well as the implementation of the Iraqi Arabisation project in the 1980s.[8] The differences between the Chaldean Church and the lay Assyrians created a disconnect, which was emphasised via the apolitical and pro-regime stance of the former in contrast to the national identity debate of the latter during the late twentieth century. Lay Assyrians focused on equal citizenship rights irregardless of religious or national affiliation, language and culture. Their most active and successful political party is the Assyrian Democratic Movement (ADM). Following the 1991 Gulf war and the removal of Hussein from power, Christian communities further fled the country or moved back north to the Kurdish-protected regions in order to

---

[5] Otmar Oehring, "Christians in Syria: Current Situation and Future Outlook", *Konrad Adenauer Stiftung*, no. 237, 2017, pp. 4-5.

[6] Farha and Mousa, "Secular Autocracy vs. Sectarian Democracy? Weighing Reasons for Christian Support for Regime Transition in Syria and Egypt", pp. 180-181.

[7] Andreas Schmoller, "Now My Life in Syria Is Finished: Case Studies on Religious Identity and Sectarianism in Narratives of Syrian Christian Refugees in Austria", *Islam and Christian–Muslim Relations*, vol. 27, no. 4, 2016, pp. 421-422.

[8] Alda Benjamen, *Assyrians in Modern Iraq: Negotiating Political and Cultural Space*, Cambridge: Cambridge University Press, 2022, pp. 223-230.

find safe haven from the Sunni-Shia civil strife and the rise in anti-Christian religious persecution and harassment.[9] The mass Christian exodus from Iraq is estimated to number one million people, with approximately 200,000 Christians still residing in the country.

One of the main downsides of the co-optation relationship in both Syria and Iraq was that in times of turmoil and civil unrest, the Christian communities would be viewed as being sympathetic to or in cahoots with the previous regimes by the Sunni or Shia population. Hence, in retrospect, on the one hand, both the 2003 Iraqi war and the subsequent 2010 Arab uprisings triggered an era where Christian persecution, harassment and violent attacks would be on the rise.[10] On the other hand, the Church leaders seemed reluctant to forgo the special status attributed to the co-optation policies in order to effectively move with the times. In other words, despite the shifts and challenges brought by the new societal narratives and priorities, and especially with the advent of a more active and Christian-supported secular civil society, the Church leadership maintained its perceived role as the acting official representative of the Christian people in Syria and Iraq. At the same time, the developments related to the Arab uprisings in Egypt and Libya, coupled with the rise of the Muslim Brotherhood and political Islam in the Middle East, deterred the Christian Churches from shifting to an anti-regime stance.[11] With the decade-long Arab uprisings having created a vacuum for new potential actors to come into play, both against the longstanding regimes and against the regional status quo as a whole, the rise of jihadist groups such as al-Qaeda and later the Islamic State (or Daesh) – as its offshoot – further deteriorated the living conditions and prospects of Christians in Iraq and Syria. The successes of the Islamic State in seizing and maintaining territories led to the creation of zones in flux between the Syrian and Iraqi borders, exacerbated even further by the capture of Raqqa in Syria as the Islamic State's first capital, and later on Mosul and its region in Iraq.[12] With the Islamic State maintaining a foothold in both countries, the remaining Christians were effectively left to their own devices by both the Syrian and Iraqi regimes, as well as by the bulk of the international response, which was primarily focused on Kurdish and

---

[9] Matthew Barber, "They That Remain: Syrian and Iraqi Christian Communities amid the Syria Conflict and the Rise of the Islamic State", in Allen D. Hertzke and Timothy Samuel Shah (eds.), *Christianity and Freedom Volume II: Contemporary Perspectives*, Cambridge: Cambridge University Press, 2016, pp. 454-456.

[10] Daniel Williams, *Forsaken: The Persecution of Christians in Today's Middle East*, New York and London: OR Books, 2016, pp. 43-46, 84-86.

[11] Samuel Lieven, "Why Syria's patriarchs back Assad", *La Croix International*, 17 April 2018. Available at: https://international.la-croix.com/news/world/why-syria-s-patriarchs-back- assad/7376.

[12] Wilson Center, "Timeline: The Rise, Spread, and Fall of the Islamic State", 28 October 2019. Available at: https://www.wilsoncenter.org/article/timeline-the-rise-spread-and-fall-the-islamic-state.

geopolitical issues, and refrained from speaking out for Christians, fearing the 'crusader label'.[13]

The Islamic State and cultural heritage destruction

The Islamic State (IS) or Daesh emerged in the late 2000s out of the al-Qaeda network, specifically from the Zarqawi-led al-Qaeda in Iraq. It split from the al-Qaeda umbrella and control in 2013 when IS leader Abu Bakr al-Baghdadi was expelled from the sorganisation's nexus. In the years that followed, the Baghdadi-led Daesh managed to establish an Islamic Caliphate within its conquered but fluid borders in Iraqi and Syrian territories, essentially forming a 'hybrid state' – as in an entity which does not fully grasp the main conditions of state sovereignty since its territoriality not established or defined in accordance with the Westphalian model – wherein Shar'ia law, coupled with aggressive jihadist ideology would be the ruling orders.[14] Eventually, during the 2013-2014 period, Islamic State fighters captured and took hold of Raqqa in Syria and Mosul in Iraq, effectively establishing both cities as the Caliphate's primary and secondary capitals. Despite the Islamic State's initial successes against the Iraqi military forces, it was the ongoing civil war and chaotic predicament in Syria that enabled it to grow further and expand its regional operations. By gaining strength through capture and subsequent looting, the Islamic State managed not only to ascertain a grip on the wider region, but also to shift to more conventional military operations rather than guerilla warfare following 2014, as well as to attract and rally both local and foreign fighters from abroad to its theatres of war.[15]

In addition, with a view to maintain its control of the seized territories and further its clout beyond the Levant and Mesopotamia, the Islamic State took advantage of both its already well-developed social media network, as well as the propaganda machine in place through the use of the Dabiq online magazine and the media production center al-Hayat.[16] In other words, iconoclasm became a means by which the continuous mediatic assaults against cultural sites turned into a daily reminder of the Islamic State's foothold on the captured territories. For the purposes of this chapter, iconoclasm is defined as a strong opposition or defiance to generally accepted beliefs and customs. Therefore, in this particular case, Islamic State

---

[13] Eliza Griswold, "Is This the End of Christianity in the Middle East", *New York Times*, 26 July 2015. Available at: https://www.nytimes.com/2015/07/26/magazine/is-this-the-end-of-christianity-in-the-middle-east.html.

[14] Simon Mabon and Stephen Royle, *The Origins of ISIS: The Collapse of Nations and Revolution in the Middle East,* London and New York: I.B. Tauris, 2017, p. 17.

[15] Ahmed S. Hashim, "The Islamic State's Way of War in Iraq and Syria: From its origins to the Post-Caliphate Era", *Perspectives on Terrorism*, vol. 13, no. 1, 2019, p. 27.

[16] Bernat Arago, "Media Jihad", *IEMed Mediterranean Yearbook,* vol. 24, pp. 109-110.

iconoclasm takes shape through the meticulous documentation, presentation and media preservation of the destruction of heritage sites and institutions which clash with its brand of jihadist ideology. Zarandona, Albarrán-Torres and Isakhan distinguish between three acts with regard to the process of destruction: the recording of the heritage site before, during and after the moment of cultural mutilation.[17] These three stages are reminiscent of theatre plays or cinema productions, thus providing, at the same time, the incentives of the narrative at play, the act itself as climax, as well as the new status quo standing as catharsis and epilogue. As a result, the performance of cultural destruction, as promoted by the social media networks of the Islamic State and exemplified by the filmmaking professionalism exhibited by all parties involved in the destructive act, is intentional, directed and instrumentalised for influence and propaganda dissemination purposes. Due to the nature of the internet, the recording of the events will remain readily available for future viewings to attract potential supporters and followers.

Both cultural destruction and its mediatisation seem key to understanding the Islamic State's motives. Although barbaric, the cultural ruin cannot be simply relegated to randomly occurring destruction. The high production values and the organisational skills at play in the mediatisation of the destruction speak volumes regarding the planning involved in all aspects of the process, the engineered state-building, as well as the cultural and religious homogeneity that is being striven for. Stein accurately describes it as 'performative destruction'.[18] At the same time, heritage destruction, especially when directed at Christianity – and the state entities, which engaged in co-optation policies – serves as a way to, at the very least, partially rationalise conflict by widening the net for potential targets, sensationalising operations and broadening the image of the omnipresent enemy that needs to be defeated and eliminated through any means necessary.

What is more, the symbolic nature of the heritage sites in question, as well as their aspect as ontic spaces for other ethnic or religious communities needs to be underlined. As a direct result, the communities' collective identity and their historical symbiotic link to the regions are traumatised or even severed, leading to the mass population exodus and internal displacement mentioned above. Moreover, heritage markers are not limited

---

[17] José Antonio González Zarandona, César Albarrán-Torres and Benjamin Isakhan, "Digitally Mediated Iconoclasm: The Islamic State and the War on Cultural Heritage", *International Journal of Heritage Studies*, vol. 24, no. 6, 2018, pp. 650-652.

[18] Gil J. Stein, "Performative Destruction: Da'esh (ISIS) Ideology and the War on Heritage in Iraq", in James Cuno and Thomas G. Weiss (eds.), *Cultural Heritage and Mass Atrocities*, California: J. Paul Getty Trust, 2022, p. 168.

to religious places of worship. Instead, they can also be pinpointed to libraries, museums, schools, art galleries or any other institution which stands as a reminder of a community's specific language, history, arts or customs. Once a symbolic connection is severed, then there is no concrete reason for a community to return to its historical cradle when things have settled down, or the status quo has been restored. In addition, since heritage markers signify a site's identity linkage to a specific population, altering and repurposing these sites effectively act as the pillars of a new under construction state identity. In other words, the end of one era signaling the beginning of another, defined by new values, principles and priorities. [19] In the same way that the state prison Bastille – a longstanding symbol of the Bourbon king dynasty in France – was demolished, with its remains and archives surviving as reminders of the seismic French revolutionary event and the abolition of monarchial rule, the alteration of heritage and institutional markers aims at shifting or downgrading their significance for political, societal and cultural priorities in favour of a new ruling order. Similarly, when the Islamic State seized Homs, Mosul or the Nineveh plains, it engaged in the thoroughly documented destruction of archaeological sites, temples and museums, stripping them of artefacts and selling them on the black market. Namely, robbing them of their cultural place in history and repurposing them by objectifying them as goods for sale to the highest bidder for the financial needs of the Caliphate.

Nevertheless, it is of note that in the case of Islamic State identity building, Christian communities are not the sole parties concerned. Any and all polytheistic sites, Yazidi, Shia Islam or other monuments or history are hence deemed as heretic and must be removed from all facets of Islamic Caliphate society. The objective was to remove religious pluralism and alternative options in order to purify and create one singular identity foundation, thus categorising, othering and fringing difference as infidelity, apostasy or dhimmitude akin to previous early centuries with regards to non-Sunni Muslims.[20] In essence, the Islamic State was in the process of redefining societal membership and, at the same, redrawing the future map of the region, away from western prerogatives as viewed through the lens of the Sykes-Picot and other post-dissolution of the Ottoman Empire agreements.[21]

---

[19] Benjamin Isakhan and Sofya Shahab, "The Islamic State's Targeting of Christians and their Heritage: Genocide, Displacement and Reconciliation", *International Journal of Heritage Studies*, vol. 28, no. 7, 2022, pp. 824-827.

[20] Pieter Nanninga, "Cleansing the Earth of the Stench of Shirk: The Islamic State's Violence as Acts of Purification", *Journal of Religion and Violence*, vol. 7, no. 2, 2019, pp. 141-143.

[21] Erin Hughes, "Nationalism by Another Name: Examining 'Religious Radicalism' from the Perspective of Iraqi Christians", *The Review of Faith & International Affairs*, vol. 15, no. 2, 2017, p. 40.

The Christian dilemma within the IS state-building process

The US Commission on International Religious Freedom reported on findings of genocide against Christians and other religious communities in 2015. Subsequently, in 2016, the US House of Representatives and Senate, the UK, European and Australian parliaments, along with other state political institutions, acknowledged the actions committed by the Islamic State against Christians, Yazidi, Shia Muslims and other religious communities located in territories under its control as amounting to genocide.[22] While Christians were no strangers to persecution, discrimination and violent crimes by radicals in the Middle Eastern region, the rise of the activities of jihadi groups in Iraq and Syria ushered an era of renewed uncertainty, promoting at the same time an unsafe and hostile environment for Christians from all walks of life, including religious leaders and Christian houses of worship. With Christians being targeted largely due to their faith, their concentrated presence in cities and villages in Mosul, Nineveh, Homs, Raqqa and Aleppo made them an easy mark for Islamic State fighters. As a result, Christians were subjected to harassment, violence, murder, kidnappings, forced conversion, along with expulsion from their home villages, cities and regions. At the same time, churches, museums, monuments and landmarks to Christianity were destroyed, looted or confiscated, leaving both no trace of their previous historical presence going back nearly two millennia, as well as no incentive for a potential future return.[23]

Originally situated in the south of Iraq and around Baghdad, the various predicaments following the 2003 Gulf war stemming from Sunni-Shia sectarian tensions, the rise of al-Qaeda and the Iraqi Kurdish question forced the majority of the Christian population to move further north to the Nineveh plains during the late 2000s. Throughout the decade of the 2010s, numerous reports have been published regarding the abduction and often the execution of prominent Christian clergy in both Iraq and Syria. For instance, during 2013 in Aleppo, Syriac Orthodox Archbishop Mar Gregorios Yohanna Ibrahim and Greek Orthodox Archbishop Boulos Yazigi were kidnapped by Syrian Jihadists and never recovered.[24] In 2013,

---

[22] Alex Whiting, "UK parliament condemns Islamic State violence as genocide", *Reuters*, 20 April 2016. Available at: https://www.reuters.com/article/us-britain-parliament-genocide-islamic-s-idUSKCN0XH 2EM.

[23] Otmar Oehring, "On the Situation of Christians in Syria and Iraq", *Konrad Adenauer Stiftung International Reports*, no. 6, 2015; Matthew Clapperton, David Martin Jones and M. L. R. Smith, "Iconoclasm and strategic thought: Islamic State and cultural heritage in Iraq and Syria", *International Affairs*, vol. 93, no. 5, 2017, p. 1219.

[24] Agenzia Fides, "Journalistic investigation: 'the 2 Bishops of Aleppo who disappeared in 2013 martyred'. But the incident is still shrouded in mystery", 15 January 2020. Available at: http://www.fides.org/en/news/67241-

Chaldean Patriarch Louis Sako stated that eighty percent of churches in Iraq were destroyed or abandoned with one of the most high-profile attacks occurring against Our Lady of Salvation Church in Baghdad.[25] Furthermore, when the Islamic State captured Mosul in 2014, it marked all Christian houses and institutions with the Arabic letter 'N'' – as in 'Nazarene', which translates to Christian – and enforced a strict ultimatum: to leave immediately, convert to its version of Sunni Islam, pay the jizya tax (dhimmi contracts) or face the sword.[26]

In contrast to al-Qaeda ideology, for the Islamic State, Middle Eastern Christianity did not necessarily equate to the United States and the West as the global enemy or the 'Crusaders'.[27] Christians were considered as 'People of the Book' and as such were allowed to coexist as second-class citizens, as long as they adhered to a number of restrictions and rules. With the same policy being enforced in the seized territories in Syria, such as Raqqa, for the Christians that chose to remain, aside from the enforced jizya tax, religious and social liberties were severely hindered.[28] In addition, Christians were not permitted to collect income from Muslims – such as rent – and were, as a result, unable to pay the obligatory dhimmi (protection) tax, facing immediate repercussions such as death, violence, and lootings, among others.[29] Christian religious crosses and symbols were swiftly removed and destroyed, while bell-ringing and demonstrations of Christian faith were forbidden from public view.[30] In other words, through the lens of the Islamic State, Christians needed to demonstrate their inferiority both to the Caliphate and Sunni Muslims through all aspects of society. Nonetheless, this ambiguous Islamic State policy with regard to the remaining Christians was not implemented uniformly throughout IS-controlled territories in Syria and Iraq.[31] To say the least, it revealed a twofold antithetic approach: on the

---

ASIA_SYRIA_Journalistic_investigation_the_2_Bishops_of_Aleppo_who_disappeared_in_2013_mart yred_But_the_incident_is_still_shrouded_in_mystery.

[25] Hughes, "Nationalism by Another Name: Examining 'Religious Radicalism' from the Perspective of Iraqi Christians", p. 38.

[26] Human Rights Watch, "Iraq: ISIS Abducting, Killing, Expelling Minorities", 19 July 2014. Available at: https://www.hrw.org/news/2014/07/19/iraq-isis-abducting-killing-expelling-minorities.

[27] Brynjar Lia and Mathilde Becker Aarseth, "Crusader Hirelings or Loyal Subjects? Evolving Jihadist Perspectives on Christian Minorities in the Middle East", *Islam and Christian–Muslim Relations*, vol. 33, no. 3, 2022, pp. 256-257.

[28] Mindy Belz, "Christians' Response to Persecution Under ISIS", *The Review of Faith & International Affairs*, vol. 15, no. 1, 2017, pp. 13-14.

[29] Georges Fahmi, "The Future of Christians in the Middle East after the Defeat of Islamic State (IS)", *IEMed. Mediterranean Yearbook*, 2014, p. 73; Barber, "They That Remain: Syrian and Iraqi Christian Communities amid the Syria Conflict and the Rise of the Islamic State", p. 471.

[30] Nina Shea, "Barbarism 2014: On Religious Cleansing by Islamists", World Affairs, vol. 177, no. 4, 2014, pp. 39-41.

[31] Hughes, "Nationalism by Another Name: Examining 'Religious Radicalism' from the Perspective of

one hand, law-abiding and jizya tax-paying Christians would be allegedly protected following the world of God; on the other hand, the living conditions of the Christians would be so drastically obstructed – beyond the limits set by the dhimmi contracts – that they would be forced to a 'voluntary' swift and mass expulsion.[32] Lending further credence to this antithesis, in other cases, such as in Sirte, Libya in 2011, the option to pay the jizya tax was never available for Christian Copts, who were instead publicly beheaded, with their filmed murders being disseminated for propaganda purposes via Islamic State social media outlets.[33]

Christians seem to have found safe havens within the Kurdistan Regional Government, Lebanon and Jordan. However, a number of Christian refugees – such as in Jordan, one of the primary recipients of the Syrian and Iraqi refugee waves – seem to opt-out from registering as such. The fear remains that they will be forced to return to their homeland and face once more either the atrocities perpetrated by radical jihadi entities or the hostile and foreign environment that has now been created.[34] The advent and successes of the Islamic State and its capture of Mosul in 2014 effectively engineered a new displacement towards the Kurdistan Regional Government (KRG).[35] The latter became the de facto 'protector' of the Christian population following the ouster of the Islamic State from the Mosul region and the Nineveh plains in 2017 in exchange for political and international support against the Baghdad government over control of the disputed Mosul region.[36]

Barber argues that the vast majority of revolutionary Syrians were Sunni, while the bulk of minority populations stood with the regime, making a case for a trade off between security and repression.[37] Christians in southwestern Syria – estimated at 500,000 people – have indeed sustained their co-optation policy with the Damascus government in exchange for protection from both the various opposition entities seeking to topple Assad, as well as from

---

Iraqi Christians", p. 39.

[32] Lia and Aarseth, "Crusader Hirelings or Loyal Subjects? Evolving Jihadist Perspectives on Christian Minorities in the Middle East", pp. 266-267.

[33] *Reuters*, "Bodies of 20 Egyptian Christians beheaded in Libya arrive in Egypt", 14 May 2018. Available at: https://www.reuters.com/article/us-libya-egypt-idUSKCN1IF0J4.

[34] Amanda Ufheil-Somers, "Christians: Egypt, Iraq, Lebanon, Palestine", *Middle East Report*, no. 267, 2013, pp. 19-20; Schmoller, "Now My Life in Syria Is Finished: Case Studies on Religious Identity and Sectarianism in Narratives of Syrian Christian Refugees in Austria", p. 434.

[35] Belz, "Christians' Response to Persecution Under ISIS", p. 16.

[36] Sotiris Roussos and Stavros Drakoularakos "Christians in Syria and Iraq: From Co-optation to Militarisation Strategies", *Studies in World Christianity*, vol. 28, no. 3, 2022, pp. 349-350.

[37] Barber, "They That Remain: Syrian and Iraqi Christian Communities amid the Syria Conflict and the Rise of the Islamic State", p. 460.

Islamic State and jihadist fighters. However, that was not the case regarding the Christians residing in the northern and eastern parts of Syria, namely the cities of Aleppo, Homs and Raqqa, which bore witness to the clashes between all involved parties and had to manage through a short-lived Islamic State rule. As a result, the cities of Damascus, Tartus and Latakia saw a considerable increase in Christian demographics in contrast to the sharp drop in Aleppo, Homs, Idlib, and Raqqa – with the latter reportedly no longer being home to any Christian inhabitants.[38] In the years prior to the Syrian civil war, Aleppo and Homs were the cities with the largest percentage of Christian citizens in the country. Hence, these Christian communities are reluctant to return to their former ancestral settlements in fear of history repeating itself, in addition to their historical presence having been expunged. Instead, the return of internally displaced persons and refugees to their cities and deserted villages will mostly depend on reassurances and conditions of both mutual peaceful coexistence with non-Christians, as well as the end of the Syrian civil war precarious and volatile environment.

The Christian predicament following the Islamic State period

Following the rise of uncertainty and fear in Syria and Iraq, the remaining Christian communities were split between regime co-optation and support for KRG or PYD.[39] With the longstanding survival strategy of co-optation with the regime no longer presenting itself as a viable or safe option, previous years saw a number of Christian paramilitary groups emerge as an alternative to ensuring the safeguarding of their people. These militias would be either self-managed and independent, absorbed as subgroups and part of the regimes' national forces, or allied with Kurdish state entities.[40]

Nonetheless, during the 2010s, the Church leaderships in both Syria and Iraq cautiously maintained the tenets of the longstanding co-optation policy with the regimes and stood firmly against the formation of Christian militias. The fear was that Christian militias would have a threefold effect: sectarian tensions would rise further due to the ethno-religious nature of the paramilitary groups;[41] the volatile environment would equate the Christian militias with the West and pit them as proxies against the brunt of jihadist

---

[38] Oehring, "Christians in Syria: Current Situation and Future Outlook", p. 15.

[39] The Kurdistan Regional Government (KRG) is the executive body of the autonomous Kurdistan Region in Iraq. The Democratic Union Party (PYD) is a political party established in Syria, at the helm of the Rojava state-building process.

[40] Barber, "They That Remain: Syrian and Iraqi Christian Communities amid the Syria Conflict and the Rise of the Islamic State", pp. 473-474.

[41] Schmoller, "Now My Life in Syria Is Finished: Case Studies on Religious Identity and Sectarianism in Narratives of Syrian Christian Refugees in Austria", pp. 421-422.

forces;[42] the future uncertain regional settlement could turn out to be disadvantageous for some of the warring parties. As a result, the Churches opted for loyalty towards the regimes, with the latter's forces being considered the sole legitimate ones to protect all Iraqis and Syrians, regardless of religious faith. Essentially, the Churches concluded that the chaotic situation at play and the potential collapse of state institutions could damage the uneasy equilibrium in effect during previous decades with regards to the relationship between Christians and the regimes, threaten the Church monopoly in acting as representatives for Christians against the state or lessen the Churches' effectiveness in their mission in the case of the ascent of a pro-Islamist regime.[43]

In western Syria, Christian paramilitary groups active under the umbrella of the pro-regime People Committees became part of Assad's regime forces and Syrian nationalist militias, such as the Syrian Social Nationalist Party. In eastern Syria, Assyrian Christians witnessed the clashes between the Islamic State and Syrian Kurdish forces, subsequently forming their own independent armed groups.[44] The latter networked with the Assyrian national movements of the previous decades – as a response to the Baathist Arabisation project – such as the Syriac Union Party, which eventually formed the Sutoro militia during 2012. Because of the shared apprehension towards the Assad regime and promises of future self-administration, the Sutoro militia cooperated closely with the Kurdish Democratic Union Party (PYD).[45] In just over a decade, the Kurdish Rojava gradually established military, political and social structures autonomous from Assad's central government. Thus, the Kurds provided an alternative form of protection for the Christians. Contrary to Assad's sectarian regime, the Christians would have equal and direct participation in the secular administrative state of Rojava. Nevertheless, this did not find all the Christians in agreement leading to a polarisation within the community. A case in point was the Sootoro militia split from Sutoro and joined pro-regime forces, in disagreement with going all in with Kurdish state-building prospects.

In contrast to Syria, Christian militias in Iraq formed earlier in light of the lukewarm success of the co-optation policy, sectarianism, and clashes

---

[42] Hughes, "Nationalism by Another Name: Examining 'Religious Radicalism' from the Perspective of Iraqi Christians", p. 41.

[43] Monier, "The Chaldean patriarch and the discourse of 'inclusive citizenship': restructuring the political representation of Christians in Iraq since 2003", p. 371; Fahmi, "The Future of Syrian Christians after the Arab Spring", pp. 10-11.

[44] Roussos and Drakoularakos, "Christians in Syria and Iraq: From Co-optation to Militarisation Strategies", p. 343.

[45] Marina Eleftheriadou, "Christian militias in Syria and Iraq: beyond the neutrality/passivity debate", *CEMMIS Middle East Bulletin*, vol. 28, 2015, pp. 13-19.

between regime and Kurdish forces. The growing presence and activities of the al-Qaeda network in the country during the 2000s raised security concerns even further and extended the drive for militarisation. With the already established since 2004, Qaraqosh Christian militia in the Nineveh Plains, the activities of al-Qaeda and the subsequent further displacement of the Christian population to the north gave way to the formation of the Nineveh Plains Guards militia, which was funded mainly by the KRG in exchange for political and electoral support towards further Kurdish autonomy from Baghdad.[46] However, the coming of the Islamic State in 2014 and the taking of Mosul led to the formation of other Christian militias, such as the Nineveh Plains Protection Units, the Babylon Brigades, Dwekh Nawsha and the Nineveh Plains Forces.[47] While some integrated with pro-regime forces and others with the Peshmerga, most Christian militias attempted to maintain autonomy and self-administration by, at times, cooperating with Baghdad but operating in areas under the control of Erbil and vice versa.[48] The relationship between the Christians in northern Iraq and the Erbil government has grown intriguingly during the end of 2010s. As a direct result of the growing tensions and hostile environment, Assyrians moved to the Kurdish region in search of protection. Soon, they were referred to as Christian Kurds since the administration did not recognise their unique Assyrian national identity.[49] Essentially exchanging guardians, the Christian population in northern Iraq, especially in Erbil, cultivated relations with the KRG and grew, despite the issues stemming from the fight against jihadist radicalism. On the other hand, the KRG counted on Christian political backing against Baghdad, as well as for rallying international Christian support for the Kurdish state-building process.[50] Hence, in 2021, Barzani claimed that Ankawa, the Christian concentrated suburb in Erbil, would become "distinct and autonomous" from the capital which would foster a safe environment for Christians, as well as foreign economic investment.[51]

---

[46] Assyrian Policy Institute, "Contested Control: The Future of Security in Iraq's Nineveh Plain", 1 June 2020, pp. 18-21. Available at: https://www.assyrianpolicy.org/contested-control.

[47] Michael Knights and Yousif Kalian, "Confidence – and Security- Building Measures in the Nineveh Plains", *Washington Institute for Near East Policy*, 14 July 2017. Available at: https://www.washington institute.org/policy-analysis/confidence-and-security-building-measures-nineveh-plains.

[48] Eliza Griswold, "Is This the End of Christianity in the Middle East", *New York Times*, 26 July 2015. Available at: https://www.nytimes.com/2015/07/26/magazine/is-this-the-end-of-christianity-in-the-middle-east.html.

[49] Judit Neurink, "Assyrians Demand Kurdish Apology for Last Century Killings", *Rudaw*, 19 August 2013. Available at: https://www.rudaw.net/english/kurdistan/19082013.

[50] Barber, "They That Remain: Syrian and Iraqi Christian Communities amid the Syria Conflict and the Rise of the Islamic State", pp. 475-476.

[51] Michael Kranz, "Safe haven: What will Ankawa's new autonomy mean for Kurdistan's Christians?", *New Arab*, 4 November 2021. Available at: https://www.newarab.com/analysis/what-will-autonomy-

Conclusion

In this chapter, I analysed the repercussions of the Islamic State in the modus vivendi of Middle Eastern Christians in Syria and Iraq. In doing this, I first provided the necessary historical background with regard to the Churches, the Christians, and their relationship with the Syrian and Iraqi regimes through the prism of the longstanding co-optation policy. Second, I examined the impact of iconoclasm, the state-building process of the Islamic State and its strategy of cultural heritage destruction in constructing religious homogeneity. Third, I articulated the Christian dilemma following the advent of the Islamic State and its capture of Raqqa and Mosul with regard to their position within the Jihadist entity, as well as the resulting refugee crisis and internal displacement. Lastly, I provided insight into the Iraqi and Syrian Christian predicament concerning choosing sides between the regimes or the Kurdish entities, the Churches' stance, and Christian militia formation.

Christians in Syria and Iraq fell victim to the Islamic State's efforts for state-building, societal cohesion engineering and territorial expansion. On the one hand, the capture by IS forces of densely-populated areas by Christian denominations led to their subsequent exodus from the region. Under threat of harassment, violence, persecution, forced marriages, rape and death, they were forced to make an impossible choice: to either flee from their homeland or stay and face the consequences. Those who stayed had to attempt to abide by second-class citizenship status and the strict rules related to the impossible of gathering jizya tribute. On the other hand, the Islamic State undertook the task of forced cultural and religious homogenisation by annihilating any and all heritage markers associated with populations of – among others – Christian, Shia, or Yazidi backgrounds. The immediate aftereffects of the cultural destruction were twofold: first, the cultural linkage of the populations with their heritage was lost; second, the destruction of sites and institutions – via its meticulous planning and digital mediatisation – and their subsequent repurposing served the Islamic State's impetus for rallying supporters from abroad, as well as for broadcasting the ontological foundations of a new state identity, free from the past.

The Christians that remained in Syria and Iraq were split among competing state entities, the Syrian or Iraqi regimes, or the KRG and PYD governments. The internal displacement to northern Iraq and southwestern Syria, along with mass regional dislocation to Jordan, Lebanon and Europe led to Christian population shrinkage in Syria and in Iraq. Those that remained eventually mobilised into Christian militia units in order to

---

mean-iraqs-largest-christian-town.

guarantee their own safekeeping, fighting under regime or Kurdish umbrella forces. In Syria, Christian support for the Assad regime is more overt due both to the concentration of the population near government-held cities, such as Damascus, the maintaining of the co-optation relationship between Church and State, and the past animosity between eastern Christians and Kurds. In Iraq, the Chaldean Church argues for sustaining Christian support for the Baghdad government and shying away from ethnic identity debates. However, internally displaced Christians to the Kurdish region and the Nineveh plains have begun integrating within Kurdish society, in exchange for future political support for further KRG autonomy. Christians have essentially hedged their bets on competing state entities. At the same time, the situation in Iraq and Syria – despite the fall of the Islamic State – remains volatile and home to sectarian and ethnic tensions, with no clear end in sight. In other words, Christian survival remains contingent on the mainstay of their chosen protector.

Bibliography

Agenzia Fides, "Journalistic investigation: "the 2 Bishops of Aleppo who disappeared in 2013 martyred". But the incident is still shrouded in mystery", 15 January 2020. Available at: http://www.fides.org/en/news/67241-ASIA_SYRIA_Journalistic_investigation_the_2 _Bishops_of_Aleppo_who_disappeared_in_2013_martyred_But_the_incident_is_still_ shrouded_in_mystery.

Arago, Bernat, "Media Jihad", *IEMed Mediterranean Yearbook*, vol. 24, pp. 108-122.

Assyrian Policy Institute, "Contested Control: The Future of Security in Iraq's Nineveh Plain", 1 June 2020. Available at: https://www.assyrianpolicy.org/contested-control.

Barber, Matthew, "They That Remain: Syrian and Iraqi Christian Communities amid the Syria Conflict and the Rise of the Islamic State", in Allen D. Hertzke and Timothy Samuel Shah (eds) *Christianity and Freedom Volume II: Contemporary Perspectives*, Cambridge University Press, 2016, pp. 453-488.

Belz, Mindy, "Christians' Response to Persecution Under ISIS", *The Review of Faith & International Affairs*, vol. 15, no. 1, 2017, pp. 12-20.

Benjamen, Alda, *Assyrians in Modern Iraq: Negotiating Political and Cultural Space*, Cambridge University Press, 2022.

Clapperton, Matthew, Jones, David Martin and Smith, M. L. R., "Iconoclasm and strategic thought: Islamic State and cultural heritage in Iraq and Syria", *International Affairs*, vol. 93, no. 5, 2017, p. 1205-1231.

Eleftheriadou, Marina, "Christian militias in Syria and Iraq: beyond the neutrality/passivity debate", *CEMMIS Middle East Bulletin*, vol. 28, 2015, pp. 13-19.

Fahmi, Georges, "The Future of Christians in the Middle East after the Defeat of Islamic State (IS)", *IEMed. Mediterranean Yearbook*, 2014, pp. 71-75.

Fahmi, Georges, "The Future of Syrian Christians after the Arab Spring", *Robert Shuman Centre for Advanced Studies*, 2018.

Farha, Mark and Mousa, Salma, "Secular Autocracy vs. Sectarian Democracy? Weighing Reasons for Christian Support for Regime Transition in Syria and Egypt, *Mediterranean Politics*, vol. 20, no. 2, 2015, p. 178-197.

France24, "Iraq fighters take 'victory selfies' at Tal Afar citadel", 28 August 2017. Available at: https://www.france24.com/en/20170828-iraq-fighters-take-victory-selfies-tal-afar-citadel.

Griswold, Eliza, "Is This the End of Christianity in the Middle East", *New York Times*, 26 July 2015. Available at: https://www.nytimes.com/2015/07/26/magazine/is-this-the-end-of-christianity-in-the-middle-east.html.

Hashim, Ahmed S., "The Islamic State's Way of War in Iraq and Syria: From its origins to the Post-Caliphate Era", *Perspectives on Terrorism*, vol. 13, no. 1, 2019, pp. 22-31.

Hughes, Erin, "Nationalism by Another Name: Examining 'Religious Radicalism' from the Perspective of Iraqi Christians", *The Review of Faith & International Affairs*, vol. 15, no. 2, 2017, pp. 34-44.

Human Rights Watch, "Iraq: ISIS Abducting, Killing, Expelling Minorities", 19 July 2014. Available at: https://www.hrw.org/news/2014/07/19/iraq-isis-abducting-killing-expelling-minorities.

Isakhan, Benjamin and Shahab, Sofya, "The Islamic State's Targeting of Christians and their Heritage: Genocide, Displacement and Reconciliation", *International Journal of Heritage Studies*, vol. 28, no. 7, 2022, pp. 820-835.

Knights, Michael and Kalian, Yousif, "Confidence – and Security- Building Measures in the Nineveh Plains", *Washington Institute for Near East Policy*, 14 July 2017. Available at: https://www.washingtoninstitute.org/policy-analysis/confidence-and-security-building-measures-nineveh-plains.

Kranz, Michael, "Safe haven: What will Ankawa's new autonomy mean for Kurdistan's Christians?", *New Arab*, 4 November 2021. Available at: https://www.newarab.com/analysis/what-will-autonomy-mean-iraqs-largest-christian-town.

Lia, Brynjar and Aarseth, Mathilde Becker, "Crusader Hirelings or Loyal Subjects? Evolving Jihadist Perspectives on Christian Minorities in the Middle East", *Islam and Christian–Muslim Relations*, vol. 33, no. 3, 2022, pp. 255-280.

Lieven, Samuel, "Why Syria's patriarchs back Assad", *La Croix International*, 17 April 2018. Available at: https://international.la-croix.com/news/world/why-syria-s-patriarchs-back- assad/7376.

Mabon, Simon and Royle, Stephen, *The Origins of ISIS: The Collapse of Nations and Revolution in the Middle East*, London/New York: I.B. Tauris, 2017.

McCallum, Fiona, "Christian Political Participation in the Arab world", *Islam and Christian–Muslim Relations*, vol. 23, no. 1, 2012, pp. 3-18.

Monier, Elizabeth, "The Chaldean patriarch and the discourse of 'inclusive citizenship': restructuring the political representation of Christians in Iraq since 2003", *Religion, State & Society*, vol. 48, no. 5, 2020, pp. 361-377.

Nanninga, Pieter, "Cleansing the Earth of the Stench of Shirk: The Islamic State's Violence as Acts of Purification", *Journal of Religion and Violence*, vol. 7, no. 2, 2019, pp. 128-157.

Neurink, Judit, "Assyrians Demand Kurdish Apology for Last Century Killings", *Rudaw*, 19 August 2013. Available at: https://www.rudaw.net/english/kurdistan/19082013

Oehring, Otmar, "Christians in Syria: Current Situation and Future Outlook", *Konrad Adenauer Stiftung*, no. 237, 2017, pp. 1-30.

Oehring, Otmar, "On the Situation of Christians in Syria and Iraq", *Konrad Adenauer Stiftung International Reports*, no. 6, 2015, pp. 64-78.

Reuters, "Bodies of 20 Egyptian Christians beheaded in Libya arrive in Egypt", 14 May 2018. Available at: https://www.reuters.com/article/us-libya-egypt-idUSKCN1IF0J4

Roussos, Sotiris and Drakoularakos, Stavros, "Christians in Syria and Iraq: From Co-optation to Militarisation Strategies", *Studies in World Christianity*, vol. 28, no. 3, 2022, pp. 334-360.

Schmoller, Andreas, "Now My Life in Syria Is Finished: Case Studies on Religious Identity and Sectarianism in Narratives of Syrian Christian Refugees in Austria", *Islam and Christian–Muslim Relations*, vol. 27, no. 4, 2016, pp. 419-437.

Shea, Nina, "Barbarism 2014: On Religious Cleansing by Islamists", *World Affairs*, vol. 177, no. 4, 2014, pp. 34-46.

Stein, Gil J., "Performative Destruction: Da'esh (ISIS) Ideology and the War on Heritage in Iraq", in James Cuno and Thomas G. Weiss (eds) *Cultural Heritage and Mass Atrocities*, J.

Paul Getty Trust, 2022, p. 168-185.

Ufheil-Somers, Amanda, "Christians: Egypt, Iraq, Lebanon, Palestine", *Middle East Report*, no. 267, 2013, pp. 18-20.

United States Commission on International Religious Freedom, *Annual Report 2021*. Available at: https://www.uscirf.gov/sites/default/files/2021-04/2021%20Annual%20Report. pdf.

Whiting, Alex, "UK parliament condemns Islamic Sttate violence as genocide", *Reuters*, 20 April 2016. Available at: https://www.reuters.com/article/us-britain-parliament-genocide-islamic-s-idUSKCN0XH2EM.

Williams, Daniel, *Forsaken: The Persecution of Christians in Today's Middle East*, New York/London: OR Books, 2016.

Wilson Center, "Timeline: The Rise, Spread, and Fall of the Islamic State", 28 October 2019. Available at: https://www.wilsoncenter.org/article/timeline-the-rise-spread-and-fall-the-islamic-state.

Zarandona, José Antonio González, Albarrán-Torres, César and Isakhan, Benjamin, "Digitally Mediated Iconoclasm: The Islamic State and the war on cultural heritage", *International Journal of Heritage Studies*, vol. 24, no. 6, 2018, pp. 649-671.

TURKISH POLICIES VIS-À-VIS CHRISTIANS: FROM EXCLUSION TO INCLUSION TO EXCLUSION AGAIN

Nikos Christofis

Introduction

The Republic of Turkey, as a direct heir of the Ottoman Empire, inherited the empire's multi-cultural, multi-religious, and multi-ethnic diversity. As a result, entering into modernity, Turkey itself is composed of several peoples with different ethnic backgrounds, among which a Christian community.[1] Christians, once an essential composite of the Ottoman administration, is now a very small percentage of the total population, with its vast majority now living in Istanbul itself.[2] With the fall of Istanbul in 1453, the proportion of the non-Muslim population in the Ottoman Empire reached 60 per cent overnight. This made it impossible for the Ottomans to rule over many different peoples through a legal system based on sharia. The millet system "set in motion the development of an order that involved autonomy and decentralisation for non-Muslim groups but within religious hierarchy".[3]

The millet system was abolished by 1839 with the Gülhane Edict, which declared all subjects of the Sultan to be equals, although this was only partially achieved without altering the mentality or practices upon/of the society.[4] Baskin Oran argues that the Ottoman notion of the *Millet-i Hakime*, i.e., those who hand down decisions or the ruling Muslim elite, and in extension, the notion of *Millet-i Mahkume*, i.e., those about whom decisions are made, continues to this day through its "cloning" in the Republic of

---

[1] For an overview and different aspects of the Christian presence in the Middle East, see Souad Abou el-Rousse Slim, *Christianity: A History in the Middle East*, Lebanon: Middle East Council of Churches, 2005; Anthony O'Mahony and Emma Loosley (eds), *Eastern Christianity in the Modern Middle East*, London: Routledge, 2010; Stephan Stetter and Mitra Moussa Nabo (eds), *Middle East Christianity: Local Practices, World Societal Entanglements*, Basingstoke: Palgrave, 2020; Sotiris Roussos, "Diaspora Politics, Ethnicity and the Orthodox Church in the Near East", *Journal of Eastern Christian Studies*, vol. 61, no. 1-2, 2009, pp. 137-148; Colin Chapman, "Christians in the Middle East – Past, Present and Future", *Transformation*, vol. 29, no. 2, 2012, pp. 91-110; Sotiris Roussos, "Globalization Processes and Christians in the Middle East: A Comparative Analysis", *The Journal of the Middle East and Africa*, vol. 5, no. 2, 2014, pp. 111-130.

[2] Bette Jane Bailey and J. Martin Bailey, *Who are the Christians in the Middle East?*, Cambridge: Eerdmans, 2003, pp. 196-197.

[3] Baskın Oran, *Minorities and Minority Rights in Turkey: From the Ottoman Empire to the Present State*, trans. John William Day, Boulder and London: Lynne Rienner, 2021, p. 13.

[4] Among several, see Carter Vaughn Findley, *Turkey, Islam, Nationalism, and Modernity: A History, 1789-2007*, New Haven and London: Yale University Press, 2010, pp. 100-102.

Turkey through several documents and/or practices that overtly established a distinction between Muslims and non-Muslims. The Republic of Turkey, by contrast, however, was designed to create a new political community based on a secular concept: "nation"; therefore, it ended the autonomy of non-Muslim minorities and explicitly denied the existence of ethnic minorities within the nation.

The present chapter focuses on the republican years and aims to provide an overview of the Turkish policies vis-à-vis the Christian minorities since 1923. In particular, the chapter will provide, firstly, a brief account of the one-party regime under the leadership of the founder of Turkey, Mustafa Kemal, and his close circle of trustees, and then, it will turn its focus on the more recent period of the Islamist Justice and Development Party (Adalet ve Kalkınma Partisi, AKP) governments. In so doing, the chapter's goal is to show the status of the minorities, particularly the Christian minorities, in Turkey throughout the past century and to identify similarities and differences between past and present governments. Finally, the core argument of the chapter is that recent policies vis-à-vis Christian minorities, despite the similarities that are presented with the past, i.e., the Kemalist past, have as an ultimate goal to securitise Turkish identity, and in particular, the Sunni-Muslim aspect of it; and therefore, should be seen through the prism of the AKP vision of constructing a *Yeni Türkiye* (New Turkey).

Kemalism, Nation-Building Process, and Minority Policies

We will remove the foreigners

dominating our market and

hand over the Turkish market to Turks.[5]

This is how Şükrü Saraçoğlu, the Republican People's Party (Cumhuriyet Halk Partisi, CHP) government's Prime Minister from 1942-46, described the "anti-minority" Wealth Tax (*Varlık Vergisi*), which was introduced during World War II. Although *Varlık Vergisi* was presented by the Turkish government as a means of countering military expenditure and economic problems derived from the World War II conditions, it "unofficially" aimed at suppressing the non-Turkish higher-class groups. Against this background, Ankara categorised the country's population as "Muslim

---

[5] Ayhan Aktar, *Varlık Vergisi ve Türkleştirme Politikaları*, İstanbul: İletişim, 2000, p. 142. See also, Ali Sait Çetinoğlu, *Varlık Vergisi 1942-1944 Ekonomik ve Kültürel Jenosid*, İstanbul: Belge Yayınları, 2009.

Turks" and "non-Muslim Turks" to classify taxpayers. More importantly, this classification helped hamper further the minorities' dominant status in the country's economy, and empower the idea of a national economy free of the control of the non-Muslim Ottomans and of its dependency on the West, which emerged during the Committee of Union and Progress rule after 1908, aimed ultimately to benefit the ethnic Turks.[6]

What is of importance here is that Saraçoğlu's statement comes in direct contravention with the official proclamations of the new government and the adoption of Article 88 in the 1924 Constitution (*Teşkilât-ı Esâsiye Kanunu*), which stated that "the people of Turkey regardless of their religion and race [are], in terms of citizenship, Turkish",[7] entitling equal rights to all of the country's citizens. Turkey's first constitution was introduced after the establishment of the Republic of Turkey – influenced also, at least regarding the protection of minorities, albeit with some differences, by the Treaty of Lausanne signed a few months earlier, according to which Turkey still bases its minority policies.[8]

The establishment of the Republic of Turkey, despite the important demographic change caused by the wars during the last years of the empire, inherited a heterogenous population including Turks, Jews and Christians, but also diverse non-Turkish Muslim groups such as Kurds, Arabs, Lazes, Muslim Georgians, Greek-speaking Muslims, Albanians, Macedonian Muslims, Pomaks, Serb Muslims, Bosnians, Tartars, Circassians, Abkhazes, and Daghestanis, among others.[9] Still, the government at the moment, as the governments that followed throughout the twentieth and twentieth-first century, continued to interpret the 1923 Treaty of Lausanne, which refers broadly to "non-Muslim minorities," as granting special legal minority status exclusively to three recognised groups: Armenian Apostolic Orthodox Christians, Jews, and Greek Orthodox Christians. Yet, these three minority groups were, and still are, recognised not as ethnic but as religious minorities.[10]

Now, Saraçoğlu's statement reveals that state practice through what has

---

[6] Kemal H. Karpat, *The Politicization of Islam: Reconstructing Identity, State, Faith, and Community in the Late Ottoman State*, Oxford: Oxford University Press, 2001, p. 371; see also, Zafer Toprak, *Türkiye'de Milli İktisat 1908-1918*, Istanbul: Doğan Kitap, 2012. About seventeen years before, similar categories were used to classify taxpayers in another law.

[7] https://www.anayasa.gov.tr/tr/mevzuat/onceki-anayasalar/1924-anayasasi/.

[8] International Helsinki Federation for Human Rights (IHF), *Turkey: A Minority Policy of Systematic Negation*, Vienna: IHF Research Foundation, 2006, p. 7 and later reports.

[9] Soner Cagaptay, "Assimilation and Kemalism: Turkish Nationalism and the Minorities in the 1930s", *Middle Eastern Studies*, vol. 40, no. 3, 2004, pp. 86-87. See also, Baskın Oran, *Minorities and Minority Rights in Turkey*.

[10] Oran, *ibid*, p. 26

been characterised as the "Turkification" process has been very different from theory, i.e., as this was defined by the constitution. The "Turkification" process has been defined as

> [T]he way in which Turkish ethnic identity has been strictly imposed as a hegemonic identity in every sphere of social life, from the language spoken in public to the teaching of history in public schools; from education to industry; from commercial practices to public employment policies; from the civil code to the re-settlement of certain citizens in particular areas. The preconditions of the implementation of Turkification policies can be summarised as follows: the emergence of Turkish nationalism as a well-structured political ideology, the recognition of this ideology by the great majority of the political elite in power, and the existence of an international political conjuncture favourable to the implementation of these policies domestically.[11]

Without the above definition losing its validity, one of the essential features of the "Turkification process" has been converting the country into a fatherland by creating a feeling of "authenticity" among the masses and converting Turkish geographical territory into exclusively Turkish.[12] Although different in character from the nationalisation movements experienced in the late Ottoman Empire in the sense that they "do not resemble neither the imperial nationalism of Sultan Abdülhamid II nor the cultural nationalism of Ziya Gökalp",[13] this process – unfolded in several stages – started with the demographic engineering that was implemented during the First World War and after and continued unabated during the Republican period marking thus, the continuities of the Kemalist state.[14]

Indeed, "Turkification" policies, as a form of assimilation, failed to recognise individuals' rights, while Turkishness came to mean, in all actuality, Turkish-speaking peoples of Turkish ethnic origin, thus deviating from the initial civic or territorial conceptualisation of Turkish national identity. Kerem Öktem argues that

---

[11] Ayhan Aktar, "'Turkification' Policies in the Early Republican Era", in Catharina Dufft (ed), *Turkish Literature and Cultural Memory: "Multiculturalism" as a Literary Theme after 1980*, Wiesbaden: Harrassowitz Verlag, 2009, p. 29; also, ibidem, "Cumhuriyetin İlk Yıllarında Uygulanan 'Türklestirme' Politikaları", *Tarih ve Toplum*, no. 156, 1996, p. 4.

[12] Ayhan Aktar, "Conversion of a 'Country' into a 'Fatherland': The Case of Turkification Examined, 1923–1934", in Ayhan Aktar, Niyazi Kızılyürek, and Umut Özkırımlı (eds), *Nationalism in the Troubled Triangle: Cyprus, Greece and Turkey*, Basingstoke: Palgrave, 2010, p. 22-23.

[13] Murat Koraltürk, *Erken Cumhuriyet Döneminde Ekonominin Türkleşmesi*, Istanbul: İletişim, 2011, p. 21.

[14] For a comprehensive account of the continuities and discontinuities between the Ottoman and early republican periods, see Erik J. Zürcher, *The Young Turk Legacy and Nation Building: From the Ottoman Empire to Atatürk's Turkey*, London and New York: I. B. Tauris, 2010.

[t]he Kemalist modernisation project paid lip-service to civic notions of Turkish identity, yet in practice, and much as in the neighbouring Balkans and Greece, created groups of 'others', who were denied full citizenship rights [… while] non-Muslims were generally seen as a potential security risk and deemed unfit for full citizenship. All of them, however, had to suffer degrees of social exclusion and state repression.[15]

In other words, the Turkish nationalists declared a permanent ideological war against the "other" ethnic, religious and linguistic groups who once lived in the same geographical location.[16] As Cagaptay argues, Ankara expected that non-Turkish Muslims would be assimilated, and while it treated Kurdish resistance with considerable force during the 1925 Kurdish insurrection led by Sheikh Said in south-eastern Turkey, Ankara's attitude was much different towards Greek and Armenian Christians. Once "these communities renounced their age-old privileges in 1925, the government resorted to various methods to alienate them. It used legal measures to make their life difficult".[17]

Discrimination against non-Muslim and non-Turkish ethnic groups intensified after the formation of the Republic in 1923. Although the recently established state guaranteed the autonomy of minorities within the framework of international law, the governments of the 1920s and 1930s explicitly pursued assimilation policies from time to time. Güven rightly argues,

> If the rights and obligations of all citizens before the laws seemed formally identical, in everyday life, belongingness to the dominant Turkish ethnic identity formed the basis of the state's identity policy. These practices intended to accelerate the processes of nation-state formation, modernisation and westernisation.[18]

With the secularisation of the Turkish legal system and the adoption of the Swiss Civil Code in 1926, the Turkish state intervened in the rights conferred by the Lausanne Treaty. The Orthodox minority, as well as the Jewish and Armenian minorities, were asked to voluntarily forgo their right to legal autonomy in issues related to family law for the state to achieve legal unity and, therefore, establish full sovereignty.[19] Still, one of the most

---

[15] Kerem Öktem, *Turkey since 1989: Angry Nation*, London and New York: Zed Books, 2011, p. 16.

[16] Aktar, "Conversion of a 'Country' into a 'Fatherland'", p. 23.

[17] Cagaptay, "Assimilation and Kemalism", p. 87.

[18] Dilek Güven, "Riots against the Non-Muslims of Turkey: 6/7 September 1955 in the context of demographic engineering", *European Journal of Turkish Studies*, vol. 12, 2011, pp. 1-2. Available at: https://doi.org/10.4000/ejts.4538.

[19] Samim Akgönül, Türkiye Rumları: Ulus-Devlet Çağından Küreselleşme Çağına bir Azınlığın Yok Oluş

important measures of the 1920s was the campaign initiated by the Law Faculty Students' Association of Istanbul University in 1928 with the motto of "Citizen, Speak Turkish!" (*Vatandaş Türkçe Konuş*)[20] to impose the universal use of Turkish by all minorities, while a series of additional measures aimed to further advance national homogenisation. As a local newspaper in Izmir wrote:

> Citizen, do not make friends with or shop from those so-called Turkish citizens who do not speak Turkish. We request from our lady citizens who work as telephone operators: Please immediately cut off conversations in Greek and Latino.[21]

The following year, in 1929, another law on Securities and Stock Market (*Menkul Kıymetler ve Kambiyo Borsaları Kanunu*) was amended so that all brokery-owners should be of Turkish origin, meaning that the ownership of Stock Market should pass to Turkish hands.[22]

While the Turkification policies implemented in the 1920s had been *de facto* administrative policies, later policies eventually acquired legal force so that the discriminatory practices against the non-Muslim minorities became *de jure* expressions of nationalist ideology.[23] The notorious law (no. 2007) passed in 1932 under the title "Restricting certain Professions and Trades to Turkish Citizens only" (*Türkiye'de Türk Vatandaşlarına Tahsis Edilen Sanat ve Hizmetler Hakkında Kanun*) is an example of this transformation with immediate repercussions in excluding the minorities from the capital, trade markets as well as the public sector.[24] The law restricted the employment of aliens, i.e., non-Muslims, in certain strategic occupations in the country, all of which were carefully listed in detail. As a result of the implementation of this law, nearly 9000 non-exchanged Greeks lost their jobs and soon thereafter migrated to Greece for good.[25]

Within the homogenisation policies employed by the Turkish state, migration and settlement policies provided additional means to create ethno-cultural unity within the borders of the newly established state. Between

---

Süreci, trans. Ceyla Gürmen, Istanbul: İletişim 2007, p. 69-74.

[20] For the student activities during the 1920s and 1930s, see Nikos Christofis, *From Kemalism to Radicalism: The Turkish Student Movement, 1923-1980*, Athens: Topos, 2021, pp. 57-65 (in Greek).

[21] Senem Aslan, "Citizen, Speak Turkish!": A Nation in the Making", *Nationalism and Ethnic Politics*, vol. 13, no. 2, 2007, pp. 245.

[22] Akgönül, *Türkiye Rumları*, p. 83.

[23] Ayhan Aktar, "Homogenising the Nation: Turkifying the Economy: The Turkish Experience of Population Exchange Reconsidered", in Renée Hirschon (ed), *Crossing the Aegean: An Appraisal of the 1923 Compulsory Exchange between Greece and Turkey*, Oxford: Berghahn, 2003, p. 93.

[24] Akgönül, *Türkiye Rumları*, p. 84.

[25] Aktar, "Homogenising the Nation", p. 32.

1929 and 1934, the local administrations compelled Armenians living in the rural areas of Asia Minor to migrate into urban centres, forcing them into a new migration wave to places like Syria.[26] By early 1934, six hundred Armenians, deported from various cities and rural areas to Istanbul within a period of two months, were settled in Armenian churches and schools and deserted houses.[27] The Jews of Turkey faced a similar fate during the pogrom-like attacks in the 1930s against them with the participation of state authorities. The pogrom-like attacks intimidated the Jews living in the cities in Thrace through threats and economic boycotts and caused, in the summer of 1934, attacks on Jewish shops, workplaces and residences.[28] The *Varlık Vergisi* mentioned above, thus, makes it just one of the measures targeting minorities, albeit perhaps the harshest one, in Turkey, showing the anti-minority policies of the state.

Following the end of World War II, Greece and Turkey entered anew a phase of rapprochement – the first one was in 1930 – resulting in both of the countries entering NATO in 1952 and the signing of the Greek–Turkish–Yugoslav Pact of Friendship and Collaboration in Ankara on 28 February 1953.[29] However, peaceful and friendly bilateral relations were tested again with the Cyprus dispute's emergence. The dispute created grave repercussions both on the relations of the two countries and the pact, but also, more importantly, to the topic at hand, regarding the treatment of the countries' minorities as both countries instrumentalised their minorities to retaliate against each other.

With the outbreak of the dispute, the anti-Greek sentiment intensified in Turkey by the provocative circulations in the Turkish Press and the declarations of several organisations and statesmen on the allegations that they were supporting Greece and providing material benefits to the guerilla fighters of the EOKA (National Organization of Cypriot Fighters) against which the reconciliatory attitude of the Greek minority press could not make any difference.[30]

Against this background, on 6-7 September, during the Tripartite

---

[26] Thomas Hugh Greenshields, *The Settlement of Armenian Refugees in Syria and Lebanon, 1915-1939*, PhD dissertation, Durham: Durham University, 1978, pp. 61-63.

[27] Güven, "Riots against the Non-Muslims of Turkey", p. 2.

[28] Analytically, see Rifat Bali, *1934 Trakya Olayları*, Istanbul: Libra, 2012.

[29] Evanthis Hatzivassiliou, *Greece and the Cold War: Frontline state, 1952–1967*, London and New York: Routledge, 2006, p. 38.

[30] Akgönül, *Türkiye Rumları*, pp. 184-189; Alexis Alexandris, *The Greek Minority of Istanbul and Greek-Turkish Relations, 1918-1974*, Athens: Centre for Asia Minor Studies, 1992, p. 254-255; Dilek Güven, *Cumhuriyet Dönemi Azınlık Politikaları ve Stratejileri Bağlamında: 6-7 Eylül Olayları*, Istanbul: Tarih Vakfı Yurt Yayınları, 2006, pp. 144ff.

Conference in London over Cyprus in 1955, the Turkish press spread the news that Ataturk's house in Thessaloniki was bombed. As a result, Cyprus is Turkish Society (*Kıbrıs Türktür Derneği*) held a demonstration on the same day, which soon turned into a pogrom destroying minority property and causing irreparable psychological cost to the Greek Orthodox population in Istanbul, and the minority population of the country, generally. Greek Orthodox exodus, however, did not end with the 6-7 September Events (6-7 Eylül Olayları). State repression and discrimination against minorities, and the Christian community, in particular, continued during the 1960s, despite the liberal atmosphere the new constitution of 1961 brought. The impasse regarding the Cyprus dispute only accelerated the situation for the Christians in Turkey. For example, in 1962, a Minority Subcommission (*Azınlık Tali Komisyonu*) was secretly established to "track all transactions of minorities contrary to the national security"[31] and, thus, serve as the modus operandi of the systematic discriminatory policies. Combined with the flaring of the crisis in Cyprus in December 1963, the Turkish Parliament passed on 16 March 1964 a decree using the Cyprus crisis as a pretext to intensify its anti-minority policies leading the Greek Orthodox population into exile and their properties to be seized, and schools and sanctuaries shut down.[32]

The AKP and Minority Policies, 2002–2011: The "Golden Age of Europeanization"

It has been claimed throughout history that the greatest conflicts separating East and West, Muslims and Christians, are the Crusades. The Crusades were also times when all these sides were acquainted with each other, communicated with each other, formed alliances, and, most importantly, exchanged science and art most intensely.[33]

By the time the still-ruling AKP came to power in 2002, the general climate seemed to change regarding the non-Muslim communities in Turkey to the extent that, as the above statement shows, the then-prime Minister Erdoğan praised the Crusades in a speech he delivered to the Parliamentary Assembly of the Council of Europe (PACE) in 2011 in an attempt to open up a dialogue among civilisations.[34] This statement came in complete compliance with the party's election manifesto through which the AKP was

---

[31] Oran, *Minorities and Minority Rights in Turkey*, p. 149.

[32] On 1964 Rum exiles, see the collection of articles in Ilay Romain Ors (ed.), *İstanbullu Rumlar ve 1964 Sürgünleri: Türk Toplumunun Homojenleşmesinde bir Dönüm Noktası*, Istanbul: İletişim, 2008.

[33] *Habertürk*, "İkinci 'one minute'", 13 June 2011. Available at: http://www.haberturk.com/dunya/haber/620412-ikinci-oneminute.

[34] In 2005, Recep Tayyip Erdoğan founded the Alliance of Civilizations Initiative with Spain's then-Prime Minister José Luis Rodriguez Zapatero.

promoting, and indeed, supported an agenda for the non-Muslims in Turkey where the latter were to be presented as "first class" and "equal citizens of the Republic and evaluated through an emphasis on "richness" deriving from "different faiths and cultures" in the AKP's election manifesto.[35]

The country's political transformation process that developed in tandem with the country's opening up to the world during the 1980s marked the questioning of the country's approach towards religious minorities. The period saw the introduction of various liberal policies and Turkey's application for EU membership, which reached a turning point when Ankara officially gained EU candidate status at the Helsinki Summit in 1999.[36] Against this background, and as Turkey-EU relations intensified, Turkish governments were forced to develop policies towards broadening the space allotted to religious minorities, as well as the recasting of religion-state relations and the parameters of freedom of religion in Turkey, which were further continued after the AKP came to power in 2002.[37]

During the first two years of AKP rule, Turkey introduced eight reform packages enhancing human rights standards in light of the Copenhagen Criteria, including extended citizenship rights, freedom of expression, and prohibitions against torture. These were accompanied by prioritising a comprehensive settlement to the Cyprus Question,[38] while at the same time, reforms were extended to the economic sphere to transform Turkey's "soft state" into an effective regulatory state that would lay the foundations of sustained economic growth without the recurrence of crises, the historical norm in Turkey.[39] Regarding religious minorities, these reform packages

---

[35] Anna Maria Beylunioğlu, "Recasting the Parameters of Freedom of Religion in Turkey: Non-Muslims and the AKP", in Bahar Başer and Ahmet Erdi Öztürk (eds.), *Authoritarian Politics in Turkey: Elections, Resistance and the AKP*, London: I. B. Tauris, 2017, p. 142.

[36] Anna Maria Beylunioğlu, "Freedom of Religion and Non-Muslim Minorities in Turkey", *Turkish Policy Quarterly*, vol. 13, no. 4, 2015, p. 140.

[37] For example, in 2002, under the second EU harmonisation package, Article 5 of the Law on Associations which prohibited associations "to protect, develop or expand languages or cultures other than the Turkish language or culture or to claim that there are minorities based on racial, religious, sectarian, cultural or linguistic differences" was repealed. Republic of Turkey Ministry of Foreign Affairs Secretariat General for EU Affairs, *Political Reforms in Turkey*, Ankara: M&B Tanıtım Hizmetleri, 2007, p. 7.

[38] Nikos Christofis and Amaryllis Logotheti, "Between Political Survival and Regional Power: The Justice and Development Party and Cyprus, 2002-2017", *British Journal of Middle Eastern Studies*, vol. 50, no. 3, 2023, pp. 1-18; Nikos Christofis, "Turkey, Cyprus and the Arab Uprisings", in Hüseyin Işıksal and Oğuzhan Göksel (eds.), *Turkey's Relations with the Middle East: Political Encounters after the Arab Spring*, New York: Springer, 2017, pp. 133-147.

[39] Ziya Öniş, "Domestic Politics, International Norms and Challenges to the State: Turkey-EU Relations in the Post-Helsinki Era", in Ali Çarkoğlu and Barry Rubin (eds.), *Turkey and the European Union: Domestic Politics, Economic Integration and International Dynamics*, London: Frank Cass, 2005, p. 11; Nikos Christofis, "Securitizing the Aegean: De-Europeanizing Greek–Turkish Relations", *Southeast European and Black Sea Studies*, vol. 22, no. 1, 2022, p. 86.

included changes introducing new measures to the laws restricting freedom of expression, minority rights, and freedom of religion, while the major amendments concerning Christian minorities were introduced in the Law on Associations, the Law on Foundations, and the Zoning Law, along with other regulations, circulars, and cabinet decrees that the government introduced in subsequent years.[40]

The AKP, a party with roots building on Islamic identity that emerged in 2001 out of a crisis within the Necmettin Erbakan-led Milli Görüş (National Vision), but also due to an organic crisis within the Kemalist *bloc* and the alienation of the masses from their political representation, giving rise to a mismatch between "represented and representatives",[41] was more than willing – and indeed, it assured the EU – to continue working on the path of the EU accession process. These reforms were followed by new legislation, including the Law on Foundations in 2008 and its amendment in 2011 – a period corresponding to the first two terms of the AKP in power – which paved the way for religious communities to re-acquire, register, and restore their properties. Furthermore, new regulations were issued to handle the issues related to private schools that belong to religious minorities. Under the AKP,

> non-minority-led foundations' acquisition of property was further facilitated; the restoration of churches, synagogues, and interreligious dialogue was encouraged; minority schools were reopened after years of closure and non-Muslim Turkish citizens' right to maintain their identity and practice their religion was repeatedly stressed.[42]

Indeed, in 2006, for the first time in Turkey's history, a Turkish Protestant (non-minority) church was opened; the following year, after three years of restoration, a historical Armenian Church in Van, the Akdamar Church, was opened as a monumental museum in 2007; the same year, the Virgin Mary Church in Bozcaada (Tenedos) was restored with the order of the then Prime Minister Erdoğan following Bozcaada's Greek Community President Simon Salto's demands; and finally, in 2011, the restoration of Sveti Stephan Bulgarian Church (non-minority church located in Istanbul) started in collaboration with Istanbul municipality and the provincial administration. The restorations were facilitated by an amendment in law in 2003, replacing the word "mosque" with "place of worship", through which

---

[40] Anna Maria Beylunioğlu, *Freedom of Religion in Turkey between Secular and Islamic Values: The Situation of Christians*, PhD dissertation, Florence: European University Institute, 2017, p. 92.

[41] Antonio Gramsci, *Selections from the Prison Notebooks*, New York: International Publishers, 1971, p. 210.

[42] Lacin Idil Oztig and Kenan Aydin, "The AKP's Approach toward Non-Muslim Minorities: Constructivist and Rationalist Insights", *Alternatives: Global, Local, Political*, vol. 42, no. 2, 2017, p. 61.

churches and synagogues gained *de jure* the same status as mosques. This meant, in all actuality, that free water and electricity facilities were provided in the same way as mosques, as well as the allocation of public real estate to those who wanted to build a place of worship.[43]

In conformity with the AKP's liberal commitments, at least in the party's early years, a dialogue process was initiated with the religious leaders of non-Muslim communities, who were promised that the government would be more determined to find lasting solutions for their long-standing problems. Towards that direction, the government founded a Council on Minority Problems (*Azınlık Sorunlarını Değerlendirme Kurulu*) aiming at enabling the government to deal with the problems of non-Muslim minorities away from the pressures that would have otherwise come from pro-establishment forces. As Soner rightly observes, these steps towards the non-Muslim minorities were part of the government's policy of de-securitisation, and as such, military and civil security institutions were excluded from the new council.[44] Thus, the Council on Minority Problems

> was charged with developing solutions to those minorities' problems, particularly their educational institutions and community foundations, in line with EU and European Court of Human Rights (ECtHR) standards.[45]

A look at the Turkish press, both pro- and anti-government, including Christian websites and organisations,[46] revealed a general optimism, and, in particular, the latter embraced the AKP initiatives and opening up towards religious communities while, at the same time, expressing their support to the Turkish government.[47] Still, the transformation process, regardless of

---

[43] Resmi Gazete, "İmar Kanunu ile İmar ve Gecekondu Mevzuatına Aykırı Yapılara Uygulanacak Bazı İşlemler ve 6785 Sayılı İmar Kanununun Bir Maddesinin Değiştirilmesi Hakkında Kanunda Değişiklik Yapılmasına İlişkin Kanun", No. 25319, Law No. 5006, 17 December 2003. Available at: https://www.resmigazete.gov.tr/eskiler/2003/12/20031217.htm#1.

[44] Around that time, the Ergenekon and Balyoz trials brought to light one or more conspiracies aimed at a coup d'état against the AKP government and a series of murders, including of the Armenian journalist Hrant Dink and that of three owners of a Christian publishing house in Malatya.

[45] Bayram Ali Soner, "The Justice and Development Party's Policies towards Non-Muslim Minorities in Turkey", *Journal of Balkan and Near Eastern Studies*, vol. 12, no. 1, 2010, p. 29.

[46] Gareth Jones, "Turkey's Christians Like AK Despite Islamist Past", *Reuters*, 20 June 2007. Available at: https://www.reuters.com/article/uk-turkey-election-christians/turkeys-christians-like-ak-despite-islamist-past-idUKL1835667220070619; World Bulletin, "Turkish Christians Favor Tolerant AK Party", 20 June 2007. Available at: https://worldbulletin.dunyabulteni.net/archive/turkish-christians-favor-tolerant-ak-party-h5482.html; "Turkey's Christians Could Face Nationalist Backlash", *International Christian Concern*, 2 January 2013. Available at: https://www.persecution.org/2013/02/07/turkeys-christians-could-face-nationalist-backlash/#.

[47] Anna Maria Beylunioglu, "Recasting the Parameters of Freedom of Religion in Turkey"; Soner Cagaptay, "Turkey's 'First Christian'", *The Washington Institute*, 3 June 2011. Available at: https://www.washingtoninstitute.org/policy-analysis/turkeys-first-christian; Mustafa Akyol, "Who Threatens Turkey's Christians?", *Al-Monitor*, 17 January 2013. Available at: https://www.al-

how positive it was, had its limitations, most notably due to Ankara's shift to a re-securitising discourse and practices and the process of de-Europeanization since the early 2010s owing to both domestic and international developments.

The Christian Minorities since Turkey's De-Europeanisation

Indeed, following the AKP's victory in the 2011 elections, and in combination with domestic developments, like the Gezi Park protests in Istanbul in May 2013 against Erdoğan's authoritarian neoliberal measures and policies, and international ones, like the Arab uprisings in the summer of 2011 through which the AKP promoted the so-called "Turkish model" for the Middle East and North African region, the started to distance itself from the country's EU accession process. What is more, perhaps, is that since the early 2010s, Turkey gradually returned to a more familiar path, that of a securitised discourse and practice and a slide to authoritarianism.[48] At that time, the anti-Christian rhetoric increased in intensity and degree and coincided with the launch of the Turkish government's *Yeni Türkiye* (New Turkey) program.[49]

The above program – the party itself coined its name[50] – is a synthesising socioeconomic and political project that aspires to an all-inclusive hegemonic narrative of the country that would replace Kemalism, draw together all the changes introduced over the AKP's administration, and present a(nother) story of how Turkish history, and the Turkish state, came about, regardless whether this version of history is correct or not.[51] What is more, as in the Kemalist period, where the constitution required non-Muslim minorities to identify as Turks,[52] the AKP era, in contrast, saw the

---

monitor.com/originals/2013/01/christians-threatened-turkey.html. *BBC*, "Turkey: First New Church in 90 Years Approved", 5 January 2015. Available at: https://www.bbc.com/news/blogs-news-from-elsewhere-30679848; *Hürriyet Daily News*, "Turkey's Christian Minority Sends Four Deputies to Parliament", 8 June 2015. Available at: https://www.hurriyetdailynews.com/turkeys-christian-minority-sends-four-deputies-to-parliament-83623.

[48] Christofis, "Securitizing the Aegean".

[49] According to the Gülen movement, anti-Christian rhetoric increased right after corruption and bribery investigations that were made public on 17-25 December 2013 and which incriminated Erdoğan, his family members and his business and political associates in an attempt to show that it was because of the movement that the previous decade Christians were treated more tolerantly. However, in this account, the movement's ills infiltration into the state apparatus and its contribution to Erdoğan's domination is consciously silenced.

[50] For the concept *Yeni Türkiye*, see Ahmet Davutoğlu, *62. Hükümet Programı,* Istanbul: AKP, September 2014. See also Ahmet Insel, *La nouvelle Turquie d'Erdoğan*, Paris: La Decouverte, 2015.

[51] Nikos Christofis, "The AKP's "Yeni Turkiye": Challenging the Kemalist Narrative?", *Mediterranean Quarterly*, vol. 29, no. 3, 2018, pp. 11-32.

[52] Kemal Kirişçi, "Disaggregating Turkish Citizenship and Immigration Practices", *Middle Eastern Studies*, vol. 36, no. 3, 2000, pp. 1-22.

construction of a Sunni nation excluding all the "foreign elements" from it,[53] a process that only accelerated after the military coup attempt on 15 July 2016.[54] In other words, the AKP promoted, and indeed, gave additional importance to, an authentic Turkish-Muslim identity, with additional emphasis on explicit Islamic codes, promoting thus, a new "civilisation" *a la Turca*, which formed around the ranks of the ruling AKP and, more importantly, around Erdoğan himself.[55]

However, as Beylunioğlu rightly points out, the increase in the emphasis on Islamic values did not have an immediate negative effect on the dialogue process; on the contrary, it increased.[56] Positive changes continued. For example, amendments on the Law on Foundations in 2011 and 2013, the introduction of a new private school regulation in 2012, and the restitution of several non-properties are some of these changes.

On that note, while the AKP puts emphasis on the nation's Sunni Muslim character, and the de-secularisation of public and cultural spaces has intensified, mixed marriages—that is, marriages and relationships within non-Muslim minority communities, as well as those between non-Muslims and Muslims—have increased in Turkey.[57] At the same time, on a symbolic level, the Turkish government invited non-Muslims to apply for public service positions, from which they have been traditionally discouraged and excluded, and on 5 July 2012, the president of religious affairs (*Diyanet İşleri Başkanlığı*), Professor Mehmet Görmez, in an unprecedented move, visited Greek Orthodox Patriarch Bartholomew I, and called for the reopening of the Halki seminary in the name of Islam, stating that "[W]e see non-Muslim citizens living in Turkey as an integral part of this country [and] we demand for them the same rights that we demand for ourselves".[58]

However, in the absence of references to EU norms, the Turkish government seems to be reshaping this equality and richness discourse by putting the religious identity of the party and its constituents forward. More importantly, though, since the early 2010s, the AKP adopted a much

---

[53] Tanıl Bora and Deniz Yonucu, "State and Civilian Violence against 'Dangerous' Others", in Esra Özyürek, Gaye Özpınar, and Emrah Altındiş (eds.), *Authoritarianism and Resistance in Turkey*, Cham: Springer, 2019, p. 230.

[54] Nikos Christofis (ed.), *Erdoğan's 'New' Turkey: Attempted Coup D'état and the Acceleration of Political Crisis*, London and New York: Routledge, 2020.

[55] Nikos Christofis, "Kemalism vs Erdoğanism: Continuities and Discontinuities in Turkey's Hegemonic State Ideology", *Middle East Critique*, forthcoming.

[56] Anna Maria Beylunioğlu, "Recasting the Parameters of Freedom of Religion in Turkey", p. 150.

[57] Anna Maria Beylunioğlu, *"Kısmet Tabii…": İstanbulun Rum Yahudi ve Ermeni Toplumlarında Karma Evlilikler*, Istanbul: İstos Yayınları, 2021.

[58] *Agos*, "Her inanç kendi din adamını yetiştirebilmeli", 5 July 2012. Available at: https://www.agos.com.tr/tr/yazi/1877/her-inanc-kendi-din-adamini-yetistirebilmeli.

stronger and tough nationalist discourse to explicitly demonise and even criminalise its critics, like the Gulen movement, let alone the minority communities of the country. Needless to say, the AKP has been violating, first and foremost, the articles of the ECtHR, which are binding on Turkey. For example, Article 9 of the ECtHR, which protects freedom of thought, conscience and religion, is considered one of the foundations of a democratic and pluralist society. Limitations on the exercise of freedom of religion must be restricted to those prescribed by law and necessary in a democratic society. The European Commission against Racism and Intolerance (ECRI) also laid out the guidelines on combatting hate speech in its general policy recommendation No.15, which was adopted on 8 December 2015.[59] Adding insult to injury, Erdoğan and his party found support more often than not in encouraging hate speech and disregarding human rights in a "rally around the flag" contest.

On 15 July 2016, Turkey experienced yet another coup attempt. Although it is beyond the scope of our analysis to fully analyse the reasons behind the coup, suffice it to say that it accelerated the country's political crisis, already in motion for more than half a decade and marked an aggressive securitisation period, including a shift towards the non-Muslim minorities of the country. Yet, it would be false to assume that the climate for the non-Muslim, particularly Christian communities, deteriorated only after the coup attempt. There were considerable signs through governmental discourses and practices marking a distancing from the earlier period. Perhaps the most striking being – in combination with the increased criticism towards the EU in general – the AKP's emphasis on the Ottoman model and the country's "deep-rooted past", implicitly or explicitly, referring to the Ottoman Empire's tolerance towards its millets. However, as Jenny White argues, "AKP politicians often refer to the millet model when discussing outreach to Christian communities. They do so largely ahistorically, without acknowledging the supremacy inherent in the historic system".[60]

Against this background, a discourse emphasising the superiority of Islam over other religions came to dominate the government's discourse employing a full-blown strategy to educate the masses to become proper Turkish citizens, i.e., Sunni-Muslim, paying additional emphasis on the youth. Indeed, although the pursuit of creating a pious generation was essentially a straightforward answer to challenge Kemalist hegemony, it implied a degree of intolerance regarding non-Muslims. As had happened

---

[59] ECRI General Policy Recommendation No. 15 on Combating Hate Speech, Adopted on 8 December 2015. Available at: https://rm.coe.int/ecri-general-policy-recommendation-no-15-on-combating-hate-speech/16808b5b01.

[60] Jenny White, *Muslim Nationalism and the New Turks*, New Jersey: Princeton University Press, 2014, p. 12.

under Kemalism, the AKP has activated the mechanisms of state power to formulate and implement the ideological transformation of the country's youth as a symbol of the "ideal new Turkish citizen". In this way, the new mythmaking in shaping the youth in AKP's Turkey entails the restructuring of collective memory around Ottoman history and Sunni Islam as foundational aspects of national identity,[61] and constructs "an ideal young person [that] carr[ies] a computer in one hand and a Quran in the other".[62]

Last but not least, shaping younger minds by constructing and promoting a new historical narrative was again in evidence in July 2020, with the reconversion of the Hagia Sophia in Istanbul into a mosque; a political Islamist and conservative ideologues claim since the 1950s.[63] The return to the top of the political agenda on turning the identically-named Hagia Sophia museums in Istanbul and Trabzon into mosques demonstrates, among other things, the AKP's perception of Christians as well. These structures were Christian sanctuaries for centuries; they were converted into mosques following the Ottoman conquest and eventually became museums during the republican era. The image of the AKP as an "imaginary Ottoman authority" prioritising Islam over Christianity was further advanced with the reopening of the Hagia Sophia museum in Trabzon as a mosque in 2013 and more recently with the re-conversion of Hagia Sophia in Istanbul into a mosque in July 2020 sharpening an already tense ideological divide between not only pious and secular Turks but also between Muslims and Christians worldwide.

Furthermore, re-converting Hagia Sophia into a mosque also served other purposes, notably, the AKP's regional ambitions for Turkey as a great Middle Eastern power.[64] Since 2014, the surrounding park area has hosted a prayer ceremony on the anniversary of Istanbul's conquest, organised by an Islamist youth organisation, which has included calls to "unchain the Hagia Sophia".[65] Thus, this decision gave Erdoğan a significant advantage in the Muslim world to present himself as a leader in the ideological and cultural war he and his party launched. As such, the museum's reconversion to a mosque status was celebrated by Erdoğan's millions of supporters, proving

---

[61] Ibid, p. 33.

[62] *İhlas Haber Ajansı*, "Başbakan'dan gençlere tavsiyeler", 27 December 2012. Available at: https://www.iha.com.tr/haber-basbakandan-genclere-tavsiyeler-256118/.

[63] Umut Azak, "'The Hagia Sophia Cause' and the Emergence of Ottomanism in the 1950s", *Turkish Historical Review*, vol. 13, no. 1-2, 2022, pp. 100-121.

[64] *BirGün*, "Erdoğan: Yeni 15 Temmuz'lara var mıyız?", 12 August 2017. Available at: https://www.birgun.net/haber/Erdoğan-yeni-15-temmuz-lara-var-miyiz-174499?__cf_chl_managed_tk__=pmd_mU_pTWA1dgIdNdPbeeHd6CqwICJ7nUvu9JPmijHKc1U-1629468162-0-gqNtZGzNAyWjcnBszQh9.

[65] Azak, "'The Hagia Sophia Cause' and the Emergence of Ottomanism in the 1950s", p. 102.

that a specific reading of the Ottoman past, imbued with a blend of Islamist, and xenophobic, ideas became the mainstream and official one. It thus reflects the political agendas of conservative nationalist and Islamist groups that imbues devout Muslim AKP voters with a sense of national pride from the imperial past, signifying, however, the militarisation of public policy and a "conquest" discourse, particularly, of Islam over Christianity. Erdoğan's statement in August 2020 is quite revealing in that respect:

> Our civilisation is one of conquest… in our civilisation, conquest is not occupation or looting. It is establishing the dominance of the justice that Allah commanded in the conquered region…. First of all, our nation removed the oppression from the areas that it conquered. It established justice. This is why our civilisation is one of conquest.[66]

While the conversion of the Hagia Sophia was the subject of a great debate centred on the topic of world cultural heritage, it becomes evident it is also part of a discussion that extends to the clash of civilisations. However, the gravity of the event and the increasing ethnoreligious authoritarianism of the AKP has stymied this debate. Unfortunately, it is not the first time that a place of worship with the status of a museum or an active place of worship has been changed into a mosque during the AKP's rule. The transformation of Armenian, Syriac, and Greek Orthodox Christian churches, either moribund or in active use, into mosques that are then placed under the auspices of the Diyanet has been a common occurrence during the AKP period. Undoubtedly, this practice indicates the relevance that Islam has achieved during the AKP's rule, both as an instrument and as an objective, i.e., to securitise the Sunni Muslim aspect of Turkishness and make it its cornerstone.

Conclusion

Over the course of two decades, the status of minorities in Turkey is directly affected by the ruling party's policies, agendas, and interests both domestically and in relation to the country's foreign affairs. This means that the minorities went through a period of reconciliation with the Turkish state after nearly 80 years with productive dialogue and openness during the first two terms of the AKP. Then, in compliance with Turkey's de-Europeanisation process and adoption of aggressive rhetoric, minorities also started to get affected.

---

[66] Cengiz Aktar, "Reconquest and De-memorization: The Fate of Hagia Sophia", in Angelos Giannakopoulos (ed.), *Politics of Memory and War: From Russia to the Middle East*, Tel Aviv: The S. Daniel Abraham Center for International and Regional Studies, 2022, p. 87.

Indeed, the AKP and, most of all, its leader, Recep Tayyip Erdoğan, has demonstrated a mixed track record about religious minorities, characterised by gestures of benevolence and egregious scapegoating and persecution of the same groups. This has been especially true in the aftermath of the failed coup in July 2016. Since then, the adoption of an authoritarian neoliberal model of governance – a seemingly inconsistent rhetoric and policy toward minorities – have been, in fact, various modalities of a coherent neo-Islamist strategy that reinforces sectarian hierarchies, institutionalises discrimination, transforming rights into discretionary benevolent acts, and solidifies majoritarian hegemony for Erdoğan at home and to pursue foreign policy goals abroad.

As Erdemir argues, a holistic and contextualised look at the AKP's rhetoric and policy regarding minorities broadly reveals the following four modalities of the Turkish government's policy:

1. Scapegoating of, and incitement against, minorities to mobilise the electorate, solidify the ranks of loyalists, and strengthen majoritarian hegemony at home.

2. Propagating conspiracy theories about minorities to divert the Turkish public's attention from the government's policy failures.

3. Performing acts of neo-Ottoman "benevolence" to portray the regime and its leadership as "tolerant" at home and abroad, while also highlighting and reinforcing sectarian hierarchies between the ruling majority and subject minorities.

4. Implementing policies ranging from benevolent to nefarious toward minorities to ensure favorable treatment or to extract concessions in international relations.[67]

Against this background, if during the early republican and later years, "Turkishness" was defined as "those who are part of the Turkish ethnic identity", during the AKP years, "Turkishness" came to mean "those who are part of the Turkish Sunni-Muslim ethnic identity". Needless to say, Christians, and minorities in general, present a threat – real or imagined – to the AKP's *Yeni Türkiye* vision.

Bibliography

Agos, "Her inanç kendi din adamını yetiştirebilmeli"', 5 July 2012. Available at:

---

[67] Aykan Erdemir, "Scapegoats of Wrath, Subjects of Benevolence: Turkey's Minorities Under Erdoğan", *Hudson Institute*, 19 April 2019. Available at: https://www.hudson.org/foreign-policy/scapegoats-of-wrath-subjects-of-benevolence-turkey-s-minorities-under-erdo-an.

https://www.agos.com.tr/tr/yazi/1877/her-inanc-kendi-din-adamini-yetistirebilmeli

Akgönül, Samim, *Türkiye Rumları: Ulus-Devlet Çağından Küreselleşme Çağına bir Azınlığın Yok Oluş Süreci*, trans. Ceyla Gürmen, Istanbul: İletişim 2007.

Aktar, Ayhan, "'Turkification' Policies in the Early Republican Era", in Catharina Dufft (ed), *Turkish Literature and Cultural Memory: "Multiculturalism" as a Literary Theme after 1980*, Wiesbaden: Harrassowitz Verlag, 2009, pp. 29-62.

Aktar, Ayhan, "Conversion of a 'Country' into a 'Fatherland': The Case of Turkification Examined, 1923–1934", in Ayhan Aktar, Niyazi Kızılyürek, and Umut Özkırımlı (eds), *Nationalism in the Troubled Triangle: Cyprus, Greece and Turkey*, Basingstoke: Palgrave, 2010, pp. 21-35.

Aktar, Ayhan, "Cumhuriyetin İlk Yıllarında Uygulanan 'Türklestirme' Politikaları", *Tarih ve Toplum*, no. 156, 1996, pp. 4-17.

Aktar, Ayhan, "Homogenising the Nation: Turkifying the Economy: The Turkish Experience of Population Exchange Reconsidered", in Renée Hirschon (ed), *Crossing the Aegean: An Appraisal of the 1923 Compulsory Exchange between Greece and Turkey*, Oxford: Berghahn, 2003, pp. 79-95.

Aktar, Ayhan, *Varlık Vergisi ve Türkleştirme Politikaları*, Istanbul: İletişim, 2000.

Aktar, Cengiz, "Reconquest and De-memorization: The Fate of Hagia Sophia", in Angelos Giannakopoulos (ed.), *Politics of Memory and War: From Russia to the Middle East*, Tel Aviv: The S. Daniel Abraham Center for International and Regional Studies, 2022, pp. 75-92.

Akyol, Mustafa, "Who Threatens Turkey's Christians?", *Al-Monitor*, 17 January 2013. Available at: https://www.al-monitor.com/originals/2013/01/christians-threatened-turkey.html.

Alexandris, Alexis, *The Greek Minority of Istanbul and Greek-Turkish Relations, 1918-1974*, Athens: Centre for Asia Minor Studies, 1992.

Aslan, Senem, "Citizen, Speak Turkish!": A Nation in the Making", *Nationalism and Ethnic Politics*, vol. 13, no. 2, 2007, pp. 245-272.

Aydinli, Ersel, "Ergenekon, New Pacts, and the Decline of the Turkish Inner State", *Turkish Studies*, vol. 12, no. 2, 2011, pp. 227–239.

Azak, Umut, "The Hagia Sophia Cause' and the Emergence of Ottomanism in the 1950s", *Turkish Historical Review*, vol. 13, no. 1-2, 2022, pp. 100-121.

Bailey, Bette Jane and J. Martin Bailey, *Who are the Christians in the Middle East?*, Cambridge: Eerdmans. 2003.

Bali, Rifat, *1934 Trakya Olayları*, Istanbul: Libra, 2012.

BBC, "Turkey: First New Church in 90 Years Approved", 5 January 2015. Available at: https://www.bbc.com/news/blogs-news-from-elsewhere-30679848;

Beylunioğlu, Anna Maria "Recasting the Parameters of Freedom of Religion in Turkey", in Bahar Başer and Ahmet Erdi Öztürk (eds.), *Authoritarian Politics in Turkey: Elections, Resistance and the AKP*, London: I. B. Tauris, 2017, pp. 141-156.

Beylunioğlu, Anna Maria, "Freedom of Religion and Non-Muslim Minorities in Turkey", *Turkish Policy Quarterly*, vol. 13, no. 4, 2015, p. 139-147.

Beylunioğlu, Anna Maria, *"Kısmet Tabii…": İstanbulun Rum Yahudi ve Ermeni Toplumlarında Karma Evlilikler*, Istanbul: İstos Yayınları, 2021.

Beylunioğlu, Anna Maria, *Freedom of Religion in Turkey between Secular and Islamic Values:The Situation of Christians*, PhD dissertation, Florence: European University Institute, 2017.

BirGün, "Erdoğan: Yeni 15 Temmuz'lara var mıyız?", 12 August 2017. Available at: https://www.birgun.net/haber/Erdoğan-yeni-15-temmuz-lara-var-miyiz-174499.

Bora, Tanil and Deniz Yonucu, "State and Civilian Violence against 'Dangerous' Others", in Esra Özyürek, Gaye Özpınar, and Emrah Altındiş (eds.), *Authoritarianism and Resistance in Turkey*, Cham: Springer, 2019, pp. 229-238.

Cagaptay, Soner, "Assimilation and Kemalism: Turkish Nationalism and the Minorities in the 1930s", *Middle Eastern Studies*, vol. 40, no. 3, 2004, pp. 86-87.

Cagaptay, Soner, "Turkey's 'First Christian'", *The Washington Institute*, 3 June 2011. Available at: https://www.washingtoninstitute.org/policy-analysis/turkeys-first-christian;

Chapman, Colin, "Christians in the Middle East – Past, Present and Future", *Transformation*, vol. 29, no. 2, 2012, pp. 91-110.

Christofis, Nikos (ed.), *Erdoğan's 'New' Turkey: Attempted Coup D'état and the Acceleration of Political Crisis*, London and New York: Routledge, 2020.

Christofis, Nikos and Amaryllis Logotheti, "Between Political Survival and Regional Power: The Justice and Development Party and Cyprus, 2002-2017", *British Journal of Middle Eastern Studies*, vol. 50, no. 1, 2023, pp. 1-18.

Christofis, Nikos, "Kemalism vs Erdoğanism: Continuities and Discontinuities in Turkey's Hegemonic State Ideology", *Middle East Critique*, forthcoming

Christofis, Nikos, "Securitizing the Aegean: De-Europeanizing Greek–Turkish Relations", *Southeast European and Black Sea Studies*, vol. 22, no. 1, 2022, pp. 83-100.

Christofis, Nikos, "The AKP's "Yeni Turkiye": Challenging the Kemalist Narrative?", *Mediterranean Quarterly*, vol. 29, no. 3, 2018, pp. 11-32.

Christofis, Nikos, "Turkey, Cyprus and the Arab Uprisings", in Hüseyin Işıksal and Oğuzhan Göksel (eds.), *Turkey's Relations with the Middle East: Political Encounters after the Arab Spring*, New York: Springer, 2017, pp. 133-147.

Christofis, Nikos, *From Kemalism to Radicalism: The Turkish Student Movement, 1923-1980*, Athens: Topos, 2021 (in Greek).

Çetinoğlu, Ali Sait, *Varlık Vergisi 1942-1944 Ekonomik ve Kültürel Jenosid*, Istanbul: Belge Yayınları, 2009.

Davutoğlu, Ahmet, *62. Hükümet Programı,* Istanbul: AKP, September 2014.

ECRI General Policy Recommendation No. 15 on Combating Hate Speech, Adopted on 8 December 2015. Available at: https://rm.coe.int/ecri-general-policy-recommendation-no-15-on-combating-hate-speech/16808b5b01.

Erdemir, Aykan, "Scapegoats of Wrath, Subjects of Benevolence: Turkey's Minorities Under Erdoğan", *Hudson Institute*, 19 April 2019. Available at: https://www.hudson.org/foreign-policy/scapegoats-of-wrath-subjects-of-benevolence-turkey-s-minorities-under-erdo-an.

Findley, Carter Vaughn, *Turkey, Islam, Nationalism, and Modernity: A History, 1789-2007*, New Haven and London: Yale University Press, 2010.

Gramsci, Antonio, *Selections from the Prison Notebooks*, NY: International Publishers, 1971.

Greenshields, Thomas Hugh, *The Settlement of Armenian Refugees in Syria and Lebanon, 1915-1939*, PhD dissertation, Durham: Durham University, 1978.

Güven, Dilek, "Riots against the Non-Muslims of Turkey: 6/7 September 1955 in the context of demographic engineering", *European Journal of Turkish Studies*, vol. 12, 2011, pp. 1-18. Available at: https://doi.org/10.4000/ejts.4538.

Güven, Dilek, *Cumhuriyet Dönemi Azınlık Politikaları ve Stratejileri Bağlamında: 6-7 Eylül Olayların*, Istanbul: Tarih Vakfı Yurt Yayınları, 2006.

Hatzivassiliou, Evanthis, *Greece and the Cold War. Frontline state, 1952–1967*, London and New York: Routledge, 2006.

Hürriyet Daily News, "Turkey's Christian Minority Sends Four Deputies to Parliament", 8 June 2015. Available at: https://www.hurriyetdailynews.com/turkeys-christian-minority-sends-four-deputies-to-parliament-83623.

International Christian Concern, "Turkey's Christians Could Face Nationalist Backlash",, 2 January 2013. Available at: https://www.persecution.org/2013/02/07/turkeys-christians-could-face-nationalist-backlash/#.

International Helsinki Federation for Human Rights (IHF), *Turkey: A Minority Policy of Systematic Negation*, Vienna: IHF Research Foundation, 2006.

İhlas Haber Ajansi, "Başbakan'dan gençlere tavsiyeler", 27 December 2012. Available at: https://www.iha.com.tr/haber-basbakandan-genclere-tavsiyeler-256118/.

İnsel, Ahmet, *La nouvelle Turquie d'Erdogan*, Paris: La Decouverte, 2015

Jones, Gareth, "Turkey's Christians Like AK Despite Islamist Past", *Reuters*, 20 June 2007. Available at: https://www.reuters.com/article/uk-turkey-election-christians/turkeys-christians-like-ak-despite-islamist-past-idUKL1835667220070619.

Karpat, Kemal H., *The Politicization of Islam: Reconstructing Identity, State, Faith, and Community in* the *Late Ottoman State*, Oxford: Oxford University Press, 2001.

Kirişçi, Kemal. "Disaggregating Turkish Citizenship and Immigration Practices", *Middle Eastern Studies*, vol. 36, no. 3, 2000, pp. 1-22.

Koraltürk, Murat, *Erken Cumhuriyet Döneminde Ekonominin Türkleşmesi*, Istanbul: İletişim, 2011.

Martin, Natalie, "Allies and Enemies: The Gülen Movement and the AKP", *Cambridge Review of International Affairs*, vol. 35, no. 1, 2020, pp. 110-127.

O'Mahony, Anthony and Emma Loosley (eds.), *Eastern Christianity in the Modern Middle East*, London: Routledge, 2010.

Oran, Baskın, *Minorities and Minority Right sin Turkey: From the Ottoman Empire to the Present State*, trans. John William Day, Boulder and London: Lynne Rienner, 2021.

Ors, Ilay Romain (ed.), *İstanbullu Rumlar ve 1964 Sürgünleri: TürkToplumunun Homojenleşmesinde bir Dönüm Noktası*, Istanbul: İletişim, 2008.

Oztig, Lacin Idil and Kenan Aydin, "The AKP's Approach toward Non-Muslim Minorities: Constructivist and Rationalist Insights", *Alternatives: Global, Local, Political*, vol. 42, no. 2, 2017, pp. 59-73.

Öktem, Kerem, *Turkey since 1989: Angry Nation*, London and New York: Zed Books, 2011.

Önis, Ziya, "Domestic Politics, International Norms and Challenges to the State: Turkey-EU Relations in the Post-Helsinki Era", in Ali Çarkoğlu and Barry Rubin (eds.), *Turkey and the European Union: Domestic Politics, Economic Integration and International Dynamics*, London: Frank Cass, 2005, pp. 8–31.

Republic of Turkey Ministry of Foreign Affairs Secretariat General for EU Affairs, *Political Reforms in Turkey*, Ankara: M&B Tanıtım Hizmetleri, 2007.

Resmi Gazette, "İmar Kanunu ile İmar ve Gecekondu Mevzuatına Aykırı Yapılara Uygulanacak Bazı İşlemler ve 6785 Sayılı İmar Kanununun Bir Maddesinin Değiştirilmesi Hakkında Kanunda Değişiklik Yapılmasına İlişkin Kanun", No. 25319, Law No. 5006, 17 December 2003. Available at: https://www.resmigazete.gov.tr/eskiler/2003/12/20031217.htm#1.

Roussos, Sotiris, "Diaspora Politics, Ethnicity and the Orthodox Church in the Near East", *Journal of Eastern Christian Studies*, vol. 61, no. 1-2, 2009, pp. 137-148.

Roussos, Sotiris, "Globalization Processes and Christians in the Middle East: A Comparative Analysis", *The Journal of the Middle East and Africa*, vol. 5, no. 2, 2014, pp. 111-130.

Slim, Souad Abou el-Rousse, *Christianity: A History in the Middle East*, Lebanon: Middle East Council of Churches, 2005.

Soner, Bayram Ali, "The Justice and Development Party's Policies towards Non-Muslim Minorities in Turkey", *Journal of Balkan and Near Eastern Studies*, 12(1), 2010, p. 23-40.

Stetter, Stephan and Mitra Moussa Nabo (eds), *Middle East Christianity: Local Practices, World Societal Entanglements*, Basingstoke: Palgrave, 2020.

Toprak, Zafer, *Türkiye'de Milli İktisat 1908-1918*, Istanbul: Doğan Kitap, 2012.

Uzgel, İlhan, "Turkey's Double Movement: Islamists, Neoliberalism, and Foreign Policy", in Pınar Bedirhanoğlu, Çağlar Dölek, Funda Hülagü, and Özlem Kaygusuz (eds.), *Turkey's New State in the Making: Transformations in Legality, Economy and Coercion*, London: Zed, 2021, pp. 64-79.

White, Jenny, *Muslim Nationalism and the New Turks*, NJ: Princeton University Press, 2014.

World Bulletin, "Turkish Christians Favor Tolerant AK Party", 20 June 2007. Available at: https://worldbulletin.dunyabulteni.net/archive/turkish-christians-favor-tolerant-ak-party-h5482.html.

Zürcher, Erik J., The Young Turk Legacy and Nation Building: From the Ottoman Empire to Atatürk's Turkey, London and New York: I. B. Tauris, 2010.

https://www.anayasa.gov.tr/tr/mevzuat/onceki-anayasalar/1924-anayasasi/.

THE GREEK/PALESTINIAN DIVIDE WITHIN THE JERUSALEM ORTHODOX CHURCH: THE INSTITUTIONAL ASPECT

Konstantinos Papastathis

Introduction

The Orthodox Patriarchate of Jerusalem is the oldest Christian institution in Palestine. It has a monastic structure via the establishment of the Brotherhood of the Holy Sepulcher, and its aim is the protection of the Orthodox custodianship rights over the Hole Places, as defined by the so-called Status Quo Agreement.[1] From the nineteenth century onwards, the national Greek element became dominant within the institution. This created an internal division between the Greek hierarchy and the Arab lay community, essentially overdetermined by the nation-building and the secularisation processes, which were the side-effects of: a) the *tanzimat* (reforms) that opened the way for the activation of the lay element in the decision-making processes of the *millet*; and b) the gradual building and crystallisation of the new collective identity, the nation.[2] The outcome of these developments was the "gradual transformation of Church administrative structures from a non-ethnic religious representation to a nationality-based religious affiliation".[3]

The Arab Orthodox movement had an ideological, economic, and social background, reflecting suppressed national and religious expectations, as well as constituting a reaction against the stereotypical orientalist discourse of the Greek religious apparatus vis-à-vis the indigenous Orthodox population. In particular, the lay community, from 1872 onwards (and with Russian support), put forward its demands to the authorities.[4] These were:

[1] Chrisostomos Papadopoulos, *Historia tis Ekklisias Hierosolymon*, Athens: Pournaras, 1970; Nikiphoros Moschopoulos, *La Question de Palestine et le Patriarcat de Jérusalem: ses Droits, ses Privilèges. Aperçu Historique*, Athens: Messager d'Athènes, 1948.

[2] Dimitris Stamatopoulos, *Metarrythmisi kai Ekkosmikeusi: Pros mia Anasynthesi tis Historias tou Oikoumenikou Patriarcheiou ton 19o Aiona*, Athens: Alexandreia, 2003, pp. 20-21.

[3] Konstantinos Papastathis and Ruth Kark, "Colonialism and Religious Power Politics: the Question of New Regulations within the Orthodox Church of Jerusalem during the British Mandate", *Middle Eastern Studies*, vol. 50, no. 4, 2014, p. 590.

[4] Derek Hopwood, *The Russian Presence in Syria and Palestine, 1843-1914: Church and Politics in the Near East*, Oxford: Clarendon Press, 1969; Theophanes G. Stavrou, *Russian Interests in Palestine, 1882-1914: A Study of Religious and Educational Enterprise*, Thessaloniki: Institute for Balkan Studies, 1963; Elena Astafieva, "La Russie en Terre Sainte: le cas de la Société Impériale Orthodoxe de Palestine (1882-1917)", *Cristianesimo*

a) the establishment of local lay councils in each ecclesiastical province; b) the establishment of a mixed council of both Greek clerical and Arab lay composition for the administration of communal affairs and the financial management of the Patriarchate; c) free admission of the Arab Orthodox to the Brotherhood; and d) active participation in the procedures for the election of the Patriarch and bishops.[5] Reading between the lines, these demands aimed at the laicisation of the communal power structures and the liberation from the foreign ecclesiastical rule. In effect, a deep-seated tension was produced between the two camps. On the one hand, the hierarchy following the ideological fallacy of Helleno-Orthodoxia, i.e., the complete equation between Greek identity and Eastern Orthodoxy, conceived the Jerusalem Patriarchate to be, by definition, a Greek national institution.[6] On the other hand, for the Arab Orthodox collective consciousness, Greek rule was conceived as the 'other' that had usurped and exploited the Arab cultural patrimony. In effect, the struggle against this form of religious imperialism became part of the overall Palestinian national cause.[7]

The area within which the two opposing camps could set their agenda and manoeuvre was defined by the regulations of the Patriarchate, which determined the internal operation of the Brotherhood, its interaction to the authorities and the laity, the management of its finances and the administration of its real estate property. The establishment, maintenance, or alteration of the regulations was, therefore, a matter of major significance in the power game between the two agents. This paper aims precisely to investigate the 'institutional' aspect of the question in contemporary times. Accordingly, the research question to be addressed is whether the Patriarchal regulations, as defined by the Charter of the Rum Orthodox Patriarchate of Jerusalem (Law 27/1958 of the Jordanian Kingdom), leave room for restructuring the power relations within the institution. To this end, the article explores the possible grey zones of the Charter as well as the possible interpretations of its clauses and the effects these produce on the overall communal operation.

---

nella Storia, vol. 24, 2003, pp. 41-68.

[5] Anton Bertram and Harry C. Luke, *Report of the Commission Appointed by the Government of Palestine to Inquire into the Affairs of the Orthodox Patriarchate of Jerusalem*, London: Oxford University Press, 1921.

[6] Pavlos Karolides, *Peri tis Ethnikis Katagogis ton Orthodoxon Christianon Syrias kai Palaistinis*, Athens: P.D. Sakellariou Press, 1909; Paraskevas Matalas, "To Patriarcheio Hierosolymon kai i Hellino-Orthodoxia", in *Orthodoxia, Ethnos kai Ideologia*, Athens: Moraiti School, 2007, pp. 113-121; Konstantinos Papastathis, "Secularizing the Sacred: the Orthodox Church of Jerusalem as a Representative of Greek Nationalism in the Holy Land", *Modern Greek Studies-Yearbook*, , vol. 30/31, 2014/2015, pp. 37-54.

[7] Noah Haiduc-Dale, "Rejecting Sectarianism: Palestinian Christians' Role in Muslim-Christian Relations", *Islam and Christian-Muslim Relations*, vol. 26, no. 1, 2015, pp. 75-88; Laura Robson, "Communalism and Nationalism in the Mandate: The Greek Orthodox Controversy and the National Movement", *Journal of Palestine Studies*, vol. 41, no. 1, 2011, pp. 6-23.

The article is divided into four parts. The first section gives a short account of the historical background of the question. The second part sketches Law 27/1958, giving special emphasis on the clauses related to the administration and hierarchy formation. Next, the article addresses the research question, referring to the various aspects of the theme, such as the national question, the financial management and the Status Quo Agreement. The last section resumes the argumentation and sets forth the conclusions.

Historical Background: The Institutional Question in Ottoman Times and the Mandate

The Fundamental Law of the Patriarchate, established in 1875, comprised 17 articles, with provisions for the administrative structures and their operation, as well as the election of the Patriarch and hierarchy.[8] The Fundamental Law was an important step towards the rationalisation of its operation. At the same time, it left many disputed aspects unclear, while the laity's involvement in the management of the institution and its finances was apparently insignificant, contrary to the system adopted in Constantinople or Antioch. The Young Turks revolution allowed a more liberal modification of the religious administration with the partial participation of the laity in the decision-making process via establishing a mixed council for supervising communal affairs.[9] On the other hand, the Turkish Order did not threaten the institutional privileges of the hierarchy, which secured the imagined Greek character of the Patriarchate, since the proposed mixed council would not participate in the electoral process of the Patriarch and the religious officials, who maintained the absolute control over the administration of the Holy Places, the extended vakf properties of the institution and the revenues derived from them.[10]

Overall, this institutional framework did not change during the Mandate.[11] The British stance may be divided into two periods in accordance with the political circumstances and the social considerations that they faced: first, from 1917 until the mid-1930s; and second, from 1938 until the end of

---

[8] Bertram and Luke, *Report*, pp. 243-249.

[9] Hopwood, *The Russian Presence*, p. 197.

[10] Konstantinos Papastathis and Ruth Kark, "Orthodox Communal Politics in Palestine after the Young Turk Revolution (1908-1910)", *Jerusalem Quarterly*, vol. 56 & 57, 2014, pp. 118-139; Evelin Dierauff, *Translating Late Ottoman Modernity in Palestine: Debates on Ethno-Confessional Relations and Identity in the Arab Palestinian Newspaper Filasṭīn (1911–1914)*, Göttingen: Vandenhoeck & Ruprecht, pp. 175-276.

[11] Antony O'Mahony, "Palestinian-Arab Orthodox Christians: Religion, Politics and Church-State Relations in Jerusalem, c. 1908-1925", *Chronos: Revue d' Histoire de l'Université de Balamand*, vol. 3, 2000, pp. 61–91; Sotiris Roussos, "How Greek, how Palestinian? The Patriarchate of Jerusalem in the mid-War Years", *Sobornost*, vol. 17, 1995, pp. 9-18; Sotiris Roussos, "The Greek Orthodox Patriarchate and Community of Jerusalem: Church, State and Identity", in Anthony O'Mahony (ed.), *The Christian Communities of Jerusalem and the Holy Land*, Cardiff: University of Wales Press, 2003, pp. 38-56.

the Mandate. On the one hand, the Administration established the Bertram-Young Commission (1925), which gave legitimacy to almost all the demands of the laity and recommended changes to the Fundamental Law in a more liberal direction that would lead to the gradual takeover of the Patriarchate by the Arab Orthodox. On the other hand, there was the necessity to maintain good diplomatic relations with Greece by protecting its interest within the British zone of control. This is the main reason why the patriarchal regulations drafted by the British in late 1930s essentially reproduced the traditional power structures within the organisation. The Administration, because of the Second World War and its future withdrawal from Palestine, did not have any interest to maintain the question in its agenda.

The partition of Palestine had as an effect on the Orthodox Patriarchate the division of the territory under its jurisdiction between two rival states. In effect, the institution had to find a *modus operandi* with both state authorities that would: a) guarantee the preservation of its rights over the Holy Places in accordance with the Status Quo agreement; and b) allow its unhampered operation in terms of administration and finances, including the management of its real estate property extended in both sides of the buffer zone. Moreover, it should be taken into account that the Patriarchate was not any more under the political supervision of an external power that ruled pragmatically its 'colony' in accordance with its own sordid ends, but under the Jordanian royal family (and bureaucracy) that gained political legitimacy through the promotion of nationalism and its opposition to Israel. The state policy, therefore, vis a vis the claims of the Arab Orthodox movement was a question of major significance, especially after the convention of the Fourth Orthodox Arab Congress (March 1956) that re-set the agenda of the lay claims.[12] To meet these demands, Amman established a Mixed Commission (consisting of the Minister of the Interior, the Governor of Jerusalem, the Muslim Judge of Jerusalem, two Brotherhood members, and two lay representatives) to inquire into the affair and propose a new set of Regulations. The Brotherhood strongly disapproved of the first draft Law and declined its institutionalisation, as being contrary to the normative framework historically being in effect within the Patriarchate.[13] The alleged violation of the Status Quo, which would work as a pretext against Jordan within the arena of international relations; the threat of disturbing the equilibrium among the Christian communities, i.e. aborting any thought of

---

[12] Daphne Tsimhoni, "The Greek Orthodox Community in Jerusalem and the West Bank 1948-1978: A Profile of a Religious Minority in a National State", *Orient*, vol. 23, no.2, 1982, pp. 284-288.

[13] Varnavas D. Tzortzatos, *Oi Vasikoi Thesmoi Dioikiseos ton Orthodoxon Patriarxceion meta Historikon Anaskopiseon*, Athens: Society for Macedonian Studies/Institute for Balkan Studies, 1972, pp. 147-149.

changing the administrative structures of other Church institutions; and the maintenance of cordial relations with Greece, which was one of the few European states that did not recognise Israel and openly supported the Arab side are possibly the factors contributed to the policy change of the Cabinet, which concluded to the enactment of the new Regulations of the Patriarchate (Law 27/1958 of the Jordanian Kingdom).

The Institutional Reform: Law 27/1958 of the Jordanian Kingdom

Overall, the new regulatory framework did not signify a thorough reform of the centralised pattern of administering the church affairs, but apparently reproduced the existing power relations both within the Brotherhood, i.e. the hierarchy vis-à-vis the monks, as well as within the community, i.e. the Greek Brotherhood vis-à-vis the Arab lay community and parish clergy. However, it should be noted that some clauses, though of secondary importance, might be seen as a step forward to promote the overall lay cause.

In particular, the new Regulations define the Patriarch as the supreme authority of the "RUM-Orthodox" Patriarchate of Jerusalem (i.e., not "Greek-Orthodox") and has general jurisdiction over all its affairs (art. 3; par. 1). The Synod decides either unanimously or by the majority on any matter affecting the Patriarchate. The Synod should be composed of 18 members, i.e., the Patriarch, and the diocesan bishops (ex officio), a number of titular bishops appointed by the Patriarch himself, and a number of archimandrites appointed by the Synod. The Patriarch maintains the power to replace the non-ex officio synodic members, in deference to the needs of the institution. In short, Law 27/1958 stipulates a centralised authoritative power structure for the Patriarchate, within which the Patriarch enjoys great power over the Synod and the institution. The Synod has complete authority to decide on and administer the affairs of the Patriarchate, to own and manage the movable and immovable property, and to receive the inheritance and the waqf endowments (art. 5). The Patriarch is the authority to implement and administer the synodal decisions.

A Mixed Council is established with a lay majority, which manages 1/3 of the general revenues of the Patriarchate (not including the donations or chantries for a specific purpose) for schooling, charity, and renovation of the parish churches. The rest 2/3 of the revenues are managed by the Patriarchal Synod. The local Council of Jerusalem will get an annual fund of 2200 dinars (Art. 7). The Mixed Council has the right to control the budget of the Patriarchate but cannot object to the managing of the financial affairs of the Patriarchate, except for the amount allotted for its use. The Regulations officially introduced the distinction between two types of endowments, i.e.

117

the so-called waqf properties: a) those donated to the Brotherhood, which is administered by the Synod; and b) those donated to the lay community, which is administered by the Mixed Council. The immovable property of the Patriarchate is entrusted to the Patriarch for its administration and management, while the government has the competency to control the proper implementation of the Law.

The patriarchal election process has four stages: a) The Synod elects as *locum tenens* one bishop, recognised by the Jordanian government (art. 18). Afterwards, the *locum tenens* invites all the bishops (either members of the holy Synod or not) and one married priest from each Local Council as representatives of the lay community (maximum number 12). This body forms the so-called "Spiritual Council". The members of the 'Spiritual Council' write on a ballot the name of the person whom they consider appropriate for the throne. Only a Jordanian citizen and a Brotherhood member is eligible to be elected as Patriarch. He should be fluent in Arabic, both spoken and written language, as well. All the proposed candidates are eligible, irrespective of the number of votes they had taken at this stage. The Jordanian government has the power to withdraw names from the catalogue of candidates. c) An assembly composed of the Synod, the bishops, the archimandrites residing in Jerusalem, and the married priests (i.e. the members of the 'Electoral Council') proceeded to choose three nominees from the list approved by the Jordanian government. d) The final stage of the election process is done by the Synod, which selects from the chosen three nominees the one to become the Patriarch. In case of a tie, the *locum tenens'* vote would be decisive (art. 21). The new Patriarch took office only after recognition of his election by the political authorities through the issuing of a *Royal Irade* (art. 23). The deposition of the Patriarch is possible, only if he is heretic or unable to properly serve his mission (e.g. mental illness). However, the deposition is valid on the condition that 2/3 of the Synodal members and 2/3 of the parish priests (who participated in his election) agree to his dethronement. Moreover, the government should acknowledge the validity of his deposition as well. If one of these conditions is not fulfilled, the act of deposition is *null and void*. The Jordanian citizenship is an eligibility criterion for the admission to the Brotherhood. Moreover, the Patriarchate should accept the admission of an appropriate number of Arab Orthodox to the Brotherhood. As regards the election of the bishops, the candidates should be Jordanian subjects, esteemed by the government and the community, as well as familiar with the Greek and Arabic languages. (art.24). The Synod should elect two Arab bishops, who will be *ex officio* members of the Synodal council.

The question that arises is whether these stipulations clarified or gave solutions to old issues or had they created further problems. The next section will endeavour to indicate the contradictory and/or ambiguous points of the Patriarchal Regulations and their effect on the overall communal operation regarding the national, financial and the so-called Status-Quo questions. In particular, it will address whether: a) the Patriarchate should be considered a Greek national institution; b) the Patriarch has the capacity to manage on his own the finances and the immovable property; and c) what is the interaction between the Regulations and the Status Quo framework, i.e. should the Regulations be considered to be part of the Status Quo and/or should the latter framework be a factor defining the internal administration of the Brotherhood?

The Gray Areas of Law 27/1958

The national question

The title of the institution is "Patriarchate of the Rum-Millet". Its alleged Greekness, therefore, is related to the definition of the term "Rum" (art. 2) and how it is interpreted by the two antagonistic sides within the Jerusalem Church. According to the hierarchy, the Greek national character of the Patriarchate has an institutional validity, which derives from the various ottoman legal decrees that defined it as 'Rum' as well as Law 27/1958.[14] This is because, according to the Greek establishment, 'Rum' for the Ottoman legal order did not mean the subject, who belonged to the Orthodox community at large, but meant those who had a Greek national consciousness and cultural belonging, spoke Greek and were loyal to the canonically recognised Church institutions. Moreover, 'Rum' was translated in this way, i.e. 'Greek', by many western sources, both diplomatic and religious, which distinguished between the Greeks and other Orthodox nations, such as the Serbs or the Georgians.[15]

On the other hand, for the Arab laity, this term should not be identified with the Greek but with the Byzantine Empire, which had a multi-ethnic state structure. The various ethnic communities subject to Constantinople, therefore, were actually "Byzantine" (Rum), regardless of their ethnic origins. In short, "Rum" should not in essence be identified with nationality, but with "citizenship", state loyalties and a sense of historical community and continuity.[16] It should be noted in this respect that the dominant

---

[14] Damaskinos Gaganiaras, *The Administrative Organization of Jerusalem Patriarchate*, unpublished PhD dissertation, Thessaloniki: Law School of Aristotle University of Thessaloniki, 2008, p. 6.

[15] Patriarchate of Jerusalem, *Refutation of the Allegations put forward by Sir Anton Bertram against the Patriarchate of Jerusalem*, Jerusalem: Greek Convent Printing Press, 1937.

[16] Sahada Khoury and Nicolas Khoury, *A Survey of the History of the Orthodox Church of Jerusalem*, Amman: Orthodox Society/Dar Al-Shorouk, 2002, p. 26.

paradigm is that the term Rum meant in the Ottoman legal order the Orthodox Ottoman subject at large without referring to any national or ethic belonging. In short, Rum was related to communal belonging and/or to the administrative centre the Orthodox subject acknowledged as its head, i.e. the Patriarchate of Constantinople or the Jerusalem Patriarchate.[17] From a historical perspective, both the Sublime Porte and the mandatory authorities did not make any distinction on the basis of national/ethnic identity between the Eastern Orthodox population, but considered all Orthodox subjects to be Rum. Bertram-Young Report verified that the term 'Rum' did not mean 'Hellene' but included all the varied Orthodox subjects of the Ottoman Empire at large. The British were against adding the term 'Greek' to Orthodox, which 'would not only run counter to tradition and precedent but would cause the gravest offence to the Arab Orthodox both in Palestine and Trans-Jordan'. In addition, it might be invoked by Athens in order to intervene at a diplomatic level in patriarchal affairs, a development that would be 'most embarrassing to the Palestine Government'.[18]

Within this framework, the use of the term Rum in Law 27/1958 should not be viewed as a recognition of the Greek national character but as manifesting the religious identity and tradition. On the other hand, the fact that the legislator uses the term "Arab Orthodox community" (art. 2) might justify the Greek view. However, this use does not indicate a contrast between "Rum", i.e. Greek, and 'Arab", but aims precisely at clarifying the ethnic origin of the lay community of Jordan. Moreover, it might be argued that since the Charter stipulates the obligation for the Patriarch to be fluent in Arabic (art. 19), the Charter implies that the Patriarch should be of another national origin, namely Greek. However, this clause neither blocks the election of an Arab or of any other nationality to the patriarchal see, nor does it confine the election only to Greeks. It simply expresses the will of the legislator to guarantee that the Patriarch should at least be able to communicate with his flock. Actually, there is not any reference to the obligation of the Patriarch to be Greek. In contrast, what eventually stipulates is that the Patriarch should be of Jordanian nationality/ citizenship (art. 24 and 28). To conclude, the only condition in relation to citizenship referred to the Charter is that the Patriarch should be of or acquire the Jordanian citizenship, which is given to all members of the Brotherhood irrespective of their national identity. He can be, therefore, of any national

---

[17] Paraskevas Konortas, *Othomanikes Theoriseis gia to Oikoumeniko Patriarheio, 17os arches 20ou Aiona*, Athens: Alexandria, 1998, pp. 303-315.

[18] C.O. 733/400/5, 'Memorandum of J. S. Bennett: Use of the Title "Greek" in the Style of the Orthodox Patriarchate of Jerusalem' (15/9/1939); Konstantinos Papastathis and Ruth Kark, "Colonialism and Religious Power Politics", p. 597.

origin. Finally, art. 28 stipulates that the Brotherhood should admit in its ranks an appropriate number of Arab Orthodox. This might imply that the Brotherhood has a different national character. However, it might also be interpreted as the legislator's will to institutionally guarantee that at least some indigenous monks are admitted. In other words, this clause does not indicate a national diversification between Greeks and Arabs, but that irrespective of the national demography and majority within the institution, the Brotherhood should have at least a minimum number of Arab nationals within its ranks. This, of course, does not mean that the indigenous can only be a minority group, but they could form the majority as well.

The property management question

Taking into account the struggle between Israel and the Palestinians for control over land, the ultimate management of the Patriarchate's considerable assets and immovable urban property is an issue of the utmost importance. The Palestinian laity considers the Greek clergy to be corrupt, irresponsible, and above all, foreign. As such, the clergy should not be permitted unrestricted management of the assets, which the Arab Orthodox regarded as belonging to them. This position was reinforced by the danger of selling the church's land to the Israelis. The question that arises, therefore, is which body has the competency to manage, lease or sell the properties. Has the Patriarch the capacity to administer on his own the finances, or is it the Synod that ultimately has this power?

The response to this question is straightforward: art. 5 of Law 27/1958 stipulates that the Synod under the chairmanship of the Patriarch is the competent authority to manage any affair related to the immovable property. The Patriarch cannot take any decision or proceed on his own regarding any transaction before acquiring the Synod's agreement. The same is defined by clause 37 of the internal Regulations of the Brotherhood as well.[19]

On the other hand, what if the Patriarch signs a sale of property without the consent of the Synod. Is such a sale legal or not? This seems to be an open question. On the one hand, it depends on state Law and the prerequisites for land transactions. This is because the Patriarch is the competent authority to sign any document related to the Brotherhood and his signature together with the Stamp of the Synod (art. 37 of the Internal Regulations) provides the necessary validity to the transaction. The vendee has not the obligation or the access to confirm that the proper process has been followed or not. As such, the transaction is valid and the Patriarch is

---

[19] Anton Bertram and John W. A. Young, *The Orthodox Patriarchate of Jerusalem: Report of the Commission Appointed by the Government of Palestine to Inquire and Report upon Certain Controversies between the Orthodox Patriarchate of Jerusalem and the Arab Orthodox Community*, London: Oxford University Press, 1926, p. 347.

exposed for maladministration to his fellow monks. On the other hand, art. 35 of Law 27/1958 stipulates that the prime minister and the cabinet are responsible for the implementation of the Law. If, therefore, the Patriarch sells a property without the consent of the Synod, this transaction is illegal and thus null and void. It should be emphasised that the Charter forms a State Law. In effect, any act contrary to its stipulations is illegal and, therefore, invalid. However, this is a Law of the Kingdom of Jordan, which is not binding for other state authorities. This question, therefore, is still open to various interpretations regarding its implementation to Israel and the Palestine Authority.

The Status Quo question

Overall, this issue is related to the dispute between the various Churches for controlling the Christian sanctuaries. It has deep historical roots and is essentially political, as a special field of interest for the external state powers and linked to the regime changes that have occurred in the area.[20] According to Cust, the term 'Status Quo' is generally defined as,

> the arrangements existing in 1852 which corresponded to the Status Quo of 1757 as to the rights and privileges of the Christian communities officiating in the Holy Places have to be most meticulously observed, and what each rite practised at that time in the way of public worship, decorations of altars and shrines, use of lamps, candelabra, tapestry and pictures, and in the exercise of the most minute acts of ownership and usage has to remain unaltered.[21]

The research question to be addressed in this respect is whether the holy places question is related to the institutional framework applied to the Orthodox Church of Jerusalem in general, as well as by Law 27/1958 in particular.

A brief and straightforward answer is yes. This is because the ranking of the Patriarchate was grounded precisely on its symbolic status as the representative of the community of the holy city, in contrast to the other religious centres whose prestige derived from their political power *per se*. Moreover, according to the Orthodox narrative, the very administrative restructuring of the institution into a Brotherhood in early Ottoman times

---

[20] Paolo Pieraccini, *Gerusalemme, Luoghi Santi e Communita Religiose nella Politica Internazionale*, Bologna: Edizioni Dehoniane, 1997; Oded Peri, *Christianity under Islam in Jerusalem: the Question of the Holy Sites in Early Ottoman Times*, Leiden: Brill, 2001; Walter Zander, "On the Settlement of Disputes about the Christian Holy Places", *Israel Law Review*, vol. 8, no. 3, 1978, pp. 331-366; Konstantinos Papastathis, "Religious Politics and Sacred Space: The Orthodox Strategy on the Holy Places Question in Palestine, 1917-1922", *Journal of Eastern Christian Studies*, vol. 65, no. 1-2, 2013, pp. 67-95.

[21] Lionel G. A. Cust, *The Status Quo in the Holy Places*, Jerusalem, 1980, p. 11.

was precisely based on the idea that its primary duty – the imagined *raison d'être* – should be the protection of the extensive Orthodox rights and privileges in the Holy Places, which were allegedly threatened by the usurping tendencies of other competing denominations.[22]

As regards particularly Law 27/1958, art. 3.2 par. a stipulates that the Patriarch should "conduct appropriately all religious ceremonies within the designated time frame in churches and shrines pertained to the Patriarchate entirely or jointly with other communities". This clause clearly implies the centrality of the Status Quo for the Church operation. This is because the terms "appropriately" and "designated time frame" should not be interpreted as merely implying the liturgical order, i.e. how to carry out the mass or lead the procession without failing to meet the specific time limits, since all the respective details are already fixed by the ritual tradition, ecclesiology and canon law. In short, these type of worship practices is self-evident, and there is no need to be regulated by state law in order to be respected. Nor could it be the duty or the will of the legislator to get involved in such questions of purely religious essence. In contrast, the legislator's intervention can only have political motives and particularly the protection of the rights and privileges of the Patriarchate, and in turn the blocking of the Brotherhood from any act that might generate a disruption of its ties with the other communities that might threaten public order. The explanation of the said provisions, therefore, should be based on the context, namely that their meaning is overdetermined by the acknowledgement by the legislator of the existence of certain holy places under the shared custodianship between the Patriarchate and other religious institutions, as noticed in the end of the clause. From this perspective, the term "appropriately" and "within the designated time frame" (which is repeated in art. 3.4 par. a as well) seem to refer precisely to the Patriarch's obligation to follow the *modus operandi* vis-à-vis the other communities (e.g. which religious head enjoys the primacy over a ceremony, or for how much time each community can use a certain shrine, etc.), which is actually defined by the Status Quo Agreement. In effect, Law 27/1958 clearly imply the Status Quo to be part of the administrative core of the Patriarchate as the framework regulating its relations with the other communities; its implementation, therefore, seems to be by law binding.

As regards the alleged incorporation of patriarchal Regulations into the Status Quo, the Greek hierarchy, on its part, maintained as early as late ottoman times that the administrative organisation of the institution should

---

[22] Kallistos Miliaras, Oi Agioi Topoi en Palaistini kai ta ep' auton Dikaia tou Hellinikou Ethnous, Thessaloniki: University Studio Press, 2002.

be considered to be part of it, because the very existence of the sanctuaries determined the monastic system as the most appropriate structure for the Patriarchate's internal operation. Moreover, this system was presented as being an everlasting historical tradition. Thus, the relevant clauses and decrees that served their proper operation cannot be subject to reform. This narrative had a political character, since it allowed the reproduction of the hierarchy's power over the lay community by preventing both a potential upgrade of the Arab lay cause versus its interests as well as a potential usurpation of the 'Greek' rights by the other Orthodox states (Russia, Romania, and Serbia), as Patriarch Damianos put it to R. Storrs.[23]

Indeed, the Status Quo framework contains certain clauses concerning the organisational character of the religious institutions involved. As Cust put it, 'the Franciscans alone of the Roman Catholic Orders are allowed to celebrate Mass independently in the Holy Places, although the clergy of any Roman Catholic Order can attend. The Patriarch himself, of course, has the right to pontificate. Similarly, of the autocephalous Orthodox Churches none other than the Orthodox Patriarchate of Jerusalem has any standing in the Holy Places.[24] Consequently, the Status Quo protected the exclusive competency and responsibility of the Patriarchate from being the only organ for ruling the affairs connected to the Orthodox rights over the sanctuaries. Any claim, therefore, raised by any other Orthodox institution (Patriarchate of Constantinople, Moscow Patriarchate, Patriarchate of Rumania, etc.) to interfere was prohibited. This regulation, however, on no occasion stipulates that the Ottoman Fundamental Law or the current Law 27/1958 should be seen as part of the Status Quo. In contrast, both codes were and/or could be subject to modifications on the condition that the existing rights and privileges of the Brotherhood over the holy places are not altered, as well as that any amendment of the Law should have the consent of the Brotherhood.

Concluding remarks

Overall, Law 27/1958 stipulates a centralised system of ecclesiastical governance, according to which the Patriarch alone or with the Synod exercises almost absolute control over all church affairs. In effect, the new Regulations could not satisfy the Palestinian Orthodox demands since they provided the Greek hierarchy with all the means for maintaining its power, such as the confinement of lay participation in patriarchal elections to the minimum. Since the laity has very little influence in the electoral result, lay

---

[23] PRO: F.O. 608/99/6.

[24] L.G.A. Cust, *The Status Quo*, p. 11.

participation seems to be in fact the pretext, the 'democratic' alibi, for the legitimisation of Greek hierarchical control rather than a substantial concession to the Palestinians. This conclusion applies to property management as well, since the religious apparatus kept absolute control over the majority of the vakf properties within and outside the Jerusalem area, irrespective of the communal claims. In short, the objections raised at that time regarding the implementation of the Law for being against Greek interests,[25] were proven to be of little value. Moreover, the state authorities involved have neither the will nor the means to reform the Law as long as the political question is not resolved, namely, which one would have the political competency over East Jerusalem. At the same time, this state of affairs allows the intervention of Jordan, Israel, and PA to their own ends since the Charter stipulates that the political authorities should officially acknowledge the elected by the Brotherhood Patriarch in order to be legally enthroned. This process, however, practically means that the state authorities have the opportunity to receive compensation in exchange for the recognition of the Patriarchal election. This mechanism has rendered the institution vulnerable to any sort of demands or 'blackmails' of political, communal and financial nature.

Bibliography

Astafieva, Elena, "La Russie en Terre Sainte: le cas de la Société Impériale Orthodoxe de Palestine (1882-1917)", *Cristianesimo nella Storia*, vol. 24, 2003, pp. 41-68.

Bertram, Anton and Luke, Harry C., *Report of the Commission Appointed by the Government of Palestine to Inquire into the Affairs of the Orthodox Patriarchate of Jerusalem*, London: Oxford University Press, 1921.

Bertram, Anton and Young, John W. A, *The Orthodox Patriarchate of Jerusalem: Report of the Commission Appointed by the Government of Palestine to Inquire and Report upon Certain Controversies between the Orthodox Patriarchate of Jerusalem and the Arab Orthodox Community*, London: Oxford University Press, 1926.

Cust, Lionel G. A., *The Status Quo in the Holy Places*, Jerusalem, 1980.

Dierauff, Evelin, *Translating Late Ottoman Modernity in Palestine: Debates on Ethno-Confessional Relations and Identity in the Arab Palestinian Newspaper Filasṭin (1911–1914)*, Göttingen: Vandenhoeck & Ruprecht, 2020.

Gaganiaras, Damaskinos, *The Administrative Organization of Jerusalem Patriarchate*, unpublished PhD, Law School of Aristotle University of Thessaloniki, 2008.

Haiduc-Dale, Noah, "Rejecting Sectarianism: Palestinian Christians' Role in Muslim-Christian Relations", *Islam and Christian-Muslim Relations*, vol. 26, 2015, pp. 75-88.

Hopwood, Derek, *The Russian Presence in Syria and Palestine, 1843-1914: Church and Politics in the Near East*, Oxford: Clarendon Press, 1969.

Karolides, Pavlos, *Peri tis Ethnikis Katagogis ton Orthodoxon Christianon Syrias kai Palaistinis*, Athens: P.D. Sakellariou Press, 1909.

Khoury, Sahada and Khoury Nicolas, *A Survey of the History of the Orthodox Church of Jerusalem*,

---

[25] Panagiotis Tzoumerkas, "O Katastatikos Nomos tou Patriarxheiou Hierosolymon(1958) kai i Diamartyria tou Patriarchou Alexandreias Christophorou pros ton Prothypourgo tis Hellados gia tin Psiphisi tou", *Ecclesiastikos Pharos*, vol. 77, 2006, pp. 145-164.

Amman: Orthodox Society/Dar Al-Shorouk, 2002.

Konortas, Paraskevas, *Othomanikes Theoriseis gia to Oikoumeniko Patriarheio, 17os arches 20ou Aiona*, Athens: Alexandria, 1998.

Matalas, Paraskevas, "To Patriarcheio Hierosolymon kai i Hellino-Orthodoxia", in *Orthodoxia, Ethnos kai Ideologia*, Athens: Moraiti School, 2007.

Miliaras, Kallistos, *Oi Agioi Topoi en Palaistini kai ta ep' auton Dikaia tou Hellinikou Ethnous*, Thessaloniki: University Studio Press, 2002.

Moschopoulos, Niciphoros, *La Question de Palestine et le Patriarcat de Jérusalem: ses Droits, ses Privilèges. Aperçu Historique*, Athenss: Messager d'Athènes, 1948.

Papadopoulos, Chrisostomos, *Historia tis Ekklisias Hierosolymon*, Athens, 1970.

O'Mahony, Antony, "Palestinian-Arab Orthodox Christians: Religion, Politics and Church-State Relations in Jerusalem, c. 1908-1925", *Chronos: Revue d' Histoire de l'Université de Balamand*, vol. 3, 2000, pp. 61–91.

Papastathis, Konstantinos and Kark, Ruth, "Colonialism and religious power politics: the question of new regulations within the Orthodox Church of Jerusalem during the British Mandate", *Middle Eastern Studies*, vol. 50, no. 4, 2014, pp. 589-605.

Papastathis, Konstantinos and Kark, Ruth, "Orthodox Communal Politics in Palestine after the Young Turk Revolution (1908-1910)", *Jerusalem Quarterly*, v. 56/57, 2014, pp. 118-39.

Papastathis, Konstantinos, "sSecularising the Sacred: The Orthodox Church of Jerusalem as a Representative of Greek Nationalism in the Holy Land", in *Modern Greek Studies-Yearbook* 2014/15, University of Minnesota, 2016, pp. 37-54.

Papastathis, Konstantinos, "Religious Politics and Sacred Space: The Orthodox Strategy on the Holy Places Question in Palestine, 1917-1922", *Journal of Eastern Christian Studies*, vol. 65, no. 1-2, 2013, pp. 67-95.

Patriarchate of Jerusalem, *Refutation of the Allegations put forward by Sir Anton Bertram against the Patriarchate of Jerusalem*, Jerusalem: Greek Convent Printing Press, 1937.

Peri, Oded, *Christianity under Islam in Jerusalem: the Question of the Holy Sites in Early Ottoman Times*, Leiden: Brill, 2001.

Pieraccini, Paolo, *Gerusalemme, Luoghi Santi e Communita Religiose nella Politica Internazionale*, Bologna: Edizioni Dehoniane, 1997.

Roussos, Sotiris, "How Greek, how Palestinian? The Patriarchate of Jerusalem in the mid-War Years", *Sobornost*, vol. 17, 1995, pp. 9-18.

Roussos, Sotiris, "The Greek Orthodox Patriarchate and Community of Jerusalem: Church, State and Identity", in A. O' Mahony (ed.), *The Christian Communities of Jerusalem and the Holy Land*, Cardiff: University of Wales Press, 2003, pp. 38-56.

Robson, Laura, "Communalism and Nationalism in the Mandate: the Greek Orthodox Controversy and the National Movement", *J. of Palestine Stud.*, v. 16, 2011, pp. 6-23.

Stamatopoulos, Dimitris, *Metarrythmisi kai Ekkosmikeusi: pros mia Anasynthesi tis Historias tou Oikoumenikou Patriarcheiou ton 19o Aiona*, Athens: Alexandreia, 2003.

Stavrou, Theophanes G., *Russian Interests in Palestine, 1882-1914: a Study of Religious and Educational Enterprise*, Thessaloniki: Institute for Balkan Studies, 1963.

Tsimhoni, Daphne, "The Greek Orthodox Community in Jerusalem and the West Bank 1948-1978: a Profile of a Religious Minority in a National State", *Orient*, vol. 23, no.2, 1982, pp. 281-298.

Tzortzatos, Varnavas D., *Oi Vasikoi Thesmoi Dioikiseos ton Orthodoxon Patriarxceion meta Historikon Anaskopiseon*, Athens: Society for Macedonian Studies/Institute for Balkan Studies, 1972.

Tzoumerkas, Panagiotis, "O Katastatikos Nomos tou Patriarxheiou Hierosolymon(1958) kai i Diamartyria tou Patriarchou Alexandreias Christophorou pros ton Prothypourgo tis Hellados gia tin Psiphisi tou", *Ecclesiastikos Pharos*, vol. 77, 2006, 145-164.

Zander, Walter, "On the Settlement of Disputes about the Christian Holy Places", *Israel Law Review*, vol. 3, 1978, pp. 331-66.

THE RUSSIAN ORTHODOX CHURCH AND THE STATE: THE MIDDLE EAST CONNECTION

Ilias Tasopoulos

Introduction

The stance of the Russian Orthodox Church (ROC) on Iraq and Syria shows several dimensions of its persistent international activities, affected by institutional aspects and geoecclesiastical considerations. The idea of a world centred around Russia that includes the Middle East intertwined with its rhetoric of protecting Christians from the unexpected developments that arose in both countries.

The greater involvement of the United States in the region reinvigorated the ROC's interest in Iraq's developments and its Christians. The strategic interaction between Russia and the United States was the crucial factor of its approach towards Iraq. At the same time, the civil war in Syria brought the ROC into a new situation where it had to balance dangers and opportunities.

This article will examine the central doctrines that run through ROC's decision-making structure in relation to Syria and Iraq in the 21st century by illustrating how the Russian Orthodox Church operates at turbulent times in the Middle East. In addition, it will discuss ROC's aims and relationship with the Russian state,[1] as its actions influence Russian domestic politics and are accordingly influenced by the Russian government.

The historical connection between the ROC and the Middle East Churches

The welfare of Orthodox Christians in the Middle East seems to have been a foreign policy concern for Russia since the times of the Ottoman Empire. The conquest of the territories hosting the four major Patriarchates had left the Russian Church as the only one free from Muslim authority.[2] As

---

[1] Martin Solik – Vladimír Baar, "Religious Component in a State's Foreign Policy. A Case Study of the Russian Orthodox Church", *Politické vedy*, vol. 23, no. 2, 2020, pp. 157-199; Robert C. Blitt, "Russia's 'Orthodox' Foreign Policy: The Growing Influence of the Russian Orthodox Church in Shaping Russia's Policies Abroad", *University of Pennsylvania Journal of International Law*, vol. 33, no. 2, pp. 364-460; Daniel Payne, "Spiritual Security, the Russian Orthodox Church, and the Russian Foreign Ministry: Collaboration or Cooptation?", *Journal of Church and State*, vol. 52, no. 4, 2010, pp. 712–27; Nikolai Petro, "The Russian Orthodox Church", in Andrei Tsygankov (eds.) *Routledge Handbook of Russian Foreign Policy*, London and New York: Routledge, 2018, pp. 217-232.

[2] Abdul Latif Tibawi, "Russian cultural penetration of Syria — Palestine in the nineteenth century (Part

a result, Russia saw itself as the protector of Orthodox Christianity and sought to expand its influence in areas where Orthodox Christians lived, including the Middle East.

As educated Russians cultivated contacts with various ethnic Christian groups in the Ottoman Empire, geopolitical developments pushed for greater Russia's political and cultural involvement in the Christian East.[3] Russia believed that it had a duty to protect and support fellow Christians living under the rule of the predominantly Muslim Ottoman Empire. The rise of the Pan-Orthodoxy doctrine brought the ROC closer to the Russian autocracy, while nationalism silently rose.[4]

Despite Soviet governments' efforts to suppress the Orthodox Church after the end of the First World War, religious institutions continued to play a significant role in Russian society, particularly among the rural population. During this time, the ROC cultivated strong ties with the Orthodox Churches in the Middle East.[5]

Safeguarding Christian communities abroad became an issue of cooperation between the ROC and the Russian state. The ROC usually presents Russia's engagement in protecting persecuted Christians in the Middle East as continuing the Russian historical mission and fulfilling historical obligations.[6]

The canonical authority of the ROC has spread far beyond the limits of the Russian empire, the Soviet Union and Russia during the last 100 years. In 2012, the ROC had over 220 dioceses, 30,000 parishes and numerous missions around the world and representation offices at the United Nations.[7] Hence, the ROC stands in a favourable position to transform its presence in these areas into political influence. Nowadays, the ROC is estimated to have between 80 and 150 million adherents, making it the largest of the recognised Orthodox church, having its seat located in one of the strongest states in the

---

I)", *Journal of The Royal Central Asian Society*, vol. 53, no. 2, 1966, pp. 66-182; Lora Gerd, "Russian policy in the Patriarchate of Antioch from the 1840s to 1914: 'soft power' in Syria and Lebanon", *Contemporary Levant*, vol. 6, no. 1, 2021, pp. 9-23; Maria Kourpa & Charitini Petrodaskalaki, "The Russian Patriarchate in the Middle East: Reclaiming an old prestige", *Middle East Bulletin*, no. 35, 2019, pp. 33-34. Available at: www.cemmis.edu.gr/index.php/en/publications/middle-east-bulletin/item/597-russia-in-the-middle-east-the-russian-bear-in-mind-middle-east-bulletin-35.

[3] Denis Vovchenko, "Modernizing Orthodoxy: Russia and the Christian East (1856–1914)", *Journal of the History of Ideas*, vol. 73, no. 2, 2012, pp. 304-307.

[4] Ibid. p. 298.

[5] Harry J. Psomiades, "Soviet Russia and the Orthodox Church in the Middle East." *Middle East Journal*, vol. 11, no. 4, 1957, pp. 371–381.

[6] Alicja Curanović, "Russia's Mission in the World", *Problems of Post-Communism*, vol. 66, no. 4, 2018

[7] Galina Petrenko, "Influence of the Russian Orthodox Church on Russia's Foreign Policy", *4th ECPR Graduate Student Conference Jacobs University Bremen*, 4-6 July 2012.

world.[8]

Since the Soviet period, the Department for External Church Relations has also had a high stature. The Church's structures abroad had to survive without Russia's protection in territories where both the Russian state and the ROC had to compete for influence. Until 2011, the foreign relations department employed over a hundred people, while the charities and educational departments staff only a dozen each.[9]

The protection of Christians in the Middle East has forged a connection between the eschatological beliefs of Eastern Christianity and the concept of the Messiah. These ideals have been incorporated into Russian foreign policy. The messianic belief that Russia has a special spiritual mission ordained by God to protect and spread Orthodoxy and promote moral and cultural values perceived as beneficial for the world is rooted in the idea that Russia is the "Third Rome."[10]

This reading of Russian identity and history has blended today's nationalistic and imperialistic ideologies. Relating a religious mission to the country's international status is a frequent feature of this sort of rhetoric, combining two top priorities: first, legitimising Russian claims to major power status; second, blending Russian nationalistic ambitions with elements from the country's tradition, showing the relevance of Orthodoxy in the idea of Russia's distinctiveness with respect to Europe.[11]

The ROC is one of the few institutions that can influence the political process nowadays, as its members regularly engage in dialogue with public authorities to develop various laws and regulations. ROC's growing influence in the country has helped transform the "Holy Rus" concept into a political instrument, just like the "Russian World" and Eurasianism.[12] As the idea that Russia is a special and unique nation with an expanded divine

---

[8] The Metropolis of Kiev and all Rus, which was recognized as the Autocephalus Church of Moscow and ruled by the Patriarch of Moscow, of the Eastern Orthodox Church. When the Russian empire was proclaimed in 1700, the Church lost its independence from the emperor and was largely under the control and pressure of the state, until the death of Joseph Stalin in 1953. Afterwards, the ROC was not seriously challenged domestically, while ROC and it came to the foreground during perestroika, remaining an established actor ever since. With the collapse of the Soviet Union, earlier laws limiting church activities and its legal status were abolished, and its resurrection began.

[9] Jane Ellis, *The Russian Orthodox Church: Triumphalism and Defensiveness*, Basingstoke: Palgrave, 2001, pp. 98-99.

[10] After the Byzantine Empire collapsed, Russian emperors were bestowed responsibility to carry on its legacy as a defender of Christianity and civilization. By upholding traditional values and moral principles, Tsars promoted a utopian vision of a pure Christian society.

[11] Betsy Perabo, "Russia's Unfinished Symphony of Church and State", *Political Theology Network*, 2 July 2018. Available at: https://politicaltheology.com/russias-unfinished-symphony-of-church-and-state/.

[12] Mikhail Suslov, "'Holy Rus': The Geopolitical Imagination in the Contemporary Russian Orthodox Church", *Russian Politics and Law*, vol. 52, no. 3, p. 67.

mission, the Church assumed a dominant role in public life, shaping the population's identity and influencing culture, politics, and foreign policy. Ever since, the protection of Christian communities and their sacred places, such as temples and worship sites, in the Middle East and beyond, has assumed a more symbolic value for Moscow.

Relations between the ROC and state under Putin: religion, ideology and foreign policy

The ROC is very active in the social, economic and educational fora of Russian politics. While at the end of the Soviet Union era, only 30 per cent of Russians identified as Orthodox Christians, today that number has risen to 70 per cent.[13] The activities abroad and the imprint of the ROC's international stature have a deep impact on domestic politics. The Russian Orthodox Church influences public discourse. In addition, access to the mass media and public opinion helps establish norms regarding Russia's foreign policy aims. In turn, utilising its revenues, ROC sets values on foreign policy and provides conceptual and ideological justifications for the Russian agenda. Apart from this, the capability to legitimise some of the Kremlin's policies renders the ROC an essential institution.[14] An example of this legitimisation is the strong Christian presence in Syria and Iraq that emerges periodically in the public discourse, linking it to contemporary political issues.

Kremlin and ROC did not always see eye to eye. On many occasions, there was friction and criticism between the Patriarchate and the Russian state authorities; however, cooperation prevails, and points of convergence are usually found. For instance, on the one hand, ever since Patriarch Kirill's leadership of ROC in 2009, his rhetoric about the Church's "independence" intended perhaps to show that the Church is distancing itself from the state.[15] On the other hand, the two find common ground on international issues. More specifically, they have a common position on what Russia's role should be in the international political scene, namely, a significant power promoting its traditionalist and conservative national identity. In this sense,

---

[13] John Hersh, "How Putin is using the Orthodox Church to build his power", Vice News, 26 March 2018. Available at: www.vice.com/en/article/gymqgb/how-putin-is-using-the-orthodox-church-to-build-his-power.

[14] Nikita Lomagin, "Interest groups in Russian foreign policy: The invisible hand of the Russian Orthodox Church", *International Politics,* no. 49, 2012, p. 504; Kadri Liik, Momchil Metodiev, Nicu Popescu, "Defender of the faith? How Ukraine's Orthodox split threatens Russia", *European Council on Foreign Relations,* 30 May 2019. Available at: www.ecfr.eu/publications/summary/defender_of_the_faith_how_ukraines_orthodox_split_threatens_russia.

[15] Mikhail Suslov, "'Holy Rus'", p. 69.

the state assists ROC in accomplishing its ecclesiastical goals abroad.[16] In turn, ROC promotes and represents Russia's interests abroad and serves its agenda.[17]

The ROC appreciates Russia's presence in the Middle East as one of the most central issues of its policy. Although there are some discontinuities, the Middle East also holds significant importance for the Russian state. The Kremlin usually prioritises issues related to its neighbouring countries and expends fewer resources abroad compared to its predecessor, the Soviet Union.[18] However, an array of factors, Islamic militancy, trade and geopolitical competition, lead Russia to deal with the Middle East.[19] ROC's involvement in key state institutions formulating Middle East policies—the president, the Duma, and the Ministry of Foreign Affairs- is noticeable.[20]

The current Russian president considers the ROC vital, as Vladimir Putin has been tightening his grip on power, giving political expression to the "true Christian church"[21] doctrine and exploiting the influence of the Russian Patriarch in the post-Soviet public space.[22] Kremlin has embraced the idea of Russia being the protector of Christians, even beyond the state's borders, where its jurisdiction ends.

The Putin government has established an understanding with the ROC to achieve spiritual security and consolidate its rule over the Russian diaspora. The signing of the 2007 Act of Canonical Communion of the Moscow Patriarchate and the Russian Orthodox Church Outside of Russia (ROCOR) epitomises the efforts of Moscow to reacquire both Russian properties and influence lost abroad during the Communist period. There is a deep belief inside the ROC that Russia is destined to protect Christians

---

[16] Dmitry (Dima) Adamsky, "Christ-loving Diplomats: Russian Ecclesiastical Diplomacy in Syria", *Survival*, vol. 61, no. 6, 2019, pp. 49-68

[17] Petrenko, "Influence of the Russian Orthodox Church on Russia's Foreign Policy".

[18] Roland Dannreuther, "Russia and the Middle East: A Cold War Paradigm?", *Russia and the World*, vol. 64, no. 3, 2012, pp. 543-560.

[19] The need to control North Caucasus, is a characteristic example. Even a low-level Islamist insurgency in Chechnya, Georgia and Abhazia, is a worrying prospect. The radicalisation and potential transnational diffusion of militant Muslims into the domestic population, including big Russian cities, which host millions of Muslim migrant workers from central Asia is something that concerns Moscow. Fred Weir, "If Kremlin doesn't fight Islamists in Syria, will it have to in Russia?", *Christian Science Monitor*, 22 October 2015. Available at: www.csmonitor.com/World/Europe/2015/1022/If-Kremlin-doesn-t-fight-Islamists -in-Syria-will-it-have-to-in-Russia. At the same time there are economic interests such as trade, along with the geopolitical competition with the West, while Moscow is also interested in upholding regional order norms.

[20] Alicja Curanović, "Russia's Mission in the World", p. 261.

[21] Anna Geifman, "Putin's "Sacred Mission" in Syria", *BESA Center Perspectives Paper*, no. 335, 2016.

[22] Max Seddon, "Putin and the Patriarchs: how geopolitics tore apart the Orthodox church", *Financial Times*, 21 August 2019. Available at: www.ft.com/content/a41ed014-c38b-11e9-a8e9-296ca66511c9.

from 'non-orthodox', who are about to destroy the Orthodox faith and force Russia to abandon its identity as an Orthodox nation.[23]

The plight of Christian communities in the Middle East and North Africa, especially in the wake of the "Arab Spring", has enhanced this trend. Deputy Chairman of the Moscow Patriarchate's Department of External Church Relations, Rev. Nikolai Balashov, has argued that the recent turmoil in the Middle East has made it more critical for the Church to become directly involved in foreign affairs.[24] According to Metropolitan Hilarion, Chairman of the Department of External Church Relations of the Moscow Patriarchate, the ROC was one of the first Russian institutions to express concern over the persecution of Christians in the Middle East.[25] The Moscow Patriarchate's efforts introduced this particular problem to the state agenda and influenced the way Kremlin dealt with this issue.

As the US invaded Iraq in 2003 and the Syrian issue came to the forefront with the Arab Spring during the last years, ROC involvement has been crucial for the domestic legitimisation of Russia's policy. According to Patriarch Kirill's take on the developments in the region, Russia's intervention in the Middle East protected Christians:[26] "just as the Russian Empire saved Assyrians from genocide at the time of the Ottoman Empire".

The ROC and the situation of Christians in Iraq

For ROC, Iraq has an immense symbolic significance as it is, situated in the land of ancient Mesopotamia where Christian communities had been living for centuries. During Saddam Hussein's era, ROC had little room to act, even when Christians became targets of the harsh dictator's Arabisation campaigns on Iraq's ethnic minorities, which were initiated in the 1970s and continued until the end of the 1980s.[27]

In hindsight, the dominant perception in the Moscow Patriarchate has been that Christians in Iraq enjoyed some basic freedoms under the Ba'athist rule as long as the government coopted them. Christian citizens exercised their right to worship freely, despite facing political marginalisation.

---

[23] Payne, "Spiritual Security, the Russian Orthodox Church, and the Russian Foreign Ministry pp. 712–717.

[24] Ellen Barry May, "Russian Church Is a Strong Voice Opposing Intervention in Syria", *New York Times*, 31 May 2012. Available at: www.nytimes.com/2012/06/01/world/europe/russian-church-opposes-syrian-intervention.html.

[25] Petrenko, "Influence of the Russian Orthodox Church on Russia's Foreign Policy", p. 5.

[26] Alicja Curanović, "Russia's Mission in the World".

[27] Shak Hanish, op. cit. Anthony O'Mahony, "Christianity in Modern Iraq", *International Journal for the Study of the Christian Church*, vol. 4, no 2, 2004, pp. 121-142.

Additionally, the growth of the Iraqi oil economy provided them with opportunities for prosperity.[28] The 1987 census estimated the Iraqi Christian population around 1.4 million, while by 2003, it had dropped to a million, according to estimates of the State Department.[29]

It appears that the Russian Orthodox Church recognised the significant risk to Christians in the region and therefore prioritised its engagement with Iraq more forcefully, particularly in response to the United States' preparations for a military operation against Baghdad during the presidency of George W. Bush. This White House's decision seemed to verify the veracity of their conviction about the wrong direction that the United States had taken. The ROC exploited the issue to show that there is an alternative to the American-Western return of imperialism in the region. Patriarch Kirill accused the United States of perpetuating Western practices and occupying foreign territories. He also argued that while the Russian Empire was not involved in the colonial system, it had been at the forefront of abolishing it worldwide after 1945.[30] The ROC was in a favourable position to benefit from the global repercussions of American intervention in Iraq.[31] Statements from ROC representatives were regularly issued, containing harsh anti-American criticism. The ROC cooperated with the Kremlin to pursue a balance in their reactions and not cross the line of attacking more fiercely to the US, having its sight on the international community's reactions.[32]

Russian Orthodox and Muslim clergy meetings with Iraqis intensified when the American attack was about to take place.[33] The ROC was careful to include Muslim clergy members in its visits and mention them explicitly in its statements[34] to show that they are represented in Russia, a place with a significant Muslim minority. This could serve as an example of multiethnic co-existence in Eurasia, in line with the Kremlin's intentions domestically.[35]

After Saddam Hussein was toppled, circumstances changed. The ROC did not see Christians challenging for a better position as the country's political system prepared to establish its first constitution. On the contrary,

---

[28] Ibid, pp. 129-130.

[29] Amanda Ufheil-Somers, "Iraqi Christians: A Primer", *Middle East Report*, no. 267, 2013, pp. 18–20.

[30] Alicja Curanović, "Russia's Mission in the World", p. 258.

[31] Roland Dannreuther, "Russia and the Middle East".

[32] Alicja Curanović, "Russia's Mission in the World", p. 258.

33 Galia Golan, "Russia and the Iraq War: was Putin's policy a failure?", *Communist and Post-Communist Studies*, vol. 37, no 4, 2004, p. 435.

[34] Dannreuther, "Russia and the Middle East".

[35] Alicja Curanović, "Relations Between the Orthodox Church and Islam in the Russian Federation", *Journal of Church and State*, vol. 52, no. 3, Summer 2010, pp. 503–539.

Christians reacted to the proposed Islamic identity of the state. The chaos from the Ba'athi collapse gave leeway to various Islamic fundamentalist groups, such as Al-Qaeda in Iraq, as well as other Sunni and Shi'a Islamist militias, to orchestrate attacks against vulnerable minorities.[36] During the war, as many as 500,000 Christians fled the country, comprising a vastly disproportionate percentage of refugees registered by the United Nations.[37] This brought the issue to the top of the ROC agenda.[38] Many Islamist organisations associated Iraqi Christians with Western colonial history in order to persecute them in the absence of a functioning state authority, driving many Christians to the neighbouring countries of Jordan, Palestine, and Syria.[39]

By the time the Arab uprisings erupted in 2010, Christians were facing insurmountable difficulties in staying in the country. The ROC maintained its focus on Iraq, even if the situation in nearby Syria deteriorated. Its reactions continued along the same lines, presenting an alternative version of events to the Western narrative. Metropolitan Hilarion attacked several times against "those who had created similar conflicts in Iraq with Syria", describing the situation in Iraq as follows: "With the help of the external military force [Saddam Hussein's] regime was overthrown, allegedly in the name of democracy. Among the results of this 'democratisation' was the persecution of Christians. Soon there were only some 100 thousand left in Nineveh, mainly in Mosul. [After living in terror and] facing threats for over a decade, over half of the countries Christians became refugees".[40]

Christians that remained in the country are concentrated in the Nineveh plain and the territory of the Iraqi Kurdistan Region. Despite their dwelling numbers, the Iraqi Christians retain a strong sense of communal identity. As this remains a concern for the ROC, it appears in its representatives' public speeches. During the Patriarch's visit to Syria, his Holiness described in dark colours the adverse effects of the crisis on the Christian communities and his concern about the events in Iraq.[41]

---

[36] Louis Elton, "Between the Devil and the Deep Blue Sea? Re- Examining Christian Engagement with Ba'athism in Syria and Iraq", *Socio- Historical Examination of Religion and Ministry*, vol. 2, no. 2, 2020, p. 61.

[37] Ibid.

[38] Sotiris Roussos, "Russia, The Middle East and the International System", in Constantinos Filis (ed.), *A Closer Look at Russia and Its Influence in the World*, New York: Nova Science Publishers, 2019, p. 352.

[39] Mohamed Kamel Doraï, "Iraqi Refugees in Syria", *Archive ouverte en Sciences de l'Homme et de la Société*, 2008. Available at: https://halshs.archives-ouvertes.fr/

[40] The Russian Orthodox Church, "Metropolitan Hilarion: Middle East and Ukraine – parts of the same strategy", 19 July 2014, Available at: https://mospat.ru/en/news/51191/

[41] The Russian Orthodox Church, "His Holiness Patriarch Kirill meets with President of Syria Bashar al-Assad", 14 November 2011. Available at: https://mospat.ru/en/news/54937/.

The ROC backed Prime Minister Putin's bid to win the 2012 presidential election. Metropolitan Hilarion supported his candidacy on the premise that it would guarantee the systematic protection of Christians subjected to persecution in different countries.[42] This issue was frequently raised during the campaign with the aim of becoming one of the trends in Russian foreign policy. Domestically, the issue of persecution against Christian minorities around the world (including the Middle East and Iraq) was of high significance, particularly among the most religious parts of Russian society.

One of the Churches' main objectives was to facilitate the return of the Christian refugees to their homeland, which was unfeasible for most refugees. With this in mind, the ROC continued to strengthen its relationship with Christian and Muslim hierarchies in Iraq, aiming to restore peaceful life in favour of ethnic and religious minorities. Metropolitan Hilarion underlined that the traditional Islamic leadership in Iraq was not hostile towards Christians, as opposed to ISIS' extreme ideology and their actions against the Christian community.[43]

As time went on, however, the Middle East and the conflict about the autocephaly of the Ukraine church became part of ROC's same strategy. Conflicts in the Middle East were linked to the escalation of violence in Ukraine, and the ROC attempted to present itself as a moral authority that responds to extremism of any nature.[44]

The anti-American critique continued unabated along the above-mentioned lines, showing the Russian commitment that supposedly contributed positively to the country. In November 2018, His Holiness Patriarch Kirill met with members of the Council of Church Leaders of Iraq-[45] on his first visit to Iraq since 2002- to announce programs for humanitarian aid. On this occasion, the Patriarch again referred to the military forces that invaded Iraq, which severely burdened Christians, while the hierarchs emphasised that Iraq had no benefit from the western

---

[42] The Russian Orthodox Church, "Russia will protect Christian minorities in the Middle East", 9 February 2012. Available at: https://mospat.ru/en/news/54549/.

[43] Metropolitan Hilarion referred to "influential leaders of traditional Islam in Iraq… that condemned the expulsion of Christians from Mosul and have been standing up against extremist ideologies… The fate of the country depends to a considerable extent on how consistent the people of traditional Islam will be in standing up against the ISIL's ideology. The Ba'ath Party in Iraq has declared a war on the ISIL. Ordinary Muslims, during an action in Bagdad, expressed support for Christians, who have lived in Iraq for almost two thousand years. The Ba'ath Party in Iraq has declared a war on the ISIL. Ordinary Muslims, during an action in Bagdad, expressed support for Christians, who have lived in Iraq for almost two thousand years", see The Russian Orthodox Church, "Metropolitan Hilarion: Middle East and Ukraine".

[44] Idem.

[45] Official website of the Moscow Patriarchate, "His Holiness Patriarch Kirill meets with members of the Council of Christian Church Leaders of Iraq", 21 November 2018. Available at: www.patriarchia.ru/en/db/text/5308832.html.

countries' policy, pinning instead great hope on Russia.[46]

The ROC and the Syrian Civil War

Despite the pressure against the Assad regime and the international isolation, the ROC was comfortable maintaining relations with Syria. Traditionally, Russian Church officials sided with Muslim leaders and Arab countries experiencing discomfort due to political and economic pressure from Western countries, even if they have amassed a poor record of human rights violations.[47] As a result, ROC representatives have enjoyed great access to Syria.

Even if the outcome of the Syrian crisis was uncertain, the international community assumed that Bashar al-Assad would retain power unless there were an outside intervention.[48] A discussion regarding a possible intervention in Syria sparked soon after NATO's intervention against Gaddafi in Libya in 2011. The Russian Church, however, strongly advocated against any Western intervention in Syria and stood by Russia's government's attempts to avert any western interference.[49]

During the Arab uprisings in 2011, Patriarch Kirill regularly visited the Middle East, promoting and portraying the ROC as the channel of communication between local Christians and the Kremlin. One of the critical ROC initiatives occurred in November of 2011 when Patriarch Kirill visited Syrian President Bashar al-Assad in Damascus. His presence at the Presidential Palace, talking about the "highly appreciate dialogue and cooperation and the example of peaceful life given by Syria", was interpreted as support to Assad,[50] although the ROC officially denied it. Its statement mentioned that when a Patriarch visits the Antioch Patriarchate, his Holiness always visits Syria and Lebanon.[51] The visit was reportedly delayed repeatedly and planned under high secrecy conditions. According to Metropolitan Hilarion, there were attempts "to dissuade the Patriarch from going ... due to disorder in Syria, that the Assad regime is in international isolation and under great pressure". At that time, the United Nations estimated that regime forces killed 3,500 protesters. The Patriarch's visit has been a

---

[46] Official website of the Moscow Patriarchate, "Representative of the Russian Orthodox Church visits Iraq", 3 April 2018. Available at: http://www.patriarchia.ru/en/db/text/5174427.html.

[47] Dannreuther, "Russia and the Middle East", p. 10.

[48] Dmitri Trenin, "The Mythical Alliance: Russia's Syria Policy", *Carnegie Moscow Center*, 12 February 2013. Available at https://carnegie.ru/2013/02/12/mythical-alliance-russia-s-syria-policy-pub-50909.

[49] Barry May, "Russian Church Is a Strong Voice Opposing Intervention in Syria".

[50] Ibid.

[51] The Russian Orthodox Church, "His Holiness Patriarch Kirill meets with President of Syria Bashar al-Assad".

significant point in introducing the issue of the protection of Syrian Christians into the Russian state agenda. In addition, deputy chairman of the Moscow Patriarchate's department of external church relations, Rev. Nikolai Balashov, said that the visit had succeeded in focusing Russia's attention on Syria, overcoming an "information blockade" of worldwide one-sided coverage of the conflict "in a biblical region".[52]

At a time when discussion worldwide revolved around a transitional government, pointing to an Assad exit, the ROC attempted to utilise its religious diplomatic clout[53] and show its indirect support towards the status quo in Syria. On February 22-23, 2012, in Larnaca of Cyprus, the Interfaith Council of the Middle East and North Africa, part of the "Religions for Peace" (RfP) World Conference, held a meeting of Muslim ulema and Christian clerics with the participation of researchers and stakeholders from Syria and other countries. The Interreligious Council of Russia, established in 1998 and representing the country's major religious communities, including Orthodox Christianity and Islam, represents Russia in RfP participated in the initiative.

The Interfaith Council for Peace in the Middle East participants issued in February 2012 a statement against any form of foreign intervention in Syria, asking for peace.[54] In addition, they rejected any form of foreign intervention declaring the Syrian crisis as an internal issue that Syrians should only resolve with the support of others. By reaffirming that Christians and Muslims are historically part of the Syrian social order, the Council complemented efforts made by state leaders and Russian diplomats to prevent active military actions against Syria.

Through the Religions for Peace World Conference, there was a call on all countries involved in economic sanctions against Syria to review these sanctions, stating that they have harmed the Syrian people, exacerbated the crisis and undermined stability and development. As per the official stance of Russia, certain countries have imposed financial and economic sanctions on Damascus without any consultation or agreement, while Christians have faced difficulties due to military operations carried out by government forces and militants of illegal armed groups, as well as due to the violent attacks perpetrated by terrorists and the constraining effect of western sanctions.

The Assad regime was primarily viewed as suppressing Islamic terrorism

---

[52] Barry May, "Russian Church Is a Strong Voice Opposing Intervention in Syria".

[53] Alicja Curanović, *The Religious Diplomacy of the Russian Federation*, Paris: Ifri, June 2012, p. 25.

[54] The Russian Orthodox Church, "The participants in the meeting between Muslim ulama and Christian clerics from Syria and other countries asked for peace in Syria" (in Russian), 2 March 2012. Available at: https://mospat.ru/ru/news/54462/.

against Christians at a time when radical Islamism gained more political visibility. "Syria lived in the atmosphere of inter-religious peace and concord for many decades while various communities of Christians, Muslims and Jews had good neighbourly relations and mutual understanding", according to a statement by the Moscow Patriarchate's Department for External Church Relations.[55] However, as time passed, concern rose in Moscow with regard to the Arab Spring shifting into a radical Islamist revolution and the Syrian conflict spreading further, which influenced the ROC's adherence to its initial stance.

Even at the height of Christian agony with regard to the abduction of two prominent hierarchs in 2013, Metropolitan Hilarion of Volokolamsk seized the opportunity to "call Western governments, supporting extremists who are eager for power, to stop this support because what is going on in Syria is not a civil war,[56] but an armed attempt to overthrow current regime with the help of external force", thus, showing that they would be against any intervention.[57]

Since 2011, the Church began pushing Kremlin to take a strong stance in defence of Syrian Christians, at a time that the regime of Vladimir Putin had been consolidating its position within the domestic sphere. The ROC highlighted the significance of the situation of the Christian community in Syria. All parishes in Russia raised and sent over 1.3 million US dollars in aid to the Orthodox Church of Antioch, under Patriarch Kirill's auspices, comprising medical equipment, clothing and food goods until 2014.[58]

The Church's insistence is said to have played a crucial role in President Vladimir Putin's justification to intervene directly in the conflict.[59] The clergy argued that protecting Christians in the Middle East amounted to something

---

[55] The Russian Orthodox Church, "On the Escalation of Violence against Christians in Syria", 27 May 2013. Available at: https://mospat.ru/en/news/52672/.

[56] The ROC didn't term the situation in Syria as a civil war. In an interview with *AsiaNews*, Metropolitan Hilarion of Volokolamsk, Head of the Moscow Patriarchate's Department for External Relations stated that he "would not term and that describing as "extremist forces seeking power"; *Asianews*, "Syria, the Pope, China: A Conversation with Orthodox Metropolitan Hilarion", 1 September 2013. Available at: www.asianews.it/news-en/Syria,-the-Pope,-China:-A-Conversation-with-Orthodox-Metropolitan-Hilarion-28880.html.

[57] The Russian Orthodox Church, "Metropolitan Hilarion of Volokolamsk: We pray for the soonest return of hierarchs abducted in Syria", 23 April 2013, https://mospat.ru/en/news/52819/.

[58] The Russian Orthodox Church, "Metropolitan Hilarion of the Russian Orthodox Church: "Persecution of Christians is Unprecedented", 29 April 2014. Available at: https://mospat.ru/en/news/51535/.

[59] Fred Weir, "Is Russia's intervention in Syria a 'holy war'? Russian Orthodox Church: 'yes'", 23 November 2015, *Christian Science Monitor*. Available at: www.csmonitor.com/World/Europe/2015/1123/Is-Russia-s-intervention-in-Syria-a-holy-war-Russian-Orthodox-Church-yes; Curanović, "Russia's Mission in the World", p. 9.

bigger. It could serve as a sign of the country's return to its spiritual roots.[60]

Doubts have been raised about whether the Russian Church and its Patriarch, Kirill, were influential enough to determine Moscow's attitude toward the civil conflict in Syria.[61] The ROC, however, was concerned with the general situation regarding Christian communities in the Middle East after the Arab Spring. At the same time, political dynamics within the ecclesiastical realm, along with the inter-church competition, provided added impetus for the Russian Orthodox Church to demonstrate its influence. Among others, the ROC intended to demonstrate its power vis-a-vis the Patriarchate of Antioch, the sole representative of Orthodox Christians in Syria, mutually recognised as autocephalous churches by the Ecumenical Patriarch of Constantinople. Even if there is "no hierarchy that could bind one group within the Church to another"[62], the ROC claims to be the prime power of Orthodoxy and desires to demonstrate its credentials.

Cordial relations with the Antioch Patriarchate were necessary as the dispute for the autocephaly of the Ukraine church intensified as the Antioch Patriarchate could play a crucial role in the conflict with the Ukraine Church.[63] Therefore, the ROC assumed that if it could help the Antioch Patriarchate in its hardship during the civil war, where the Antioch Church had sided with the Assad regime, it could count on its help on other ecclesiastical fronts, primarily in Ukraine. Disputes about jurisdictional boundaries and the recognition of new churches would soon arise.

Had the ROC successfully brought Russia to Assad's side during the civil war, ostensibly to protect Christians, it would show that it could deliver results to its allies. It did so in 2015. The symbolic significance of bringing Russia in to defend Christians needing protection was high for the Russian Patriarchate in its struggle for influence within ecclesiastic circles.

The Russian Orthodox Church backed the country's parliamentary decision to allow President Vladimir Putin to use military force in Syria, describing the fight against terrorism as a "holy war", a term that it had refrained from using for a long time. The Interfaith Council of Russia, a public body that unites leaders from Russia's four main religious traditions: Orthodox Christianity, Islam, Judaism, and Buddhism, also released a

---

[60] Adamsky, "Christ-loving Diplomats", passim.

[61] Nikolay Kozhanov, "Russian-Syrian Dialogue: Myths and Realities", *The Journal of the Middle East and Africa*, vol. 5, no 1, 2014, pp. 1-22.

[62] Ibid., p. 7

[63] Alekseï Makarkin, "What will happen to the ROC and its parishioners. Five Questions About Church Crisis", (in Russian), *Vedomosti.ru*, 16 October 2018. Available at: www.vedomosti.ru/opinion/articles/2018/10/16/783837-chto-budet-rpts-ee-prihozhanami-pyat-voprosov-tserkovnom.

statement supporting military operations against terrorism in the Middle East.

The ROC positioned itself as the protector of Christians of all denominations and began engaging hierarchs and communities within and beyond the Orthodox world. At a time when the Putin regime had prioritised its domestic consolidation, setting religious matters on the side,[64] the ROC managed to present itself as an indispensable institution of the country's spiritual rebirth. While the Russian Patriarchate continuously pressed for more substantial support to Arab Christians, cooperation between the ROC and the Kremlin was very tight. Whenever the Russian Church raised the Syrian issue, it was usually a follow-up to statements by secular officials.[65]

The Russian intervention helped the ROC upgrade its importance in the region. The Church supported and provided justification for Russia's official position on Syria, promoting the view that an operation is not only strategically desirable, but also morally legitimate.[66] Stopping "Christian genocide" was a more persuasive aim both domestically and internationally, rather than lending any support to the Assad regime.[67] The Russian state could argue that it opposed militant Islamism, while at the same time cooperating with the ROC to protect the Eastern Christian presence in Syria. This helped Moscow properly link its foreign policy with Christianity's future in Russia.[68] The military operation propped up the Kremlin and contributed to the steep rise of Vladimir Putin's approval rating to an all-time high, despite the fact that Russian troops abroad often accumulate quite low support.

Most of the population followed the developments in Syria,[69] while numerous local Christian communities in Russia have been traditionally concerned with the fate of Syrian Christians. Religious communities in Russia, along with Christian and Muslim clergy in Syria, helped restore

---

[64] John Anderson, "Putin and the Russian Orthodox Church: Asymmetric Symphonia?", *Journal of International Affairs*, vol. 61, no. 1, 2007, pp. 186–187.

[65] Kozhanov, "Russian-Syrian Dialogue".

[66] PONARS Eurasia, "The Role of the Russian Orthodox Church in Moscow's Syrian Campaign", 10 February 2020. Available at: www.ponarseurasia.org/the-role-of-the-russian-orthodox-church-in-moscow-s-syrian-campaign/.

[67] Leonid Issaev & Serafim Yuriev "The Christian Dimension of Russia's Middle East Policy", *Alsharq Forum Expert Brief*, no. 6, 2017. Available at: www.hse.ru/mirror/pubs/share/217045866.

[68] Andrew Ashdown, *An exploration of Christian-Muslim relations in Syria. 2000 - 2018. Contextualising the religious landscape, historic and contemporary dynamics in Christian-Muslim relations, and eastern Christian frameworks of engagement*, PhD dissertation, Winchester: University of Winchester. pp. 91-92.

[69] PONARS Eurasia, "The Role of the Russian Orthodox Church in Moscow's Syrian Campaign".

schools in Damascus[70] and churches[71], carried humanitarian work and dispatched aid,[72] acknowledged by leaders of the Syrian state.[73] By demonstrating proficiency in securing and sending humanitarian aid, independently of the Russian state, and participating enthusiastically in operations in the Middle East[74], the Church showed a strong desire to utilise all available resources in aiding the Christian community.

The ROC cooperated with the Russian state in the field of humanitarian aid. After the 2015 military intervention, Moscow tried to develop foreign assistance conduits through many organisations.[75] The ROC's experience and interest in such a sensitive issue meant that several Churches were mobilised to this cause, while the Patriarchate assisted and promoted participation in aid initiatives.

The expanded network in areas such as Latakia, where Greek-Orthodox communities have bonds with the ROC, facilitated Russian policy goals in Syria. ROC's actions could be interpreted as both a display of power and exploitation of opportunities presented during the civil conflict. The ROC showed that it could offer tangible help to the Christian cause. This Russian presence in Latakia had another significant dimension, as humanitarian aid reached Alawites, in a region earlier regarded as a regime stronghold, when the population faced real difficulties. As the Assad regime predominantly consists of Alawites, Damascus appreciated the humanitarian aid.[76]

---

[70] The Russian Orthodox Church, "A boarding school in Damascus receives aid from Russian religious communities", 16 January 2019. Available at: https://mospat.ru/en/news/46761/; The Russian Orthodox Church, "Religious communities in Russia begin joint efforts for restoring schools in Syria", 30 March 2019. Available at: https://mospat.ru/en/news/46493/

[71] Official website of the Moscow Patriarchate, "Orthodox Church of Antioch receives aid from Russia for restoring churches in Syria destroyed during the hostilities", 30 November 2018. Available at: www.patriarchia.ru/en/db/text/5315227.html; The Russian Orthodox Church, "Russian delegation visits Syria to discusses the issue of restoration of ancient convent in Maaloula", 21 March 2018. Available at: https://mospat.ru/en/news/47592/.

[72] The Russian Orthodox Church, "Orthodox children in Syrian Latakia received Christmas gifts from Moscow parish", 8 January 2018. Available at: https://mospat.ru/en/news/47799/; The Russian Orthodox Church, "Children from Sunday schools in Latakia receive presents from Russia", 25 October 2017. Available at: https://mospat.ru/en/news/48093/; The Russian Orthodox Church, "Interreligious working group completes unprecedented humanitarian action in Syria and Lebanon", 9 February 2018. Available at: https://mospat.ru/en/news/47712/.

[73] The Russian Orthodox Church, "Church-state delegation visits Syria", 13 April 2016. Available at: https://mospat.ru/en/news/49610/.

[74] Issaev& Yuriev, "The Christian Dimension of Russia's Middle East Policy".

[75] Jonathan Robinson "Russian aid in Syria: An underestimated instrument of soft power", *Atlantic Council*, 14 December 2020. Available at: www.atlanticcouncil.org/blogs/menasource/russian-aid-in-syria-an-underestimated-instrument-of-soft-power/; Marika Sosnowski and Jonathan Robinson, "Mapping Russia's soft power efforts in Syria through humanitarian aid", *Atlantic Council*, 25 June 2020. Available at: www.atlanticcouncil.org/blogs/menasource/mapping-russias-soft-power-efforts-in-syria-through-humanitarian-aid/.

[76] Fabrice Balanche, "Latakia Is Assad's Achilles Heel", 23 September 2015, *The Washington Institute for*

The Kremlin saw the ROC as an indispensable pillar in its endeavour in Syria, as Moscow sought to use foreign aid for political purposes. Its military presence allowed it to increase its influence and institutionalise ways to establish humanitarian aid flows. A soft power campaign designed to increase pro-Russian sympathies was soon implemented. As Russia decided to move on its own, outside of the UN framework,[77] the inclusionary element of religious co-existence was instrumental in accomplishing its targets.

As Russia attempted to bring closer Muslim populations along with protecting Christians, the ROC was a valuable player. Helping Christians or individuals with an Islamic background, who had converted to Christianity could prove the Church's adherence to the tenets of the religion. Reportedly, converts were brought under the protection of the Church to apply for religious asylum, while the Russian Orthodox Patriarchate initiated a program that would cover the costs of their emigration to Russia.[78]

Confronting "Christianophobia",[79] the persecution and discrimination of Christians, remained a top priority for the Church.[80] The ROC even organised an international conference, which was titled 'The Problem of the Persecution of Christians', bringing together world religious leaders and experts and painting an image of Russia as the protector of the region's Christians. Furthermore, the Russian Church managed to secure the support of the Russian muftis for the cause of Christians of the Middle East.[81]

According to its statements, the ROC also wanted to bring the West to its cause, presumably to show that its main aim was to help Christians in the region by any means necessary. Even if it failed, it would demonstrate that the main players were either indifferent or inefficient.

Metropolitan Hilarion argued on several occasions that Western countries, which had helped Christians for centuries -pointing to France-have denied them support, leading them outside the region. Therefore, according to the official line, Russia's persistence showed that they were the

---

Near East Policy. Available at: www.washingtoninstitute.org/policy-analysis/latakia-assads-achilles-heel.

[77] Ishtar Al Shami, "How Religion and Money Shape Russian Soft Power in Syria", 26 May 2022, *The Washington Institute for Near East Policy.* Available at: www.washingtoninstitute.org/policy-analysis/how-religion-and-money-shape-russian-soft-power-syria.

[78] Ibid.

[79] Nataliya S. Semenova, Ekaterina V. Kiseleva, Aleksandr M. Solntsev, "The Trend to Discriminate Christians: Shifting from the 'Post-Christian' West to the Global South", *Religions,* vol. 12, no. 108, 2021. Available at: https://doi.org/10.3390/rel12020108.

[80] The Russian Orthodox Church, "Metropolitan Hilarion: Middle East and Ukraine".

[81] Curanović, "Russia's Mission in the World", p. 261.

only force in which Christians had placed their hopes. [82]

The ROC did, however, acknowledge serious European attempts that showed "the steadfast resolve of many European countries to come to the defence of persecuted Christians"; showcasing the Greek initiative in October 2015, held in Athens, which organised a high-level forum on Religious and Cultural Pluralism and Peaceful Co-existence in the Middle East and a second forum in October 2017.[83]

Regularly highlighting the situation of the Middle East Christians on the agenda of international events and meetings with religious and political leaders has been a prime ROC objective. In March 2015, during a session of the UN Human Rights Council, sixty-five countries adopted the first resolution of its kind on supporting Middle Eastern Christians, having as initiators Russia, the Vatican, Lebanon and Armenia.

ROC's appeals to the world community, international organisations and political and religious leaders drew the attention of public opinion across the globe. In contrast, the mass media, as the ROC reiterated, initially were silent about this problem as if it did not exist. The restoration of churches and infrastructure, security guarantees and development of international relations play an essential role in the cause of facilitating return to the Middle East and preserving Christian presence.

The Russian Orthodox Church, committed to defending conservative values, has maintained its fundamental objective of incorporating Christian principles in the decision-making process for critical public matters, both on a national and international level.[84] The spread of its influence across the spectrum of the Russian state, such as the military, was often mentioned in its public statements to illustrate that key public institutions share their perspective. This was also depicted in Syria praising Russian military action "as a part of the Church's adaptive effort",[85] while Orthodox priests blessed missiles destined for Syria.[86] ROC's impact on foreign policy culminated in Russia's intervention in Syria. The interconnectedness of the Russian

---

[82] The Russian Orthodox Church, "Metropolitan Hilarion of the Russian Orthodox Church"

[83] Official website of the Moscow Patriarchate, "Address by Metropolitan Hilarion of Volokolamsk, chairman of the Department for External Church Relations of the Moscow Patriarchate, at the 2nd International Conference on Christian Persecution held in Budapest", 29 November 2019. Available at: www.patriarchia.ru/en/db/text/5539063.html.

[84] Gregory L. Freeze, "Russian Orthodoxy and Politics in the Putin Era", *Carnegie Endowment for International Peace*, 9 February 2017. Available at: https://carnegieendowment.org/2017/02/09/russian-orthodoxy-and-politics-in-putin-era-pub-67959.

[85] Curanović, "Russia's Mission in the World", p. 261.

[86] Boris Knorre, Aleksei Zygmont, "'Militant Piety' in 21st-Century Orthodox Christianity: Return to Classical Traditions or Formation of a New Theology of War?", *Religions*, vol. 11, no. 2, 2020, pp. 1-17.

Orthodox Church and the country's military complex has created an environment conducive to reviving a traditionalist ethos and nationalist sentiment, both domestically and internationally.[87]

Conclusions

The greater involvement of the United States in the region reinvigorated the Russian Orthodox Church's interest regarding Christians in Iraq and the country's development. The ROC attempted to exploit the repercussions of American endeavours and help Christians handle the difficulties they faced. The strategic interaction between Russia and the United States was the crucial factor of its decisions in Iraq.

At the same time, the Russian Church had new dilemmas in the face of the Syrian civil war, where it had to balance between dangers and opportunities. The Church promoted its own narrative in international relations, while attempting to influence the greater involvement of the Russian state in the conflict.

Relating a religious mission to Russia's international status is a frequent feature of the Russian state's rhetoric that helps it legitimise its claim to major power status, concurrently promoting its nationalistic outlook. This highlights the relevance of Orthodoxy in the idea of Russia's distinctiveness with respect to Europe and the West in general. Its rhetoric was based on the idea of a Russian-centered world that includes the Middle East, following the imperative of protecting Christians from the unexpected developments that arose in both countries. The Russian Orthodox Church helped in the legitimisation of Kremlin's policy, highlighting the anti-western stance of the Kremlin.

Bibliography

Adamsky, Dmitry (Dima), "Christ-loving Diplomats: Russian Ecclesiastical Diplomacy in Syria", *Survival*, vol. 61, no. 6, 2019, pp. 49-68.

Adamsky, Dmitry, *Russian Nuclear Orthodoxy: Religion, Politics, and Strategy*, Stanford: Stanford University Press, 2019.

Al-Khateb, Khaled "Russia plays up ties to Syrian Christians", *Al-Monitor*, 11 February 2021. Available at: www.al-monitor.com/originals/2021/02/russia-syria-iran-christians-orthodox-religion.html

Al Shami, Ishtar "How Religion and Money Shape Russian Soft Power in Syria", 26 May 2022, *The Washington Institute for Near East Policy* Available at: www.washingtoninstitute.org/policy-analysis/how-religion-and-money-shape-russian-soft-power-syria.

Ashdown, Andrew, *An exploration of Christian-Muslim relations in Syria. 2000 - 2018.*

---

[87] Dmitry Adamsky, *Russian Nuclear Orthodoxy: Religion, Politics, and Strategy*, Stanford: Stanford Press, 2019.

Contextualising the religious landscape, historic and contemporary dynamics in Christian-Muslim relations, and eastern Christian frameworks of engagement, PhD dissertation, Winchester: University of Winchester.

Anderson, John, "Putin and the Russian Orthodox Church: Asymmetric Symphonia?", *Journal of International Affairs*, vol. 61, no. 1, 2007, pp. 185-201.

Balanche, Fabrice, "Latakia Is Assad's Achilles Heel", *The Washington Institute for Near East Policy*, 23 September 2015. Available at: www.washingtoninstitute.org/policy-analysis/latakia-assads-achilles-heel.

Barry May, Ellen, "Russian Church Is a Strong Voice Opposing Intervention in Syria," *New York Times*, 31 May 2012. Available at: www.nytimes.com/2012/06/01/world/europe/russian-church-opposes-syrian-intervention.html.

Blitt, Robert C., "Russia's 'Orthodox' Foreign Policy: The Growing Influence of the Russian Orthodox Church in Shaping Russia's Policies Abroad", *University of Pennsylvania Journal of International Law*, vol. 33, no. 2, pp. 364-460.

Curanović, Alicja, "Relations Between the Orthodox Church and Islam in the Russian Federation", *Journal of Church and State*, vol. 52, no. 3, Summer 2010, pp. 503–539.

Curanović, Alicja, "Russia's Mission in the World", *Problems of Post-Communism*, vol. 66, no. 4, 2018, pp. 253-267.

Curanović, Alicja, *The Religious Diplomacy of the Russian Federation*, Paris: Ifri, June 2012.

Dannreuther, Roland, "Russia and the Middle East: A Cold War Paradigm?", *Russia and the World*, vol. 64, no. 3, May 2012.

Doraï, Mohamed Kamel, "Iraqi Refugees in Syria", *Archive ouverte en Sciences de l'Homme et de la Société*, 2008. Available at: https://halshs.archives-ouvertes.fr/.

Ellis, Jane, *The Russian Orthodox Church: Triumphalism and Defensiveness*, Basingstoke: Palgrave, 2001.

Elton, Louis, "Between the Devil and the Deep Blue Sea? Re-Examining Christian Engagement with Ba'athism in Syria and Iraq", *Socio-Historical Examination of Religion and Ministry*, vol. 2, no. 2, 2020, pp. 88-110.

Freeze, Gregory L., "Russian Orthodoxy and Politics in the Putin Era", *Carnegie Endowment for International Peace*, 9 February 2017. Available at: https://carnegieendowment.org/2017/02/09/russian-orthodoxy-and-politics-in-putin-era-pub-67959.

Geifman, Anna, "Putin's 'Sacred Mission' in Syria", *BESA Center Perspectives Paper*, no. 335, 2016.

Gerd, Lora, "Russian policy in the Patriarchate of Antioch from the 1840s to 1914: 'soft power' in Syria and Lebanon", *Contemporary Levant*, vol. 6, no. 1, 2021, pp. 9-23.

Golan, Galia, "Russia and the Iraq War: was Putin's policy a failure?", *Communist and Post-Communist Studies*, vol. 37, no 4, 2004, pp. 429-459.

Hersh, John, "How Putin is using the Orthodox Church to build his power", *Vice News*, 26 March 2018. Available at: www.vice.com/en/article/gymqgb/how-putin-is-using-the-orthodox-church-to-build-his-power.

Hussain, Shahid, "Deconstructing Russia's Response to the Hagia Sophia", 17 August 2020, *Modern Diplomacy*. Available at: https://moderndiplomacy.eu/2020/08/17/deconstructing-russias-response-to-the-hagia-sophia/.

Issaev, Leonid & Yuriev, Serafim, "The Christian Dimension of Russia's Middle East Policy", *Alsharq Forum Expert Brief*, no. 6, 2017. Available at: www.hse.ru/mirror/pubs/share/217045866.

Knorre, Boris & Zygmont, Aleksei, "'Militant Piety' in 21st-Century Orthodox Christianity: Return to Classical Traditions or Formation of a New Theology of War?", *Religions*, vol. 11, no. 2, 2020, pp. 1-17.

Kozhanov, Nikolay, "Russian-Syrian Dialogue: Myths and Realities", *The Journal of the Middle East and Africa*, vol. 5, no 1, 2014, pp. 1-22.

Kourpa Maria & Petrodaskalaki, Charitini, "The Russian Patriarchate in the Middle East: Reclaiming an old prestige", *Middle East Bulletin*, no 35, 2019, pp. 33-34. Available at:

www.cemmis.edu.gr/index.php/en/publications/middle-east-bulletin/item/597-russia-in-the-middle-east-the-russian-bear-in-mind-middle-east-bulletin-35.

Liik, Kadri & Metodiev, Momchil & Popescu, Nicu, "Defender of the faith? How Ukraine's Orthodox split threatens Russia", *European Council on Foreign Relations*, 30 May 2019. Available at: www.ecfr.eu/publications/summary/defender_of_the_faith_how_ukraines_orthodox_split_threatens_russia.

Lomagin, Nikita, "Interest groups in Russian foreign policy: The invisible hand of the Russian Orthodox Church", *International Politics*, no. 49, 2012, pp. 498-516.

Makarkin, Alekseĭ, "What will happen to the ROC and its parishioners. Five Questions About Church Crisis", (in Russian), *Vedomosti.ru*, 16 October 2018. Available at: www.vedomosti.ru/opinion/articles/2018/10/16/783837-chto-budet-rpts-ee-prihozhanami-pyat-voprosov-tserkovnom.

O'Mahony, Anthony, "Christianity in Modern Iraq", *International Journal for the Study of the Christian Church*, vol. 4, no 2, 2004. pp. 121-142.

Payne, Daniel, "Spiritual Security, the Russian Orthodox Church, and the Russian Foreign Ministry: Collaboration or Cooptation?", *Journal of Church and State*, vol. 52, no. 4, 2010, pp. 712–727.

Perabo, Betsy, "Russia's Unfinished Symphony of Church and State", *Political Theology Network*, 2 July 2018. Available at: https://politicaltheology.com/russias-unfinished-symphony-of-church-and-state/.

Petrenko, Galina, "Influence of the Russian Orthodox Church on Russia's Foreign Policy", 4th ECPR Graduate Student Conference, *Jacobs University*, Bremmen, 4-6 July 2012.

Petro, Nikolai, "The Russian Orthodox Church" in Andrei Tsygankov (ed.), *Routledge Handbook of Russian Foreign Policy*, Abingdon, New York: Routledge, 2018, pp. 217-232.

Psomiades, Harry J., "Soviet Russia and the Orthodox Church in the Middle East." *Middle East Journal*, vol. 11, no. 4, 1957, pp. 371–381.

Robinson, Jonathan, "Russian aid in Syria: An underestimated instrument of soft power", *Atlantic Council*, 14 December 2020. Available at: www.atlanticcouncil.org/blogs/menasource/russian-aid-in-syria-an-underestimated-instrument-of-soft-power/.

Roussos, Sotiris, "Russia, The Middle East and the International System", in Filis, Constantinos (ed.) *A Closer Look at Russia and Its Influence in the World*, New York: Nova Science Publishers Inc, 2019, pp. 347-360.

Seddon, Max "Putin and the Patriarchs: how geopolitics tore apart the Orthodox church", *Financial Times*, 21 August 2019. Available at: www.ft.com/content/a41ed014-c38b-11e9-a8e9-296ca66511c9.

Semenova, Nataliya S., & Kiseleva, Ekaterina V. & Solntsev, Aleksandr M., "The Trend to Discriminate Christians: Shifting from the 'Post-Christian' West to the Global South", *Religions*, vol. 12, no. 108, 2021. Available at: https://doi.org/10.3390/rel12020108.

Solik, Martin, Baar, Vladimír, "Religious Component in a State's Foreign Policy. A Case Study of the Russian Orthodox Church", *Politické vedy*, vol. 23 no. 2, 2020, pp. 157-199.

Sosnowski, Marika & Robinson, Jonathan, "Mapping Russia's soft power efforts in Syria through humanitarian aid", 25 June 2020, *Atlantic Council*. Available at: www.atlanticcouncil.org/blogs/menasource/mapping-russias-soft-power-efforts-in-syria-through-humanitarian-aid/.

Suchkov, Maxim A., "Why did Moscow call Ankara's Hagia Sophia decision "Turkey's internal affair"?", 14 July 2020, *Middle East Institute*. Available at: www.mei.edu/publications/why-did-moscow-call-ankaras-hagia-sophia-decision-turkeys-internal-affair.

Suslov, Mikhail, "'Holy Rus': The Geopolitical Imagination in the Contemporary Russian Orthodox Church", *Russian Politics and Law*, vol. 52, no. 3, pp. 67-86.

Tibawi, Abdul Latif, "Russian cultural penetration of Syria—Palestine in the nineteenth century (Part I)", *Journal of The Royal Central Asian Society*, vol. 53, no. 2, 1966, pp. 66-182.

Trenin, Dmitri, "The Mythical Alliance: Russia's Syria Policy", *Carnegie Moscow Center*, 12

February 2013. Available at: https://carnegie.ru/2013/02/12/mythical-alliance-russia-s-syria-policy-pub-50909.

Ufheil-Somers, Amanda "Iraqi Christians: A Primer," *Middle East Report*, no. 267, Summer 2013, pp. 18–20.

Vovchenko, Denis, "Modernizing Orthodoxy: Russia and the Christian East (1856–1914)", *Journal of the History of Ideas*, vol. 73, no. 2, April 2012, pp. 295-317.

Weir, Fred, "If Kremlin doesn't fight Islamists in Syria, will it have to in Russia?", *Christian Science Monitor*, 22 October 2015. Available at: www.csmonitor.com/World/Europe/2015/1022/If-Kremlin-doesn-t-fight-Islamists-in-Syria-will-it-have-to-in-Russia.

Weir, Fred, "Is Russia's intervention in Syria a 'holy war'? Russian Orthodox Church: 'yes'", 23 November 2015, *Christian Science Monitor*. Available at: www.csmonitor.com/World/Europe/2015/1123/Is-Russia-s-intervention-in-Syria-a-holy-war-Russian-Orthodox-Church-yes.

Internet Sources

Middle East Media Research Institute, "Russia's Reactions To Turkey's Decision To Turn Hagia Sophia Back Into A Mosque, Part I: The Kremlin's Muted Response", 29 July 2020. Available at: https://memri.org/reports/russias-reactions-turkeys-decision-turn-hagia-sophia-back-mosque-part-i-kremlins-muted#_ednref9.

PONARS Eurasia, "The Role of the Russian Orthodox Church in Moscow's Syrian Campaign", 10 February 2020. Available at: www.ponarseurasia.org/the-role-of-the-russian-orthodox-church-in-moscow-s-syrian-campaign/.

Official Sources

Official website of the Moscow Patriarchate, "Representative of the Russian Orthodox Church visits Iraq", 3 April 2018. Available at: www.patriarchia.ru/en/db/text/5174427.html.

Official website of the Moscow Patriarchate, "His Holiness Patriarch Kirill meets with members of the Council of Christian Church Leaders of Iraq", 21 November 2018. Available at: www.patriarchia.ru/en/db/text/5308832.html.

Official website of the Moscow Patriarchate, "Orthodox Church of Antioch receives aid from Russia for restoring churches in Syria destroyed during the hostilities", 30 November 2018. Available at: www.patriarchia.ru/en/db/text/5315227.html.

Official website of the Moscow Patriarchate, "Address by Metropolitan Hilarion of Volokolamsk, chairman of the Department for External Church Relations of the Moscow Patriarchate, at the 2nd International Conference on Christian Persecution held in Budapest", 29 November 2019. Available at: www.patriarchia.ru/en/db/text/5539063.html.

The Russian Orthodox Church," His Holiness Patriarch Kirill meets with President of Syria Bashar al-Assad", 14 November 2011. Available at: https://mospat.ru/en/news/54937/.

The Russian Orthodox Church, "Russia will protect Christian minorities in the Middle East", 9 February 2012. Available at: https://mospat.ru/en/news/54549/.

The Russian Orthodox Church, "The participants in the meeting between Muslim ulama and Christian clerics from Syria and other countries asked for peace in Syria" (in Russian), 2 March 2012. Available at: https://mospat.ru/ru/news/54462/.

The Russian Orthodox Church, "Metropolitan Hilarion of Volokolamsk: We pray for the soonest return of hierarchs abducted in Syria", 23 April 2013. Available at: https://mospat.ru/en/news/52819/.

The Russian Orthodox Church, "On the Escalation of Violence against Christians in Syria", 27 May 2013. Available at: https://mospat.ru/en/news/52672/.

The Russian Orthodox Church, "Metropolitan Hilarion of the Russian Orthodox Church:

"Persecution of Christians is Unprecedented", 29 April 2014. Available at: https://mospat.ru/en/news/51535/.

The Russian Orthodox Church, "Metropolitan Hilarion: Middle East and Ukraine – parts of the same strategy", 19 July 2014. Available at: https://mospat.ru/en/news/51191/.

The Russian Orthodox Church, "Church-state delegation visits Syria", 13 April 2016. Available at: https://mospat.ru/en/news/49610/.

The Russian Orthodox Church, "Children from Sunday schools in Latakia receive presents from Russia", 25 October 2017. Available at: https://mospat.ru/en/news/48093/.

The Russian Orthodox Church, "Orthodox children in Syrian Latakia received Christmas gifts from Moscow parish", 8 January 2018. Available at: https://mospat.ru/en/news/47799/.

The Russian Orthodox Church, "Interreligious working group completes unprecedented humanitarian action in Syria and Lebanon", 9 February 2018. Available at: https://mospat.ru/en/news/47712/.

The Russian Orthodox Church, "Russian delegation visits Syria to discusses the issue of restoration of ancient convent in Maaloula", 21 March 2018. Available at: https://mospat.ru/en/news/47592/.

The Russian Orthodox Church, "A boarding school in Damascus receives aid from Russian religious communities", 16 January 2019. Available at: https://mospat.ru/en/news/46761/.

The Russian Orthodox Church, "Religious communities in Russia begin joint efforts for restoring schools in Syria", 30 March 2019. Available at: https://mospat.ru/en/news/46493/.

CHRISTIAN RIGHT AND US MIDDLE EAST POLICY: FOREIGN POLICY IN THE SERVICE OF GOD'S WILL

Marina Eleftheriadou

Introduction

Religion has always been an integral feature of Unites States (US) socio-political landscape, even though the US were the first polity to ban the establishment of an official state-endorsed religion. The influence of religion in US policy-making has ebbed and flowed over time. Yet, it always lingered in what Huntington dubs as 'American Civil Religion',[1] which rests on a pervasive—trans-religious and extra-religious—belief that Americans are 'chosen' people destined to play a unique role in the world. On top of this creeping religiosity, which manifests in the religious references, symbols and performative functions that 'embellish' various public rituals, actors across the religious spectrum have strived to influence policy-making on state and federal level. Their ability to do so suffered under the advent of modernity's crushing rationality in the 19th and religiously-diverse migration in the early 20th century. Scopes trial (1925), best known as Monkey trial, was the symbolic turning point in the struggle between the forces of modernity and religion. The latter's ridicule in the courtroom and the frontpages of national press spearheaded a period of geographical, social and political retreat. The secularisation thesis—a dominant paradigm within sociology of religion for the better part of the 20th century— theorised a deterministic drive to secularism, culminating in the eventual demise of religion as a potent socio-political force. In reality, US religious actors' retreat lasted less than half a century.

The forceful return of religion to the public sphere and politics rode on the wave of religious constituencies' political reactivation in the mid to late 1970s, which led to the establishment of the Christian Right as a distinct and increasingly influential socio-political block. The Christian Right consists of groupings and networks of socially conservative and politically active individuals, who draw most of their socio-political views from their religious beliefs.[2] Even though the Christian Right is not denomination-specific, in

---

[1] Samuel P Huntington, *Who are we?: The Challenges to America's National Identity*, New York: Simon and Schuster, 2004.

[2] The Christian Right is a subgroup of the Religious Right, which includes similarly conservative and religion-driven groups and individuals from other religious traditions, such as Judaism and Islam.

the US, it is dominated by white evangelicals, particularly the fundamentalist, pentecostal and charismatic trends within evangelicalism.[3]

The influence of the Christian Right in US domestic politics has been widely documented, particularly in relation to the methodical dismantlement of secular values and rights. The Christian Right's influence in US foreign policy has received far less attention,[4] even though it has also grown in the past decades and its impact has been mostly damaging. The purpose of this chapter is to examine the role of the Christian Right in US foreign policy in the Middle East; a region of high importance to the US (at least until the recent pivot to Asia), as well as the Christian Right, which has directed most of its foreign policy advocacy to the Middle East. The chapter demonstrates that Christian Right's Middle East 'foreign policy' has developed along three prongs: Christian persecution, proselytisation and Israel. Rather surprisingly, as it may seem at first glance, Israel and issues related to Israel's security (e.g. Iranian nuclear program) is the Christian Right's primary foreign policy concern and the field where it has been most influential and has scored most of its successes.

The remaining chapter is structured as follows. The first section provides a brief overview of the consolidation of Christian Right's influence in US foreign policy-making, dating back to the late 1970s. It does not aspire to offer an exhaustive and detailed overview of Christian Right 'foreign policy' over these years, but merely to trace the political and institutional evolution of its capacity to set an agenda and promote specific policies. Thus, certain periods (and Administrations) are brushed over compared to others. The second—and main—section of this chapter examines the role of the Christian Right in US foreign policy in the Middle East. It is divided into two subsections. The first explores the first two prongs of Christian Right foreign policy in the region—that is, Christian persecution and proselytisation—and demonstrates how the former has served and eventually has been sacrificed to promote the latter. This is best evident in the Christian Right's involvement in Iraq since 2003, which has contributed in the dwindling of the indigenous Christian population. The second subsection examines the roots and evolution of Christian Right's, and particularly Christian Zionist's, interest in Israel and its impact on US policy towards the Israeli state and the

---

[3] Clyde Wilcox and Carin Robinson, *Onward Christian Soldiers?: The Religious Right in American Politics*, Philadelphia: Westview Press, 2011, p. 8. Hence, in this chapter, unless otherwise stated, the term Christian Right will primarily refer to evangelicals.

[4] The subject attracted the interest of scholars primarily after the election of George W. Bush in 2001. Several books and articles were published on the topic in early to mid-2000s, but interest has waned in the past decade, with some notable exceptions, such as Andrew Preston, *Sword of the Spirit, Shield of Faith: Religion in American War and Diplomacy*, New York: Knopf, 2012; Gregorio Bettiza, *Finding Faith in Foreign Policy: Religion and American Diplomacy in a Postsecular World*, Oxford: Oxford University Press, 2019.

Arab-Israeli peace process.

The rise and consolidation of Christian Right influence in US foreign policy

Two developments were key in the nationwide remobilisation of the Christian community in the US and the return of religion to the public sphere and politics: the 1963 prohibition of state-sponsored prayer in schools and the 1973 legalisation of abortion in the Roe v. Wade Supreme Court decision. The latter, in particular, alarmed an assortment of religious interest groups, which perceived it as a direct attack on their core beliefs; one that could be countered only by widespread and systematic political remobilisation.[5] Evangelicals—rather than the organised Catholic and Mainline Protestant churches—were better at organising this return to politics by effectively mobilising their diffuse networks. Education (e.g. Liberty University), media (e.g. CBN) and voter mobilisation were the three prongs of this effort. In 1979, Jerry Falwell founded Moral Majority as a political platform for millions of frustrated Christians. It was pivotal in channelling the religious vote to Ronald Reagan, inaugurating an era where the evangelical vote came to play an increasingly decisive role in the election of all subsequent Republican candidates, turning into an important constituency that even Democratic candidates and presidents could not disregard.

At the conclusion of the Reagan administration, Moral Majority gave way to the Christian Coalition, which in the following years rendered the Christian Right a permanent feature of the American political process.[6] Christian Coalition was founded in the wake of Pat Robertson's unsuccessful campaign to challenge George H.W. Bush for the Republican candidacy in the 1988 presidential elections. George H.W. Bush's victory came at a cost. In return for support, he was obliged to publicly acknowledge his connection to the evangelical core and lend a friendly ear to their concerns. Notably, he had to 'sacrifice' his son and future president, George W., who equipped with his personal story of born-again redemption, became his father's main liaison with the Christian Right.[7]

---

[5] For a brief, yet concise, overview of the return of religion across all major global religions, including American evangelicals, see Gilles Kepel, *The Revenge of God: The Resurgence of Islam, Christianity, and Judaism in the Modern World*, University Park, Pennsylvania: Pennsylvania State University Press, 1994, pp. 100-139. See also Nancy T. Ammerman, "Re-awakening a Sleeping Giant: Christian Fundamentalists in Late Twentieth-century US Society", in Gerrie Ter Haar and James Busuttil (eds.) *The Freedom to do God's Will: Religious Fundamentalism and Social Change*, London: Routledge, 2003.

[6] Lee Marsden, *For God's Sake: The Christian Right and US Foreign Policy*, London: Zed Books, 2008, p. 16.

[7] Ibid., pp. 32-33.

In the interregnum between the Bush Sr. and Bush Jr. presidencies, the Clinton administration was far more amenable to religious pressure than often assumed. If Bush Sr. administration was the one to solidify the unofficial influence of the Christian Right, the Clinton administration institutionalised this influence. At the same time, during the Clinton administration, the Christian Right had the opportunity to (re)invent its foreign policy advocacy. In the past, groups from the Christian Right were primarily concerned with domestic issues, and particularly moral values, showing limited interest in foreign policy. Those that did, such as Phyllis Schlafly's Eagle Forum, were driven by resolute anti-communism.[8] The end of the Cold War inevitably rendered anti-communism less pressing and ultimately less appealing in the corridors of the White House and State Department. Thus, the internationally-oriented evangelicals needed a new agenda that was more in harmony with post-Cold War US position and policies.

The (re)invention of foreign policy concerns was spearheaded by an unlikely alliance, consisting of Nina Shea, a Catholic that made a name for herself with her work against liberation theology in Latin America, and Michael Horowitz, a Jewish neo-conservative, who would publish in 1995 what would become the defining article for Christian Right's post-Cold War foreign policy engagement. Titled "New Intolerance Between the Crescent and the Cross",[9] it set the tone for the redirection of Christian Right's foreign advocacy to the (supposedly prevalent) worldwide persecution of Christians, who, as Horowitz suggested in a subsequent piece, were "the Jews of the 21st century".[10] A couple of years later, Nina Shea, detailed, in her book *In the Lion's Den,*[11] the 'martyrdom' of contemporary Christians, which according to Shea in the 20th century alone resulted in more Christian deaths than in the previous 19 centuries combined. In the second half of the 1990s, Shea collaborated with Horowitz on several projects designed to popularise and politicise the notion of Christian persecution. This new foreign policy focus was innately appealing to evangelical groupings, such as the National Association of evangelicals,[12] which saw in this shift more opportunities for proselytising, particularly in

---

[8] Ibid., pp. 27-32.

[9] Michael Horowitz, "New Intolerance between the Crescent and the Cross", *The Wall Street Journal,* 5 July 1995.

[10] Quoted in Stuart Croft, "'Thy will be done': the new foreign policy of America's Christian Right", *International Politics,* vol. 44, no. 6, 2007, p. 700.

[11] Nina Shea, *In the Lion's Den,* Nashville: Broadman & Holman Publishers, 1997.

[12] Croft, "'Thy will be done': the new foreign policy of America's Christian Right", p. 694.

the 10/40 Window,[13] where most of the persecution was supposed to take place and where the first cause célèbre of the new Christian Right foreign policy was born. The Christian predicament in South Sudan drew unprecedented support from US evangelicals and was the driving force behind the "International Religious Freedom Act" (1998), which at the end of the Clinton Presidency, had set in place the first and foremost institutional springhead of Christian Right's foreign policy: the *Commission on International Religious Freedom*. The Commission's Annual Reports on International Religious Freedom have been ever since a key tool for lauding and condemning countries according to their record in religious freedom, which in reality as many have noted, often reads as Christian freedom.[14]

The election of George W. Bush Jr. launched a new period in Christian Right's involvement in foreign policy. Religiosity was omnipresent in the Bush Administration. Cabinet meetings opened in prayer, while "attendance at Bible study was, if not compulsory, not quite uncompulsory", as one of George Bush Jr. former speechwriters, David Frum, pointedly noted.[15] Bush's personal religious beliefs often figured high in his interactions with the media and foreign political leaders. Mahmoud Abbas recounts an indicative interaction in a meeting between the two in 2003. Bush allegedly told Abbas: "God told me to strike at al Qaida and I struck them, and then he instructed me to strike at Saddam, which I did, and now I am determined to solve the problem in the Middle East".[16] Bush not only normalised the religious discourse, but he and his neo-conservative entourage also opened the gates of decision-making to direct evangelical influence. Numerous prominent members of the Christian Right were appointed in key positions across the administration, while dozens of internships were held by students from evangelical colleges, such as Patrick Henry College, which at one point boasted of having secured 100 places for their evangelical students in various posts in the Bush Administration.[17] The influence of the Christian Right extended to more unexpected places, like the Pentagon[18] or even the

[13] The 10/40 Window is a term used by evangelicals to refer to those regions lying between the 10th and 40th parallel north of the equator, covering the eastern hemisphere and parts of South Europe and north-of-the-equator Africa. The term 10/40 Window is a politically correct version of the older term 'resistant belt', which spanned the same area and denoted the region's challenges—and thus higher rewards—for missionary work.

[14] Michelle Boorstein, "Agency that Monitors Religious Freedom Abroad Accused of Bias", 17 February 2010. Available at: https://www.washingtonpost.com/wp-dyn/content/article/2010/02/16/AR20100 21605517.html.

[15] David Frum, *The Right Man: The Surprise Presidency of George W. Bush*, London: Weidenfeld & Nicolson, 2003, pp. 4, 13.

[16] Quoted in Stephen R. Rock, *Faith and Foreign Policy: The Views and Influence of US Christians and Christian Organizations*, New York: Bloomsbury Publishing, 2011, p. 28.

[17] Croft, "'Thy will be done': the new foreign policy of America's Christian Right", p. 698.

[18] Nothing illustrates the influence of religion in the military better than the case of General Jerry Boykin,

battlefields of Iraq and Afghanistan,[19] where conservative evangelicals took over 50 per cent of the military chaplaincy posts.[20]

The 'war against terrorism' was a mixed blessing for the Christian Right. On the one hand, the intricacies of the war required the US to extend "the hand of friendship to precisely the countries the [Christian Right] opposed—notably Sudan, Pakistan and Uzbekistan".[21] On the other hand, democracy promotion and state-building that soon substituted the poorly-conceived 'war against terrorism' paved the way for more opportunities to proselytise. To placate the Christian Right for its choice of allies in the 'war against terrorism', the Bush administration "level[ed] the playing field"[22] for evangelical missionary groups in the management of foreign assistance. This was mainly achieved through the establishment of the *Center for Faith-Based and Community Initiatives* (CFBCI) within USAID in late 2002, with the declared purpose to promote faith-based organisations (FBOs) in USAID programs. At the end of the Bush administration, approximately a quarter of all USAID partners were faith-based.[23] In fact, Christian FBOs received up to 98 per cent of USAID funds reserved for FBOs, even though over half of aid-receiving countries had a majority Muslim population.[24] This was barely surprising, considering that Bush appointed Andrew Natsios, the former vice president of the evangelical Christian humanitarian organisation (and largest Christian Right recipient of USAID funds) World Vision, as head of USAID.[25]

The Obama administration did little to change this imbalance.[26] Similar

---

who in 2002 was appointed as Deputy Undersecretary of Defense for Intelligence and was in charge of tracking Osama bin Laden. Before he was eventually replaced in 2007, Boykin on occasions had recounted his deployment in Somalia in 1993, painting a picture of a rather supernatural experience guided by Boykin's conviction that "my God was bigger than his [General Aidid's]. I knew that my God was real and his was an idol". Marsden, *For God's Sake*, p. 233. On Boykin remarks see also Esther Kaplan, *With God on their side: George W. Bush and the Christian Right*, New York: The New Press, 2005, pp. 20-23.

[19] A very interesting—yet under-researched—field of Christian Right influence is private military companies (PMC). For instance, Erik Prince, the founder of Blackwater, has served at the board of Christian Freedom International, a missionary evangelical organisation. Jeremy Scahill, *Blackwater: The Rise of the World's Most Powerful Mercenary*, New York: Nation Books, 2007, p. 223.

[20] Marsden, *For God's Sake*, pp. 234-235. For more on the role of religion in the U.S. military, see Ronit Y. Stahl, *Enlisting Faith: How the Military Chaplaincy Shaped Religion and State in Modern America*, Cambridge, Mass.: Harvard University Press, 2017.

[21] Joshua Green, "God's Foreign Policy", 1 November, 2001. Available at: https://washingtonmonthly. com/2001/11/01/gods-foreign-policy/.

[22] Marsden, *For God's Sake*, p. 124.

[23] David J. Wright, "Taking stock: The Bush faith-based initiative and what lies ahead", *Nelson Rockefeller Institute of Government*, 2009, 36able at: http://research.policyarchive.org/20306.pdf.

[24] Marsden, *For God's Sake*, p. 125.

[25] Ibid., p. 126.

[26] Lee Marsden, "Bush, Obama and a faith-based US foreign policy", *International Affairs*, vol. 88, no. 5,

to other foreign policy fields (e.g. the use of drones in counterterrorism), Obama to a large extent preserved the policies of his predecessor, despite the significant changes in terms of rhetoric and semantics. Hence, religious actors from the Christian Right retained their access to foreign policy institutional channels and tools (e.g. USAID) that allowed them to conserve their capacity to influence policy-making. Hence, it was Obama's reluctance to fully break with Bush's legacy that, to some extent, eased the way for Donald Trump to essentially close the Evangelical-Republican *deal*.

Trump, who in 2016 attracted 81 per cent of White evangelical Protestant vote, forged an ostensibly unholy alliance with the Christian Right and evangelicals in particular, which withstood moral and political scandals and only increased in the 2020 elections (85 per cent of the evangelical vote).[27] This alliance manifested in the domestic field, in issues such as Supreme Court nominations and the issue of abortion. In terms of foreign policy, it was best *performed* in the opening ceremony of the US Embassy in Jerusalem (May 14, 2018), which sealed Trump's decision to succumb to Israel's and Christian Zionist longstanding demand to relocate the US Embassy from Tel Aviv to Jerusalem, offering thus indirect recognition of Israel's claim to the whole city as its capital. At the ceremony, Trump and his daughter, Ivanka, were surrounded by a large assortment of influential (and controversial) evangelicals, such as Robert Jeffress and John Hagee. Hagee, the chairman of the Christian Zionist organisation Christians United for Israel, set the tone for the occasion and its host: "We thank you, O Lord, for President Donald Trump's courage in acknowledging to the world a truth that was established 3,000 years ago – that Jerusalem is and always shall be the eternal capital of the Jewish people".[28] Joe Biden, who as a Catholic already faces an impossible balancing act with the evangelicals, has largely focused on the domestic front and, much like his other Democratic predecessors, seems to opt for preserving the legacy of his immediate predecessor in foreign policy fields that are dear to the evangelical community.

2012, pp. 960-965.

[27] Pew Research Center, "How the faithful voted: A preliminary 2016 analysis", 2016. Available at: https://www.pewresearch.org/fact-tank/2016/11/09/how-the-faithful-voted-a-preliminary-2016-analysis/; Pew Research Center, "Most White Americans who regularly attend worship services voted for Trump in 2020", 2021. Available at: https://www.pewresearch.org/fact-tank/2021/08/30/most-white-americans-who-regularly-attend-worship-services-voted-for-trump-in-2020/.

[28] Matt Korade, Kevin Bohn, and Daniel Burke, "Controversial US pastors take part in Jerusalem embassy opening", *CNN*, 14 May 2018. Available at: https://edition.cnn.com/2018/05/13/politics/hagee-jeffress-us-embassy-jerusalem/index.html.

The Christian Right in the Middle East

Christian Right's interest in the Middle East is hardly surprising; after all, it is where the Holy Land is. This is enough to mobilise even the most domestic-oriented US evangelical. Hence, notwithstanding US foreign policy's Pivot to Asia or, more recently, East Europe, the Christian Right's influence remains anchored in the Middle East. It has little to say and little at stake in Ukraine or any other international hotspot. Reviving anti-communism would be of little relevance in the fight against an equally fervently religious Russia. The Middle East, in contrast, continues to offer the evangelical Christian Right bountiful opportunities to exert influence in the fulfilment of what many among them, primarily those related to Christian Zionism, believe to be God's plan. Christian Right's Middle East 'foreign policy' rests on three main prongs: Christian persecution, proselytisation and Israel. Christian persecution and proselytisation are interlinked in the sense that the former is perceived primarily as a vehicle for the latter. Israel, on the other hand, is a self-contained policy field that, as the discussion below demonstrates, largely dominates Christian Right's foreign policy concerns and engagement in the Middle East.

Christian Right's efforts to 'save' Middle East Christians (and Muslims)

Christian Right was primarily interested in the 'salvation' of Middle East Christians in the context of the mid-1990's re-direction of foreign policy advocacy to Christian persecution worldwide. As mentioned in the section above, South Sudan was the first cause célèbre of the Christian Right post-Cold War foreign policy engagement. Given that the Christian Right's mobilisation around the persecution of Christians in South Sudan was responsible for establishing the mechanisms and processes governing its foreign policy engagement, one would expect that Christian persecution would continue to dominate the evangelical foreign policy agenda. However, after Sudan, Christian persecution ceased to figure high in Christian Right's foreign policy in the region, at least until the rise of ISIS in 2014.

The 9/11 attacks and the US invasion of Afghanistan and Iraq, in 2001 and 2003 respectively, were undoubtedly a milestone for Christian Right's influence in Middle East foreign policy.[29] The attacks and US response had an earth-shattering effect on the opportunity environment in terms of

---

[29] In the wake of the 2001 attacks, prominent (tel)evangelists, such as Franklin Graham, Jerry Falwell and Pat Robertson were often quoted blaming the non-godly ways of modern American society for the 9/11 attacks. Equally as often they pushed anti-Islamic rhetoric to its limits, describing Prophet Muhammad as "a terrorist" and Islam as "a very evil and wicked religion", thus contributing to the normalisation of Islamophobic discourse in the US. Quoted in Marsden, *For God's Sake*, p. 198.

influence and reach. Evangelicals were among the most fervent supporters of the Iraq war. A survey of 350 top evangelical leaders, taken prior to the Iraq invasion, found that 59 per cent approved the use of military force against Saddam Hussein in Iraq, while only 19 per cent opposed it.[30] In contrast, mainline Protestant and Catholic leaders were far less supportive of the war or often vehemently opposed it.[31] Evangelicals also provided some of the most bizarre readings of the Just War theory to legitimise the war in Iraq.

For instance, Richard Land from the Southern Baptist Convention drafted a letter co-signed by other prominent evangelicals, such as Chuck Colson and Bill Bright, stating that a pre-emptive military strike on Iraq would be legitimate under Just War Theory.[32] On March 2003, Larry King hosted on his CNN show, *Larry King Live*, a discussion on 'What would Jesus do about war with Iraq?' The Catholic and (mainline) Protestant panellists suggested that Jesus would be against the war, projecting his peaceful teachings. In contrast, all three evangelical guests said that while Jesus did not condone war, he most certainly did not oppose it either.[33] Jerry Falwell painted the image of an even more belligerent God in his 2004 essay "God is Pro-War", where he not only condoned the war in Iraq but stated that the Bible is equally replete with references to God-ordained war and depictions of Jesus bearing a "sharp sword" and ruling over nations with "a rod of iron".[34]

The change to a more aggressive stance in foreign policy issues conflicted with the more defensive and somehow helpless tone of the past, when the focus was on Christian persecution. The 'war against terrorism' allowed the Christian Right to go on the offensive; alas not to protect Christians from persecution. For mission-orientated evangelicals, Iraq was a prized field for proselytisation; one that could act as a springboard for further missionary expansion in the Middle East. Proselytisation in this regard rested on successful 'democracy promotion', which for US Christian Right meant more access and more proselytisation opportunities in territories hitherto

---

[30] Beliefnet, "Evangelical Views of Islam", *Ethics & Public Policy Center*, 2003. Available at: https://www.beliefnet.com/news/politics/2003/04/evangelical-views-of-islam.aspx.

[31] Interestingly, one of the most stridently anti-war denominations was the United Methodist Church, which counted among its members President Bush and Vice President Dick Cheney. Rock, *Faith and Foreign Policy*, pp. 1-3.

[32] Marsden, *For God's Sake*, p. 227.

[33] Bill Broadway, "TV Debate Delineates Christian Divide on War", *Washington Post*, 14 March 2003. Available at: https://www.washingtonpost.com/archive/local/2003/03/15/tv-debate-delineates-christian-divide-on-war/a488a3e7-15de-426c-bd16-69f08a83d0a5/.

[34] Jerry Falwell, "God is Pro-War", *World Net Daily*, 31 January 2004. Available at: https://www.wnd.com/2004/01/23022/.

closed to evangelical message.

Hence, proselytisation by—democracy promotion—proxy became the second and dominant at that time prong of Christian Right's Middle East foreign policy. As shown in the previous section, USAID's hijacking by faith-based organisations was designed to ease their proselytising activities. By 2004, more than 900,000 Bibles in Arabic had been sent to Iraq. On the ground, at least nine evangelical churches had opened in Baghdad alone and no less than 30 evangelical missionaries were working in the city, while dozens of other missionaries had visited Iraq in the months after the invasion.[35] However, in retrospect, their copious efforts to convert Muslims to Christianity proved futile; attesting to 10/40 Window's renown resistance to proselytising. If anything, they changed the way Muslims in the region viewed the US; not any more as "a secular republic containing many religious Christians… [but as] a specifically Christian entity".[36]

Worse than that, they deteriorated conditions for the indigenous Iraqi Christian population.[37] The Christian community in Iraq has been decimated since 2003. Even before ISIS stormed the Nineveh Plains, out of the 1.4 million Christians in 2003, two-thirds had already left the country. In 2014, approximately 200,000 Christians were displaced from Mosul and other areas that came under ISIS control.[38] The plight of Christians and other religious minorities, such as Yazidis, in Syria and Iraq belatedly pivoted Christian Right's focus from offering *salvation* to Muslims to the actual salvation of indigenous Christian communities, which was not on the agenda of the evangelical missionaries that flocked into Iraq in 2003. It produced a series of interesting (in terms of breaking with the past), yet eventually abortive initiatives during and after ISIS rule. To a large extent, indigenous Christians rejected the Christian Right outreach. If anything, it was met with scepticism or profound animosity, mainly because it was under a proselytisation leash. In North Iraq, missionary (mainly evangelical) groups mushroomed under the ISIS emergency and Kurdistan Regional

---

[35] Charles Duhigg, "Evangelicals Flock Into Iraq on a Mission of Faith", *Los Angeles Times*, 18 March 2004. Available at: https://www.latimes.com/archives/la-xpm-2004-mar-18-fg-missionary18-story. html.

[36] Tim Winter, "America as a Jihad State: Middle Eastern Perceptions of Modern American Theopolitics", *The Muslim World*, vol. 101, no. 3, 2011, p. 403.

[37] The following paragraphs draw from the author's past research, namely Zakia Aqra and Marina Eleftheriadou, "Untying the Knots of Religious Diversity in Iraqi Kurdistan: Deploying Pluralism against Barbarism", *Centre for Religious Pluralism in the Middle East (CRPME)*, 2016. Available at: https://cemmis.edu.gr/images/CRPME/crpme_report_2.pdf; Marina Eleftheriadou, "Christian militias in Syria and Iraq: beyond the neutrality/passivity debate," *Middle East Bulletin*, vol. 28, 2015.

[38] Recent estimates bring the Christian population to below 275,000 and it is expected to further decrease as Iraq continues its downward spiral of political instability. Aqra and Eleftheriadou, "Untying the Knots", p. 15.

Government's (KRG) open-doors policy. Local Christian leaders described evangelical presence as prying on the insecurity and desperation of those displaced by ISIS.[39] More strikingly, KRG's tolerance towards evangelical missionary activities was absent when it came to indigenous churches' liberty to evangelise; an unmistakable exhibition of double standards, which was duly noted by indigenous Christians and other minority members.

The issue of external (Christian) influence and assistance concerned stakeholders outside the realm of possible church antagonism for the faithful. Christian political parties and local militias have been equally divided on this issue. The Assyrian Democratic Movement (ADM), which after 2003 had managed to secure the majority of the Assyrian vote, has been staunchly opposed to external interference in Iraqi affairs. In the same vein, the Nineveh Plain Protection Units (NPU), the militia formed by ADM in the wake of ISIS takeover, has been firm in its insistence to accept members and funds exclusively from the local Christian community and the Assyrian diaspora.[40] In fact, Restore Nineveh Now, a fund-raising initiative organised by the US-based Assyrian diaspora, allegedly played a key role in the funding of NPU's non-military needs, including the procurement of uniforms and protection gear.[41] More controversial have been the allegations that NPU sought the help of a relatively unknown US-registered private military company (PMC), Sons of Liberty International (SOLI), who was allegedly contracted by Restore Nineveh Now and the American Mesopotamian Organisation (AMO), a California-based group of Assyrian-Americans, to boost NPU's military capacity. SOLI's head, Matthew Van Dyke, who rose to fame after he joined the Libyan opposition and was imprisoned by the Qaddafi regime in 2011, claimed to have recruited western ex-military to train NPU.[42] Restore Nineveh Now acknowledged VanDyke's involvement in the training program but claimed that it had to terminate his contract on the account that he attempted "to use the NPU to promote his business".[43]

Another Christian militia, Dwekh Nawsha, and her parent organisation Assyrian Patriotic Party (APP), have been more open about their willingness to work with foreign fighters. Contrary to the NPU, though, Dwekh Nawsha's foreign regiment was not led by a PMC. Instead, it comprised of

---

[39] Ibid., p. 12-13.

[40] Ibid., p. 16-17.

[41] Eleftheriadou, "Christian militias in Syria and Iraq", p. 16.

[42] Ibid., p. 16. Agence France-Presse, "American Christians heading up private militias fighting jihadists in Iraq", *Raw Story*, 26 February 2015. Available at: http://www.rawstory.com/2015/02/american-christians-heading-up-private-militias-fighting-jihadists-in-iraq/.

[43] Agence France-Presse, "American Christians heading up private militias fighting jihadists in Iraq". See also SOLI's website, which mentions North Iraq and NPU among its past missions https://www.sonsoflibertyinternational.com/missions/

mainly American self-motivated ex-soldiers, who travelled thousands of miles to join its ranks, often guided by an explosive mix of religious, patriotic and PTSD-fuelled motivations. Some openly brandished overtly Christian-themed tattoos and often had previous experience as US soldiers in Iraq or fighting with Kurdish forces in Syria. The latter joined Dwekh Nawsha because they 'discovered' that Kurds in Syria were "a bunch of damn Reds".[44] Christian foreign fighters saw little (if any) combat during the liberation of Nineveh from ISIS,[45] but the image of armed cross-bearing foreigners further deteriorated the environment for indigenous Christians, who had to navigate through the increasing suspicion of local actors that viewed the Christian community as the fifth column of the US.

Christian Right's limited (and eventually negative) impact on the *salvation* of Christianity in Iraq and Syria was most evident in the debate around the creation of an autonomous Christian zone in the Nineveh Plains. The idea of an autonomous zone that would host Christians and possibly other religious minorities after the liberation of Nineveh circulated in the period before and briefly after the liberation of Nineveh from ISIS. One of the plans that were examined at that time envisaged the creation of an autonomous zone under international protection;[46] a proposal supported by some minority, including Christian, groups in Iraq.[47] The US Christian Right, and other foreign Christian groups, advocated the creation of an autonomous entity. However, they often favoured solutions that ran the risk of disproportionately benefiting the Christians; thus, reaffirming the view that the international community cares about Christians, and not the Yazidi or Turkmen.

In any case, the post-ISIS realities of Iraq could not accommodate such an entity. The Baghdad-Kurdish *bras de fer* for the control of disputed territories in northern Iraq, persistent intra-Shia rivalries that prevent the formation of a stable government and Sunni collective punishment leave little room for religious minorities.[48] External religious actors, including the

---

[44] A fellow foreign fighter, who stayed with the Kurdish-led forces, was more acerbic in his evaluation, claiming that those who left got cold feet when they felt the intensity of actual fighting. Middle East Eye, "Western volunteers rally to Iraq Christian militia", *Middle East Eye*, 18 February 2015. Available at: https://www.middleeasteye.net/news/western-volunteers-rally-iraq-christian-militia; Eleftheriadou, "Christian militias in Syria and Iraq", p. 17.

[45] It is noteworthy that Christian foreign fighters are an Iraqi phenomenon. There are numerous cases of western fighters, who joined Kurdish-led groups to fight ISIS in Syria, but very few examples of foreign fighters, who have joined Christian militias. Eleftheriadou, "Christian militias in Syria and Iraq", p. 17.

[46] For an overview of different plans see Zakia Aqra, Stavros I. Drakoularakos, Marina Eleftheriadou et al., "Religious Pluralism in the Middle East", *Centre for Religious Pluralism in the Middle East (CRPME)*, no. 4, 2017, pp. 12-14. Available at: https://cemmis.edu.gr/images/CRPME/crpme_report_4.pdf.

[47] Aqra and Eleftheriadou, "Untying the Knots", pp. 16-17.

[48] Aqra et al., "Religious Pluralism in the Middle East", pp. 4-6.

US Christian Right, did not have the power (or interest, for that matter) to push for solutions that could help preserve the Christian presence, which dwindled further in the post-ISIS years amidst a wave of Christian exodus from the region. In sum, the factsheet of the 20 years of Christian Right involvement in the *salvation* of Muslims and indigenous Christians in Iraq and Syria has little to show besides unsuccessful and eventually harmful attempts at proselytisation and influence. It has been much more successful in its third foreign policy prong: Israel.

Israel and the 'end of times'

Undoubtedly, it comes as a surprise that Israel, rather than Christian persecution, features on the top of the Christian Right's agenda and represents the foreign policy field where it has scored most of its successes. This ostensible paradox is less surprising in light of the US public's overwhelming support for Israel dating back to the establishment of the Israeli state.[49] Subsequent polls have shown that this support has been more pronounced among white evangelicals and while it has fluctuated in other religious communities, white evangelicals have gradually become the second most pro-Israel population after American Jews. A 2022 Pew Research poll shows that 68 per cent of white evangelicals have a favourable view of the Israeli government (and 86 per cent of the Israeli people) compared to only 50 percent of Catholics. More tellingly, 70 percent of white evangelicals believe that God gave the land of Israel to the Jewish people; a belief shared only by half as many US Jews.[50]

This support and, by extension, the centrality of pro-Israel foreign policy in the Christian Right is a corollary of the influence of Christian Zionism within the US Christian Right and a series of (un)fortunate developments that fostered its growth in the US. Christian Zionism has its roots in the dispensationalist movement that emerged in Britain in the 18th century. It is closely linked to the ideas of 'British Israelism', which is centred on the belief that Great Britain and the British people as direct descendants of the Lost Tribes of Israel.[51] Premillennial dispensationalism was popularised by the teachings of Louis Way and John Darby in mid–19th century Britain and by the end of the century, it expanded to the United States, where it assumed

---

[49] A Gallup poll, shortly after Israel was established in 1948, showed that American support for Jews was about three times greater than support for Arabs/Palestinians. Mark R. Amstutz, *Evangelicals and American Foreign Policy*, Oxford: Oxford University Press, 2014, p. 130.

[50] Becka A. Alper, "Modest Warming in U.S. Views on Israel and Palestinians", *Pew Research Center*, 26 May 2022. Available at: https://www.pewresearch.org/religion/wp-content/uploads/sites/7/2022/05/PF_05.26.22_Israel_report.pdf.

[51] For the history and impact of British Israelism, see Aidan Cottrell-Boyce, *Israelism in Modern Britain*, London: Routledge, 2020.

its current form. At its core, dispensationalism holds an eschatological view of history; one that retains a special place for Israel and Jews worldwide. It teaches that human history can be divided into seven time periods (aka dispensations); from the Garden of Eden until the Second Coming of Jesus. Christian Zionism believes that we are closing on the end of the sixth period, which means that the Second Coming is imminent and Israel is prophesised to play a key role in the events to come.[52] The specifics are often a matter of debate within Christian Zionism. Nevertheless, they share a set of core beliefs that run across all Christian Zionist variants. Jewish 'restoration' is universally perceived as a necessary historical and political process in God's plan and the path to the Second Coming. Deeply eschatological, Christian Zionism encourages the careful search for signs in present-day events pointing to the *end of times*. In this regard, historic Palestine and Israel become the epicentre of biblical prophecies signalling Jesus' return to earth. After all, the Valley of Megiddo in north-central Israel is the foretold land of the ultimate historic showdown between the forces of good and evil in the Battle of Armageddon.[53]

Even though only about 10 percent of US evangelicals are dispensationalists,[54] Christian Zionists have become an increasingly important subgroup within the Christian Right, particularly after Jerry Falwell and Moral Majority rose to dominate the politically active evangelicals.[55] According to Donald Wagner, the rise of Christian Zionism in the US was accelerated by the convergence of five trends and/or developments.[56] First, despite their initially low numbers, the conservative evangelical and charismatic movements, where premillennial dispensationalism was rooted, were the fastest-growing branch of US Christianity. Second, evangelical political participation was boosted when Jimmy Carter, a Southern Baptist, was elected in the 1976 presidential elections. Third, by the mid-1970s the impact of another development, the 1967 War, had modified the map of the pro-Israel lobby networks in the United States. Dispensationalists perceived Israel's victory in the Six Days War as a sign that the end of times was approaching, which increased their interest in the events and the level of support for Israeli encroachment in the Occupied Territories, particularly Jerusalem. Israel's occupation of Arab

[52] Marsden, *For God's Sake*, p. 8.

[53] Donald Wagner, "Reagan and Begin, Bibi and Jerry: the theopolitical alliance of the Likud party with the American Christian 'right'", *Arab Studies Quarterly*, vol. 20, no. 4, 1998, p. 37.

[54] *Christianity Today*, "What It Means to Love Israel", 5 September 2007. Available at: https://www.christianitytoday.com/ct/2007/september/16.24.html.

[55] Marsden, *For God's sake: the Christian right and US foreign policy*, p. 8.

[56] Wagner, "Reagan and Begin, Bibi and Jerry", pp. 41-42.

lands and the exponential growth of the settler movement, on the other hand, had created tensions in the relations of many Jewish organisations with the mainline Protestant, Eastern Orthodox, and Catholic communities. As a consequence, by the 1980s, Jewish lobby groups such as the American-Israel Political Affairs Committee (AIPAC) turned to the growing evangelical community for support in navigating US (foreign) policy-making. Dependency on evangelicals only grew in the following years, as many American Jews, both from Reform and ultra-Orthodox anti-Zionist Judaism, reduced their financial contributions and overall support, in disagreement with their unconditional support of Israel's policies.

The fourth factor that accelerated the emerging evangelical Christian Zionist political agenda was the end of Labour's dominance in Israel's political system. Likud's victory in the 1977 elections under the leadership of Menachem Begin signalled the emergence of an interlocutor that spoke the language of Christian Zionists. The final, fifth development that sealed the Likud-Christian Right alliance, was Jimmy Carter's March 1977 speech, merely two months before Likud came to power, in which he supported Palestinian "right to a homeland". Carter's 'betrayal' spurred the first massive mobilisation of US evangelicals for a foreign policy issue. Full-page advertisements, co-sponsored by evangelical and Jewish groups, appeared in major newspapers across the US In direct reference to Carter's speech, the advertisements stated: "We affirm as evangelicals our belief in the promised land to the Jewish people… [and] we would view with grave concern any effort to carve out of the Jewish homeland another nation or political entity". In what can be read in retrospect as a warning for future presidents, they added: "The time has come for evangelical Christians to affirm their belief in biblical prophecy and Israel's divine right to the land".[57]

The advertisement campaign was the first concrete and successful demonstration of Likud Christian-Zionist alliance. It set a precedent for similar interventions, including ad and mail campaigns, scripted to the slightest detail visits to local representatives[58] and the mobilisation of pastors and Jewish pressure groups, against what they perceived as anti-Israeli US foreign policies. From that first challenge of White House's policy towards Israel under Carter administration up until Trump's decision to relocate the US embassy to Jerusalem, Christian Zionism's influence has only grown in importance and has had a damaging impact on the prospects of Israeli-Palestinian conflict resolution.

---

[57] Both quoted in ibid., p. 42.

[58] Christian Zionist activists are provided with an exhaustive list of instructions detailing steps prior, during and after the meeting, from dress code and using key phrases to employing coloured paper in thank you letters. Marsden, *For God's Sake*, pp. 37-39.

Israeli (aspiring) leaders know very well that the approval of the Christian Right and its powerful Christian Zionist faction is often more important than good relations with the occasional resident of the White House. When Israel bombed in 1981 Iraq's nuclear plant, Menachem Begin dialled the phone of Jerry Falwell before calling Reagan or anyone else in the administration.[59] More indicatively, Benjamin Netanyahu's first tenure as Israel's Prime Minister was marked by his visit to Washington, D.C. in January 1998, where shortly after arriving he was introduced to a Christian Right gathering by Jerry Falwell as "the Ronald Reagan of Israel".[60] Under this evangelical shield, Netanyahu could easily withstand the pressure in his subsequent meeting with Clinton, who unsuccessfully attempted to persuade him to abstain from sabotaging the Oslo Accords.

Christian Right's indirect corroding effect on the peace process occurred on several junctions of its decades-long course. In the process, it deteriorated—once again—the conditions for indigenous Christians, whose continuous presence in the Holy Land attested to its Christian history. Palestinian Christians, on either side of the 1967 borders, suffered the consequences of Christian Zionist complicity in Israel's spoiling of the peace process. For instance, in 1997 a report circulated in Israeli media and Christian Zionist circles claiming that the Palestinian Authority (PA) persecuted local Christians. Subsequent investigation revealed that a Christian Zionist group, the International Christian Embassy-Jerusalem, cooperated with the office of the Israeli Prime Minister Netanyahu's Spokesperson, David Bar-Ilan, to exaggerate and often fabricate accounts of Christian persecution.[61]

Nevertheless, Christian Zionist impact has nowhere been more damaging than in its political and financial support to Jewish settlements in the Occupied Territories. Christian Zionist groups, such as the Christian Friends of Israeli Communities (CFIC) and International Fellowship of Christians and Jews (IFCJ), have poured millions of US dollars in the construction and support of settlements in the West Bank and the encouragement of Jewish immigrants from the former Soviet Union to settle there.[62] In conjunction with the continuous lobbying efforts in the US Congress to increase the economic and military assistance and the multi-pronged pressure to minimise White House's pressure on Israel, Christian Right's direct involvement in creating facts on the ground render the two-state solution,

---

[59] Wagner, "Reagan and Begin, Bibi and Jerry", p. 43.

[60] Ibid., p. 33.

[61] Ibid., p. 46-48.

[62] Marsden, *For God's Sake*, p. 192.

which has been the preferred peace process recipe, not only a distant but an increasingly unfeasible goal.

Conclusions

After decades of neglect, the role of religion in international politics has captivated the imagination of scholars. The rise of the Christian Right in the US and the spillover of its influence from domestic to foreign policy issues was one of the main drivers of this interest in how religious beliefs and actors affect politics outside state borders. The purpose of this chapter was not as much to engage with the theoretical debate,[63] but to explore in depth how this influence manifested in one of the key fields and regions of US foreign policy, that is the Middle East.

Christian Right's influence in US Middle East foreign policy-making grew out a process of re-invention of foreign policy advocacy after the end of Cold War, which rendered anti-communism and anti-Soviet policies obsolete. In light of the above, Christian persecution, which according to Christian Right accounts was prevalent across the globe, became the main prism through which the Christian Right, and evangelicals who dominate the Christian Right, would approach foreign policy issues and build the institutional tools that would enable them to have an impact of foreign policy agenda and decision-making.

Indeed, one can identify Christian persecution as one of the main themes/prongs of Christian Right foreign policy engagement in the Middle East. However, under the surface, as this chapter demonstrates, Christian persecution is by no means the most important issue of concern and, by extension. it is not the foreign policy field that presents the most initiatives and successes. On the contrary, Christian persecution has been used as a battering ram to improve access to territories that are considered traditionally resistant to proselytisation. In the wake of the 9/11 attacks and the subsequent 'war against terrorism' and 'democracy promotion' in the Middle East, proselytisation-by-proxy turned into a key prong of Christian Right foreign policy in the region and particularly Iraq.

Christian Right's ability to promote this goal was vastly enhanced by the involvement of faith-based organisations (FBOs) in USAID operations and the appointment of individuals from the Christian Right in key political and administrative positions. The opening of the gates of foreign-policy making is often attributed to the George W. Bush Administration, but in reality, the

---

[63] For theoretical accounts see Nukhet Sandal and Jonathan Fox, *Religion in International Relations Theory: Interactions and Possibilities*, New York: Routledge, 2013; Jack Snyder (ed.), *Religion and International Relations Theory*, New York: Columbia University Press, 2011.

first steps towards this direction date back to the Clinton Administration, while subsequent Presidents, including Barack Obama, largely preserved the Bush legacy on this matter. The primacy of proselytisation was retained even during the ISIS takeover of territories in Syria and northern Iraq, even though Christian persecution returned as a theme in the Christian Right discourse.

Nevertheless, the policy concern that has been throughout these years at the top of Christian Right's foreign policy agenda in the Middle East is rather unrelated to the plight of Christians. Instead, Israel and issues related to its security have preoccupied Christian Right's foreign policy in the Middle East. This 'fixation' is directly linked to the influence of Christian Zionism within US Christian Right. Driven by eschatological beliefs that place Israel at the centre of events leading to the Second Coming, US evangelicals, among other things, promote the immigration of Jews to Israel, exert pressure on the US government to follow pro-Israeli policies and funnel funds to settlements in the Occupied Territories as a means to precipitate the end of times.

In sum, in over twenty years of active involvement in US foreign policy in the Middle East, Christian Right's track-record is highly problematic. Not only did it not achieve its goal of 'Christianising' the Middle East by proselytising the Muslims of the region, but it deteriorated the conditions for the indigenous Christian communities, who continue to flee their ancestral homes, erasing the centuries-long presence of Christianity in the region. In the same vein, their policy towards Israel, guided by eschatological perceptions of God's plan, not only tarnishes the image of the US and Christianity for that matter, but contributes to the creation of facts on the ground and unbearable conditions for the local population, including Palestinian Christians, that are against any God's will.

Bibliography

Agence France-Presse, "American Christians Heading up Private Militias Fighting Jihadists in Iraq", *Raw Story*, 26 February 2015. Available at: http://www.rawstory.com/2015/02/american-christians-heading-up-private-militias-fighting-jihadists-in-iraq/.

Alper, Becka A., "Modest Warming in U.S. Views on Israel and Palestinians", *Pew Research Center*, 26 May 2022. Available at: https://www.pewresearch.org/religion/wp-content/uploads/sites/7/2022/05/PF_05.26.22_Israel_report.pdf.

Ammerman, Nancy T., "Re-Awakening a Sleeping Giant: Christian Fundamentalists in Late Twentieth-Century Us Society", in Gerrie Ter Haar and James Busuttil (eds.) *The Freedom to Do God's Will: Religious Fundamentalism and Social Change*, London: Routledge, 2003, pp. 89-110.

Amstutz, Mark R., *Evangelicals and American Foreign Policy*, Oxford: Oxford University Press, 2014.

Aqra, Zakia, Stavros I. Drakoularakos, Marina Eleftheriadou, *et al.*, "Religious Pluralism in the Middle East", *Centre for Religious Pluralism in the Middle East (CRPME)*, no. 4, 2017. Available at: https://cemmis.edu.gr/images/CRPME/crpme_report_4.pdf.

Aqra, Zakia, and Marina Eleftheriadou, "Untying the Knots of Religious Diversity in Iraqi Kurdistan: Deploying Pluralism against Barbarism", *Centre for Religious Pluralism in the Middle East (CRPME)*, 2016. Available at: https://cemmis.edu.gr/images/CRPME/crpme_report_2.pdf.

Beliefnet, "Evangelical Views of Islam", *Ethics & Public Policy Center*, 2003. Available at: https://www.beliefnet.com/news/politics/2003/04/evangelical-views-of-islam.aspx.

Bettiza, Gregorio, Finding Faith in Foreign Policy: Religion and American Diplomacy in a Postsecular World, Oxford: Oxford University Press, 2019.

Boorstein, Michelle, "Agency That Monitors Religious Freedom Abroad Accused of Bias", 17 February 2010. Available at: https://www.washingtonpost.com/wp-dyn/content/article/2010/02/16/AR2010021605517.html.

Broadway, Bill, "Tv Debate Delineates Christian Divide on War", *Washington Post*, 14 March 2003. Available at: https://www.washingtonpost.com/archive/local/2003/03/15/tv-debate-delineates-christian-divide-on-war/a488a3e7-15de-426c-bd16-69f08a83d0a5/.

Christianity Today, "What It Means to Love Israel", 5 September 2007. Available at: https://www.christianitytoday.com/ct/2007/september/16.24.html.

Cottrell-Boyce, Aidan, *Israelism in Modern Britain,* London: Routledge, 2020.

Croft, Stuart, "'Thy Will Be Done': The New Foreign Policy of America's Christian Right", *International Politics*, vol. 44, no. 6, 2007, pp. 692-710.

Duhigg, Charles, "Evangelicals Flock into Iraq on a Mission of Faith", *Los Angeles Times*, 18 March 2004. Available at: https://www.latimes.com/archives/la-xpm-2004-mar-18-fg-missionary18-story.html.

Eleftheriadou, Marina, "Christian Militias in Syria and Iraq: Beyond the Neutrality/Passivity Debate", *Middle East Bulletin*, vol. 28, 2015, pp. 13-19.

Falwell, Jerry, "God Is Pro-War," *World Net Daily*, 31 January 2004. Available at: https://www.wnd.com/2004/01/23022/.

Frum, David, *The Right Man: The Surprise Presidency of George W. Bush*, London: Weidenfeld & Nicolson, 2003.

Green, Joshua, "God's Foreign Policy", 1 November 2001. Available at: https://washington monthly.com/2001/11/01/gods-foreign-policy/.

Horowitz, Michael, "New Intolerance between the Crescent and the Cross", *The Wall Street Journal*, 5 July 1995.

Huntington, Samuel P., *Who Are We?: The Challenges to America's National Identity*, New York: Simon and Schuster, 2004.

Kaplan, Esther, With God on Their Side: George W. Bush and the Christian Right, New York: The New Press, 2005.

Kepel, Gilles, *The Revenge of God: The Resurgence of Islam, Christianity, and Judaism in the Modern World*, University Park, Pennsylvania: Pennsylvania State University Press, 1994.

Korade, Matt, Kevin Bohn, and Daniel Burke, "Controversial Us Pastors Take Part in Jerusalem Embassy Opening", *CNN*, 14 May 2018. Available at: https://edition.cnn.com/2018/05/13/politics/hagee-jeffress-us-embassy-jerusalem/index.html.

Marsden, Lee, "Bush, Obama and a Faith-Based Us Foreign Policy," *International Affairs*, vol. 88, no. 5, 2012, pp. 953-74.

———. *For God's Sake: The Christian Right and Us Foreign Policy*, London: Zed Books, 2008.

Middle East Eye, "Western Volunteers Rally to Iraq Christian Militia," *Middle East Eye*, 18 February 2015. Available at: https://www.middleeasteye.net/news/western-volunteers-rally-iraq-christian-militia.

Pew Research Center, "How the Faithful Voted: A Preliminary 2016 Analysis", 2016. Available at: https://www.pewresearch.org/fact-tank/2016/11/09/how-the-faithful-voted-a-preliminary-2016-analysis/.

———, "Most White Americans Who Regularly Attend Worship Services Voted for Trump in 2020," 2021. Available at: https://www.pewresearch.org/fact-tank/2021/08/30/most-white-americans-who-regularly-attend-worship-services-voted-for-trump-in-2020/.

Preston, Andrew, *Sword of the Spirit, Shield of Faith: Religion in American War and Diplomacy*, New York: Knopf, 2012.

Rock, Stephen R., *Faith and Foreign Policy: The Views and Influence of Us Christians and Christian Organizations*, New York: Bloomsbury Publishing, 2011.

Sandal, Nukhet and Jonathan Fox, *Religion in International Relations Theory: Interactions and Possibilities*, New York: Routledge, 2013.

Scahill, Jeremy, *Blackwater: The Rise of the World's Most Powerful Mercenary*, New York: Nation Books, 2007.

Shea, Nina, *In the Lion's Den,* Nashville: Broadman & Holman Publishers, 1997.

Snyder, Jack, (ed.), *Religion and International Relations Theory*, NY Columbia Univ. Press, 2011.

Stahl, Ronit Y., *Enlisting Faith: How the Military Chaplaincy Shaped Religion and State in Modern America*, Cambridge, Mass.: Harvard University Press, 2017.

Wagner, Donald, "Reagan and Begin, Bibi and Jerry: The Theopolitical Alliance of the Likud Party with the American Christian 'Right'," *Arab Studies Quarterly*, 20(4), 1998, pp. 33-51.

Wilcox, Clyde, and Carin Robinson, *Onward Christian Soldiers?: The Religious Right in American Politics,* Philadelphia: Westview Press, 2011.

Winter, Tim, "America as a Jihad State: Middle Eastern Perceptions of Modern American Theopolitics," *The Muslim World*, vol. 101, no. 3, 2011, pp. 394-411.

Wright, David J., "Taking Stock: The Bush Faith-Based Initiative and What Lies Ahead," *Nelson Rockefeller Institute of Government,* 2009. Available at: http://research.policyarchive.org/20306.pdf.

CHRISTIANITY IN THE MODERN MIDDLE EAST: CURRENT SITUATION AND FUTURE CHALLENGES

Anthony O'Mahony

Introduction

Christian presence across the Middle East (West Asia) region is facing a variety of acuate challenges which are increasingly considered as existential.[1] In terms of history the current situation might be considered similar to that faced by Eastern Christianity as a consequence of the geopolitical changes in the late period of the Ottoman rule including World War I,[2] the Armenian Genocide,[3] the Syriac Sayfo,[4] and the displacement of the entire Eastern Orthodox population during the early 1920's with the establishment of the modern states of Greece and Turkey.[5] With the collapse of Ottoman Empire, the wider geopolitical and ecclesial situation significantly changed across Europe, Russia and the former Ottoman territories directly having an impact upon Eastern Christianity this included the Bolshevik Revolution which brought about the near destruction of the Russian Orthodox Church.[6] This in turn severed the historic ties with Eastern Churches in the Middle East until after World War II.[7] In the aftermath of these traumatic events determined efforts were made by the Christian communities in the region to

---

[1] Tigrane Yégavian, "Les chrétiens d'Orient ont-ils encore un avenir?", *Études*, no. 6, 2022, pp. 67-78. The 'bench-mark' for the current concern for the future of the Middle East is the wide-ranging study published nearly three decades ago Jean-Pierre Valognes, *Vie et mort des chrétiens d'Orient des origines à nos jours*, Paris: Fayard, 1994.

[2] Benny Morris and Dror Ze'evi, *The Thirty-Year Genocide: Turkey's Destruction of Its Christian Minorities, 1894–1924*, Harvard: Harvard University Press, 2019.

[3] Raymond Kévorkian, *The Armenian Genocide: A Complete History*, London: Taurus, 2011.

[4] David Gaunt, Naures Atto & Soner O. Barthoma (eds.), *LET THEM NOT RETURN: Sayfo – The Genocide Against the Assyrian, Syriac, and Chaldean Christians in the Ottoman Empire*, Oxford: Berghahn, 2017.

[5] Nikodemos Anagnostopoulos, *Orthodoxy and Islam: Theology and Muslim-Christian Relations in Modern Greece and Turkey*, London: Routledge, 2017.

[6] Daniel Kalkandjieva, *The Russian Orthodox Church, 1917-1948: From Decline to Resurrection*, London: Routledge, 2015.

[7] Anthony O'Mahony, "The Greek Orthodox Patriarchates in the Middle East", in Anthony O'Mahony (ed.), *Eastern Christianity and the Cold War, 1945-91*, London: Routledge, 2010, pp. 240-252; Kjartan Anderson, "Pilgrims, Property and Polities: The Russian Orthodox Church in Jerusalem", in Anthony O'Mahony (ed.), *Eastern Christianity: Studies in Modern History, Religion and Politics*, London: Melisende, 2004, pp. 388-430. However, the Church of England attempted renewed ecclesial engagement with the Eastern Churches in accordance with these new geopolitical realties Pandora Dimanopoulou-Cohen, *Rendez à César ce qui est à César et à Dieu ce qui est à Dieu?: le rapprochement des Églises anglicanes avec l'Église orthodoxe grecque, 1903-1930*, Paris: Cerf, 2016.

rebuild the Eastern Orthodox, Armenian and Syriac and the Eastern Catholic churches in the context of new nation-states and mandatory governance in the interwar Middle East. World War II followed by the imposition of Communist rule in the Eastern European states and the Cold War impacted upon all Eastern Christians in the Middle East.[8] Regional conflict across the Middle East also felt upon all Christians from the Arab–Israeli conflict in the post war era to conflict in Iraq and Syria, the effects of war have challenged Christianity in the Middle East to the point that many are concerned for its survival. This has included the forced displacement and emigration of Christian from across the entire region. It is critical to understand the dynamics of Christian emigration from the Middle East, the first phase of which began in the later part of the nineteenth century and continued until World War I. During that time, thousands of Christians left the Ottoman Empire in search of economic opportunities, including greater religious freedom and political tolerance. After World War II, socio-economic factors continued to influence the emigration of Christians and to a lesser extent, of non-Christians. In the post-independence period, from the late 1940s to the present time, Christian emigration continued to rise, primarily due to economic insecurity but also due to political instability and military conflicts: the 1948 Palestinian–Israeli conflict, the Lebanese Civil War (1975–1990), the Islamic revolution in Iran, and the series of wars in the Persian Gulf—the Iran–Iraq War (1980–1989), the First Gulf War (1990–1991), and the US lead invasion of Iraq, which began in 2003. To this should be added the Russian Federations invasion of the Ukraine in February 2022 which has an impact on the Eastern Christian churches in the Middle East sharpening relations between the Patriarchates of Constantinople and Moscow and allowing for an increasing influence by the various states in the region on ecclesial affairs in a changing geopolitical situation. Patriarch Sako of the Chaldean Catholic Church centred on Iraq stated "The world economic crisis and the global situation marked by the Russian military invasion in Ukraine are also having serious effects on the network of charitable and social works promoted by the Churches in the Middle East. This circumstance is driving the exodus of Christians from the region of the world where Jesus was born, died and rose again."

In the same statement Patriarch Sako provided details to illustrate the direct effects of the world crisis and the ongoing war in Europe also on the economic stability of the ecclesial solidarity networks active in the Middle

---

[8] See the various contributions on the Armenian, Coptic, Syriac, and Assyrian Church of the East in the collections: Lucian N. Leustean (ed.), *Eastern Christianity and the Cold War, 1945-91*, London: Routledge, 2010; Lucian N. Leustean (ed.), *Eastern Christianity and Politics in the Twenty-First Century*, London: Routledge, 2014; Anthony O'Mahony and Emma Loosley (eds.), *Eastern Christians in the modern Middle East*, London: Routledge, 2010.

East… [The Cardinal explained that] "this situation has a negative impact on the economic state of the Church in Iraq, Syria and Lebanon", where the entire population is affected by unemployment, poverty or limitations in water and electricity services. "The economic resources of the dioceses are limited. The charities that helped us are now focusing their efforts on Ukraine".[9]

Added to this is the rise of radical currents including forms of 'religious nationalism' which offer no account of Christianity as a sustaining difference to the religious, cultural, and societal character of the region.[10] Therefore, to focus on emigration[11] and persecution in isolation from the demographic and socioeconomic factors, regional conflicts, the lack of human rights, religious tolerance and freedom, plus the rule of law is to risk viewing Christians solely as victims of persecution and mere relics of a fading past. Such a narrow focus robs Christians of agency as significant actors in their own societies.[12] The future of Christian presence in the Middle East has become inseparably from the wider geopolitical context in the region. Antoine Audo, S.J. Chaldean Bishop of Aleppo, has correctly opined: 'If we want to reflect on the future of Christians in the Middle East, we cannot ignore the strategic, economic and religious interests that encompass the entire region, both regionally and internationally'.[13] Religious actors have long been aware of the acute situation and challenges Christians in the region

---

[9] Agenzia Fides, "The alarm of Chaldean Patriarch Sako: world crisis and war in Ukraine aggravate the 'alarming' exodus of Christians from the Middle East", 23 August 2022. Available at: http://www.fides.org/en/news/72688

[10] Joseph Yacoub, *Une diversité menacée. Les chrétiens d'Orient face au nationalisme arabe et à l'islamisme*, Paris: Salvator, 2018; Brynjar Lia & Mathilde Becker Aarseth, "Crusader Hirelings or Loyal Subjects? Evolving Jihadist Perspectives on Christian Minorities in the Middle East", *Islam and Christian–Muslim Relations,* vol. 33, no. 3, 2022, pp. 255-280.

[11] Bernard Heyberger provides an overview on Christian migration in "Migration of the Middle Eastern Christian and European Protection: a long History", in Andreas Schmoller (ed.), *Middle Eastern Christians and Europe Historical Legacies and Present Challenges*, Vienna: Lit Verlag, 2018, pp. 23-42; Kristian Girling, "Displaced Populations", in Kenneth R. Ross, Mariz Tadros, and Todd M. Johnson (eds.), *Christianity in North Africa and West Asia*, Edinburgh: Edinburgh University Press, 2018, pp. 427-438. Scholarly studies have been rightly preoccupied with the migration of Christians from the Middle East for a number of decades: Elie Austen, "L'émigration massive des chrétiens d'Orient", *Etudes*, vol. 373, no. 1-2, 1990, pp. 101-106; Hermanus Teule, "Middle Eastern Christians and Migration: Some Reflections", *The Journal of Eastern Christian Studies*, vol. 54, 2002, pp. 1-23.

[12] In contrast to this perspective, the theological and ecclesial thought of Antoine Audo offers a reflection which is both creative and imbued with courage: "The Current situation of Christianity in the Middle East, especially Syria, after the Synod of the Middle East's Final Declaration (September 2012) and the Papal Visit to Lebanon", in *Living Stones Yearbook 2012*, London: Melisende, 2012, pp. 1-17; Mar Antoine Audo, "Reflections on the Apostolic Exhortation of Benedict XVI and the Papal Visit to Lebanon", in Dietmar Winkler (ed.), *Towards a Culture of Co-Existence in Pluralistic Societies: The Middle East and India*, Piscataway, NJ: Gorgias Press, 2021, pp. 135-148.

[13] Antoine Audo, "The Church in the Middle East. The Future of Christians in the Region", in Harald Suermann and Michael Altripp (eds.), *Orientalisches Christentum. Perspektiven aus der Vergangenheit für die Zukunft*, Leiden: Brill/Schöningh, 2021, p. 52.

face.[14] The Holy See considers the present situation and future of Christianity in the Middle East of importance and significant for the character and identity of the Christian tradition, Global Christianity, and the Catholic Church in world today[15] In fact, Pope Francis and the Ecumenical Patriarch have made Christianity in the Middle East a central element in their joint diplomatic and religious action.[16] Frans Bouwen outlined the various contexts for Christian in the Middle East – the geopolitical context, of which the Christian are an integral part and in which they have to build their future; the impact of religious 'radicalization and exclusivism'; the resources that the Christian communities and churches have at their disposal; and challenges that they have to face and the commitments that they have to make.[17]

Catherine Mayeur-Jaouen sums up the current situation and attendant challenges:

> The taking of Mosul by the Islamic State (Daesh) led to a massive exodus of Christians from the plain of Nineveh to Iraqi Kurdistan. The payment of a tribute (jizya) imposed on the last Christians of Raqqa in Syria in February 2014 by a 'pact', then the beheading of 21 Copts in Libya a year later, together with the ostentatious destruction of churches, indicate the Christianophobia at work in the ideology of Daesh. It is important to always bear in mind that the refugees (11 million displaced people out of 22 million Syrians) and victims of the war are largely Muslims, that destruction has affected

---

[14] Vatican News, "Continental Synodal Assembly for the Middle East opens in Lebanon", 14 February 2023. Available at: https://www.vaticannews.va/en/church/news/2023-02/continental-synodal-assembly-for-the-middle-east-opens.html.

[15] Francesca Merlo, "Pope: 'Never forget plight of Syria and Christians in Middle East'", *Vatican News*, 20 June 2022. Available at: https://www.vaticannews.va/en/pope/news/2022-06/pope-francis-discourse-greek-melkite-synod.html.

[16] "The grave challenges facing the world in the present situation require the solidarity of all people of good will, and so we also recognize the importance of promoting a constructive dialogue with Islam based on mutual respect and friendship. Inspired by common values and strengthened by genuine fraternal sentiments, Muslims and Christians are called to work together for the sake of justice, peace and respect for the dignity and rights of every person, especially in those regions where they once lived for centuries in peaceful coexistence and now tragically suffer together the horrors of war. Moreover, as Christian leaders, we call on all religious leaders to pursue and to strengthen interreligious dialogue and to make every effort to build a culture of peace and solidarity between persons and between peoples. We also remember all the people who experience the sufferings of war. In particular, we pray for peace in Ukraine, a country of ancient Christian tradition, while we call upon all parties involved to pursue the path of dialogue and of respect for international law in order to bring an end to the conflict and allow all Ukrainians to live in harmony. "It might be noted that both Pope and Patriarch noted in 2014 the conflict in the Ukraine had repercussions for Christians in the Middle East. Asia News, "Pope and Ecumenical Patriarch: May the martyrdom of the Middle East nourish the journey of Christian unity", 30 November 2014. Available at: https://www.asianews.it/news-en/Pope-and-Ecumenical-Patriarch:-May-the-martyrdom-of-the-Middle-East-nourish-the-journey-of-Christian-unity-32836.html.

[17] Frans Bouwen, "For the future of Christian presence in the Middle East", *One in Christ: A Catholic Ecumenical Review*, vol. 50, no. 2, 2016, p. 174.

Muslim holy places as well as ancient sites, and that the taking of Mosul was accompanied by the decapitation of recalcitrant Sunni imams: Daesh and the wars of the region are a catastrophe for everyone. And we can fear that enforced departure and massacres may end by emptying these countries of their Christians, already few in number. Confronted with a general wave of migration, which for Christians seems like a haemorrhaging, prophets of the 'death' of 'Eastern Christians' - a literary genre in a West which feels itself threatened- are not short of arguments for condemning the millions of Christians living in the Near East to imminent disappearance.

How is it possible, in such a climate of violence, to escape a logic of victimisation which leads to separation or departure, but also to avoid a logic of denial which hides reality? In fact, Christianity has become an ultra-minority in the Near East, its historic birthplace. In Egypt, Palestine and Lebanon, the departure of the educated and dynamic middle classes, especially for economic reasons, has long been happening. To these original reasons is added the rapid confessionalisation of conflicts, aggravated by the American invasion in 2003. The role of local actors (Saudi Arabia, Turkey, Iran, Qatar, Israel) has followed community and confessional lines. In the current regional confrontation between Shi'a and Sunnis, beginning in 2005, concerns for the future of a multi-confessional Lebanon have increased. In Egypt, the rise of a 'Coptic question' and the exercise of power by the Muslim Brotherhood (2011-2013) have altered the traditional image of peaceful coexistence. The oasis of Jordan looks fragile. Palestinian Christians have long suffered from the political impasse, the economic crisis, and in general from the violence in the occupied Palestinian territories. Today, with the rise of political Islam and jihadism, Christians are threatened or killed in the Middle East because they are Christians, like the Yazidis, even more harshly treated and exterminated by Daesh. Are the increasing attacks on Middle Eastern Christians the inescapable continuation of the 1915 genocide, and proof of the deadly threat which Islam represents for Christians? Has the life of Eastern Christians come down to a series of death throes? Have they not left simply because they have been persecuted? How then do we explain that they survived until now, and prospered during certain periods? Their history amounts neither to their relations with Muslims, nor to their recourse to the assistance of a sympathetic West. The current ultra-confessionalisation and communitarianism do not explain the whole of a long history. We need to turn our attention to Eastern Christians themselves, who are neither a fifth column of the West, as the jihadists accuse them, nor the eternal victims of Muslims, as a number of Islamophobic Western sites claim.[18]

The trend towards the study of 'world Christianity' with a focus on Asia, Africa, and Latin America has in recent times emerged, however, little attention has been given to the Eastern Christian churches despite the fact that the Eastern Christians constitute one of largest Christian traditions in the world.[19] Dyron B. Daughrity, however, has posed a prudent consideration: "the `North to South' metaphor has been helpful and challenging, but before we adopt it as rigid paradigm, we must face up to the absence of the East in that typology".[20] Eastern Christian churches are mainly concentrated in Russia, Eastern Europe, the Middle East, East Africa and in diasporas in the West.[21] Eastern Christianity have somewhere between 250-300 million members worldwide, estimates can vary; which makes one of largest-Christian traditions with approximately 12 per cent of

---

[18] Catherine Mayeur-Jaouen, "Les chrétiens au Moyen-Orient à l'heure de Daesh", *Annuaire français des relations* internationales, vol. XVII, 2016, p. 681.

[19] Scott M. Kenworthy, "Beyond Schism: Restoring Eastern Orthodoxy to the History of Christianity", *Reviews in Religion and Theology*, vol. 15, no. 2, 2008, pp. 171-178. See also Charles Miller and Anthony O'Mahony (eds.), "The Orthodox Churches in Contemporary Contexts", *International Journal for the Study of the Christian Church*, vol. 10, no. 2-3, 2010, pp. 82-89; Anthony O'Mahony and John Flannery (eds.), "Eastern Orthodoxy: Modern History and Contemporary Theology", *Journal of Eastern Christian Studies*, vol. 63, no. 1-2, 2011, pp. 125-126; Anthony O'Mahony and John Flannery (eds.), *The Catholic Church in the Contemporary Middle East*, London: Melisende, 2010.

[20] Dyron B. Daughrity, "Christianity Is Moving from North to South – So What About the East?", *International Bulletin of Missionary* Research, vol. 35, no. 1, 2011, p. 21. See the trilogy by Philip Jenkins, *The Next Christendom: The Coming of Global Christianity*, Oxford: Oxford University Press, 2002; *The New Faces of Christianity: Believing the Bible in the Global South*, Oxford: Oxford University Press, 2006; *God's Continent: Christianity, Islam and Europe's Religious Crisis*, Oxford: Oxford University Press, 2007.

[21] See the Pew Foundation report on "Global Christianity: A Report on the Size and Distribution of the World's Christian Population", 19 December 2011, Available at: https://assets.pewresearch.org/wp-content/uploads/sites/11/2011/12/Christianity-fullreport-web.pdf (hereinafter *Report*). The *Report* estimated that there are some 2.18 billion Christians, representing nearly a third of the estimated 2010 global population of 6.9 billion. Christians are to be found across the globe which today means that no single region can indisputably claim to be the centre of global Christianity; which is not the case for other religious traditions. This is in contrast to the past when Europe held that position, for example in 1910 about two-thirds of the world's Christians lived within the continent. Today, however, approximately one quarter of all Christians live in Europe (26%); the Americas (37%); in sub-Saharan Africa (24%), in Asia and the Pacific (13%). The *Report* noted extraordinary changes in the global configuration of Christianity – in sub-Saharan Africa a 60-fold increase, from fewer than 9 million in 1910 to more than 516 million in 2010, and in the Asia-Pacific region, a 10-fold increase, from about 28 million in 1910 to more than 285 million in 2010. In China today it is estimated that up to ten per cent of the population is Christian, which is set to increase dramatically making this country, in due course, having the largest concentration of Christians in the world outstripping the US. There is a growing awareness of the Eastern Christian tradition today among Chinese Christian intellectuals as the first Christian encounter with Chinese culture and civilization: Benoît Vermander, "The Impact of Nestorianism on Contemporary Chinese Theology", in Roman Malek and Peter Hofrichter (eds.), *Jingjiao: The Church of the East in China and Central Asia*, London: Routledge, 2006, pp. 181-194; Jeremias Norman, "Eastern Christianity in China", in Ken Parry (ed.), The Blackwell Companion to Eastern Christianity, Oxford: Wiley/Blackwell, 2007, pp. 280-290.

the global Christian population.[22]

Eastern Christianity in its various traditions is the dominant character of Christianity in the Middle East.[23] The churches of the Middle East can be grouped into five families: Oriental Orthodox – Armenian, Coptic and Syriac; Eastern Catholics – Armenians, Chaldeans, Copts, Latins, Maronites, Melkites and Syriacs; Eastern Orthodoxy – the patriarchates of Constantinople, Antioch, Alexandria and Jerusalem; The 'Assyrian' Church of the East; and the various Protestant dominations.[24]

The ecclesial context for Middle Eastern Christianity is one of great complexity. Its origins are those of Christianity itself expressed in deep cultural, linguistic and theological diversity.[25] Middle Eastern Christianity, despite being a small part of Global Christianity, certainly less than one per cent, has a significance and importance for the wider Christian tradition. Sidney H. Griffith, however, locates the Middle East for the history of Christianity:

> It is important to take cognizance of the seldom acknowledged fact that after the consolidation of the Islamic conquest and the consequent withdrawal of 'Roman/Byzantine' forces from the Fertile Crescent in the first half of the seventh century perhaps 50 per cent of the world's confessing Christians from the mid-seventh to the end of the eleventh centuries found themselves living under Muslim rule.[26]

Samir Khalil Samir, S.J.[27] of the Pontifical Oriental Institute positions the

---

[22] Pew Foundation, "Global Christianity: A Report on the Size and Distribution of the World's Christian Population", 19 December 2011. Available at: http://www.pewforum.org/Christian/Global-Christianity-orthodox.aspx.

[23] Dietmar W. Winkler, "Christianity in the Middle East: Some Historical Remarks and Preliminary Demographic Figures", in Dietmar Winkler (ed.), *Syriac Christianity in the Middle East and India*, Piscataway, NJ: Gorgias Press, 2013, pp. 107-125; Herman Teule, "Christianity in West Asia", in Felix Wilfred (ed.), *The Oxford Handbook of Christianity in Asia*, New York: Oxford University Press, 2014, pp. 17-29.

[24] Anthony O'Mahony, "Christianity in the Middle East: Modern History and Contemporary Theology and Ecclesiology: An Introduction and Overview", *Journal of Eastern Christian Studies*, vol. 63, no. 3-4, 2013, pp. 231-260; Anthony O'Mahony, "Christianity in the wider Levant Region: Modern History and Contemporary Context", in Kail Ellis (ed.), *Secular Nationalism and Citizenship in Muslim Countries: Arab Christians in the Levant*, Basingstoke: Palgrave, 2018, pp. 61-88; Anthony O'Mahony, "Christianity in the Middle East: The Challenge of Coexistence", in Edward G. Farrugia and Gianpaolo Rigotti (eds.), *A Common Mission: The Oriental Congregation and the Oriental Institute (1917-2017)*, Rome: Orientalia Christiana Analecta, 2020, pp. 425-468.

[25] Frans Bouwen, "The Churches in the Middle East", in Lawrence S. Cunningham (ed.), *Ecumenism. Present Realities and Future Prospects*, Indiana: University of Notre Dame Press, 1998, pp. 25-36.

[26] Sidney H. Griffith, *The Church in the Shadow of the Mosque: Christians and Muslims in the World of Islam*, New Jersey: Princeton University Press, 2008, p. 11.

[27] Samir Khalil Samir has sought to develop a Christian theology in the context of the historic encounter with Islam from the perspective of contemporary times, see Zeljko Pasa (ed.), *Between the Cross and Crescent:*

significance of Middle Eastern Christianity due their cultural richness, proud of their apostolic origins at the beginning of Christianity; a rejection of the term 'minority'; an understanding of their vocation to be a unifying bridge between cultures, civilizations, religions East and West.[28] The idea that the Christians in the Middle East are representatives of a minority is very much contested as reduction of the character of the region which is defined by its religious plurality not just by majority-minority markers. That said, Todd M. Johnson, has noted that one of the most profound changes to have taken place in the global religious landscape has been `the unrelenting proportional decline of historic Christian communities in the Middle East'.[29]

Contemporary challenges of Christian presence in the region might be liaised with a crisis in the imagination of global Christianity in understanding the implications of this reality despite the fact that today we live in an extraordinary moment when it is estimated that Christians today account for close to over a third of humanity.[30] At no point in historical memory has one religious tradition, as Christianity is today, been so vast, so geographically spread. This crisis is not mirrored for Judaism of whom one third live in Israel or small clusters in Iran, Morocco and Turkey; or for Islam with approximately 20 per cent of Muslims live in the Middle East. The sacred spaces of Judaism in Jerusalem and for Islam in the holy places in the Arabian Peninsula are assured of a living and strong co-religious presence, however, this cannot be said for Christian Holy Places and territory which are seeing their communities decline in number leading to a less secure future.

In the history religious landscape of the Middle East in 1910 Christians composed 13.6 per cent of the population in the region; however only 4.2 per cent by 2010. Johnson considers that this proportion could decline to 3.6 per cent by 2025 – whilst noting that this figure could be much lower if the flight of Christians Iraq and Syria continues. In fact, the Middle East is becoming more Muslim with the percent increasing from 85 per cent in 1990 to 92.3 per cent in 2010 – the de-pluralization of the region is one of the principal forces for change and destabilization.[31]

Studies in Honor of Samir Khalil Samir, S.J. on the Occasion of His Eightieth Birthday, Rome: Orientalia Christiana Analecta, 2018; Wakif Nasry (ed.), *Samir Khalil Samir, S.J. on Islam and the West*, San Francisco: Ignatius Press, 2008.

[28] Samir Khalil Samir, *Rôle culturel des chrétiens dans le monde arabe*, Beirut: Cahiers de l'Orient Chrétien, 2003.

[29] Todd M. Johnson and Gina A. Zurlo, "Ongoing Exodus: Tracking the Emigration of Christians from the Middle East", *Harvard Journal of Middle Eastern Politics and Politics*, vol. 3, 2013-2014, p. 39.

[30] See the overview provided by Sebastian Kim and Kirsteen Kim, *Christianity as a World Religion*, London: Bloomsbury, 2016.

[31] Johnson and Zurlo, "Ongoing Exodus", p. 44.

Christianity in the Near and Middle East today in terms of numbers are a minority tradition.[32] In Egypt,[33] Lebanon[34] and among Palestinian Christians,[35] the departure of the educated and dynamic middle classes, especially for economic reasons, has long been a trend.[36] We might add to these reasons the rapid spread of underlining communal and religious conflicts, aggravated by the US led western invasion of Iraq in 2003. The Christians of Iraq have been one of the main communal causalities of the breakdown in civil and political order in the country. Christians have found it difficult to hold a position as a minority community spread across the country with the carving-up of the regions between the various ethnic and religious groups – Sunni, Shiite and Kurd.[37] The Church in Iraq, comprising the Assyrian Church of the East,[38] the Ancient Church of the East,[39] and the Chaldean Church,[40] represented a historic Christian culture which had

---

[32] In a series of studies Bernard Heyberger describes the modern historical and scholarly context for the study of Christianity in the Middle East, "Le christianisme oriental à l'époque ottomane: du postcolonial au global (1960-2020)", *Annales. Histoire, Sciences Sociales*, vol. 76, no. 2, 2021, pp. 301-337; Bernard Heyberger and Nathalie Vergeron, "Les Minorités Chrétiennes d'Orient Au Cœur Des Tensions Liées à La Question Nationale", *Diplomatie*, vol. 93, 2018, pp. 58–61; Bernard Heyberger, "La France et la protection des chrétiens maronites. Généalogie d'une representation", *Relations internationales*, vol. 173, no. 1, 2018, pp. 13-30; Bernard Heyberger and Aurélien Girard, "Chrétiens Au Proche-Orient", *Archives De Sciences Sociales Des Religions*, vol. 171, no. 3, 2015, pp. 11-35; Bernard Heyberger, *Les chrétiens au Proche-Orient. De la compassion à la compréhension*, Paris: Payot, 2013.

[33] Francine Costet-Tardieu, offers a portrait of Christianity in Egypt before the great transformation brought about by economic, social, cultural and demographic change in the middle of the twentieth century, *Les minorités chrétiennes dans la construction de l'Égypte modern 1922-1952*, Paris: Karthala, 2016.

[34] Boutros Labaki, "The Christian Communities and the Economic and Social Situation in Lebanon", in Andrea Pacini (ed.), *Christian Communities in the Arab Middle East: The Challenge of the Future*, Oxford: Clarendon Press, 1998, pp. 222-258; Boutros Labaki, "Les chrétiens du Liban (1943-2008). Prépondérance, marginalisation et renouveau", *Confluences Méditerranée*, vol. 66, 2008, pp. 99-116.

[35] Bernard Sabella, "Palestinian Christian Emigration from the Holy Land", Proche-Orient Chrétien, vol. 41, 1991, pp. 74-85; Bernard Sabella, "Socio-Economic Characteristics and Challenges to Palestinian Christians in the Holy Land", in Anthony O'Mahony (ed.), *Palestinian Christians: Religion, Politics and Society in the Holy Land*, London: Melisende, 1999, pp. 222-251.

[36] Bernard Sabella, "L'émigration des arabes chrétiens: dimensions et causes de l'exode", *Proche-Orient Chrétien*, vol. 47, 1997, pp. 141-169.

[37] Herman Teule, "Christians in Iraq: An Analysis of Some Recent Political Developments", *Der Islam*, vol. 88, no. 1, 2012, pp. 179-98; Herman Teule, "Christianity in Iraq and its Contribution to Society", in Dietmar W. Winkler (ed.), *Syriac Christianity in the Middle East and India: Contributions and Challenges*, Piscataway, NJ: Gorgias Press, 2013, pp. 23-42.

[38] Dietmar Winkler with Wilhelm Baum, *The Church of the East. A Concise History*, London: Routledge, 2003.

[39] Dahlia Khay Azeez, "The Schism of the Eastern Syriac Church (the 'Nestorian Church') in the Twentieth Century", *Orientalia Christiana Periodica*, vol. 87, no. 2, 2021, pp. 453-493.

[40] Kristian Girling, *The Chaldean Catholic Church: Modern History, Ecclesiology and Church-State Relations*, London: Routledge, 2017; Kristian Girling, "Engaging 'the Martyred Church' – The Chaldean Catholic Church, Assyrian Church of the East and the Holy See in Ecumenical Dialogue 1994-2012 and the Influence of the Second Vatican Council", in *Living Stones Yearbook 2012*, London: Melisende, 2012, pp. 38-64; Kristian Girling, "To Live within Islam: The Chaldean Catholic Church in modern Iraq, 1958–2003", *Studies in Church History*, vol. 51, 2015, pp. 366-384; Kristian Girling, "Patriarch Louis Raphael I Sako and Ecumenical Engagements between the Church of the East and the Chaldean Catholic Church",

evolved beyond the confines of the Roman Empire in almost total isolation from the influences of Hellenistic culture. Their distinctive rite is considered the product of a fusion between Judeo-Christianity and Assyro-Babylonian and Iranian cultures. The rite uses Syriac, a language close to Aramaic, the language used by Christ and the disciples. These Churches were culturally embedded in the landscape of Mesopotamia.[41] The loss of Christians in Iraq profoundly alters not just the character of those lands but also their future.[42]

The conflict in Syria has generated a justified concern that the fate of Christians in Iraq is one that they might also share as a consequence of religious and ethnic confrontation.[43] The Melkite Greek Catholic Archbishop of Aleppo, Jeanbart, stated in January 2012: 'We are very worried about the consequences of an overthrow of the regime which will drive many of our faithful to emigrate, just as in Iraq after the fall of Saddam Hussein. Christians have no confidence in an extremist Sunni power. We fear the domination of the dogmatic Muslim Brotherhood'.[44] The Syrian crisis in began in March 2011 since which approximately half the Christian population has left Syria, some 600,000 out of a total of 1.2 million have either left or have been displaced within the country or to Lebanon. As in Iraq, significant damage has been done to the infrastructure of the Christian communities – destruction of churches, schools, communal property this has encouraged many to consider that they have no future and have left.[45]

One in Christ, vol. 50, 2016, pp. 100-121.

[41] Mar Awa Royel, "The Pearl of Great Price: The Anaphora of the Apostles Mar Addai & Mar Mari as an Ecclesial and Cultural Identifier of the Assyrian Church of the East", *Orientalia Christiana Periodica*, vol. 80, 2014, pp. 5-22.

[42] Joseph Yacoub, *Babylone chrétienne. Géopolitique de l'Église de Mésoptamie*, Paris: Desclée de Brouwer, 1996.

[43] See the study by Antoine Audo, "Christianity in the Middle East: Current Challenges and Opportunities for the Future, through the Experience of Syria", in *Living Stones Yearbook 2022*, London: Melisende, 2022, pp. 136-141. Andrew Ashdown reflects on the possibilities of Christian thought in the region, especially in the context of Syria and the 'Church of Antioch', "Eastern Christian Mystical Traditions and the Development of Ecumenical and Interreligious Dialogue: Louis Massignon, Olivier Clement, Georges Khodr and Paolo Dall 'Oglio, with a Protestant Contribution", in *Living Stones Yearbook 2020*, London: Melisende, 2020, pp. 86-118.

[44] Fabrice Balanche, "Un scénario à l'irakienne pour les chrétiens de Syrie", in Marie-Hélène Robert and Michel Younès (eds), *La vocation des chrétiens d'Orient. Défis actuels et enjeux d'avenir dans leurs rapports à l'islam*, Paris: Karthala, 2015, p. 27. For an overview account see Andrew Ashdown, *Christian–Muslim Relations in Syria: Historic and Contemporary Religious Dynamics in a Changing Context*, London: Routledge 2020.

[45] Religious discourses of the Syrian conflict are increasingly generalized as they seek refuge elsewhere Andreas Schmoller, "Now My Life in Syria Is Finished: Case Studies on Religious Identity and Sectarianism in Narratives of Syrian Christian Refugees in Austria", *Islam And Christian–Muslim Relations*, vol. 27, no. 4, 2016, pp. 419-437; Andreas Schmoller, "Anti-Islamic Narratives of Middle Eastern Diaspora Christians: An Interdisciplinary Analytical Framework", in Herman Teule and Joseph Verheyden (eds.), *Eastern and Oriental Christianity in the Diaspora*, Leuven: Peeters, 2020, pp. 189-214. For an account on the eve of internal conflict in Syria, see Annika Rabo, "We Are Christians, and We Are Equal Citizens: Perspectives on Particularity and Pluralism in Contemporary Syria", *Islam and Christian–Muslim Relations*, vol. 23, no. 1, 2012, pp. 79-93.

In the zones held by the opposition or by radical Islamists groups, the Christian population has almost completely disappeared, relocating into the government-held areas.[46] In the Syrian Government zones due to the movement of populations since 2011 has seen a rise in the percent of minority communities present – Alawites, Shiites, Druze, Christians and others. In previous crises many Christians from across the region took refuge in Lebanon to settle and rebuild communal and religious life;[47] however, for many Christians who are leaving Iraq and Syria regard their stay as a stepping to exile, emigration and diaspora.[48] Lebanese Christians are now concerned as they consider that they could be the next victims of this historical process of the elimination of Christians from the Middle East which begun with the Armenian and Syriac Christian massacres of the end of the 19th century.

The challenge for Christians in the region has been how to position themselves in relation to a host of regional actors in particular that of Saudi Arabia, Turkey, Iran, Gulf Arab states, which has developed around religious-communal associations. In the current regional confrontation between Shi'a and Sunnis concerns for the future of a multi-confessional states such as Iraq, Lebanon and Syria have increased. In Egypt, the rise of a 'Coptic question' and the exercise of power by the Muslim Brotherhood (2011-2013) have altered the traditional image of peaceful coexistence.[49] The 'oasis' of Jordan looks fragile due to on-going tensions between society, government, on-going environmental and economic stresses and a growing Islamist current also accompanied by large numbers of mainly Sunni Muslim displaced in the border areas with Syria.[50] That said, the monarchy in Jordan

---

[46] Balanche, "Un scénario à l'irakienne pour les chrétiens de Syrie", p. 28.

[47] This is well described for the Armenian community by Nicola Migliorino and Ara Sanjian, "Les communautes armeniennes du Proche-Orient arabe", *Confluences Méditerranée*, vol. 66, 2008, pp. 73-82; Ara Sanjian, "The Armenian Minority Experience in the Modern Arab World", *Bulletin of the Royal Institute for Inter-Faith Studies*, vol. 3, no. 1, 2001, pp. 149-179; Ara Sanjian, "The Armenian Church and Community in Jerusalem and the Holy Land (From their origins until the modern era)", in Anthony O'Mahony (ed.), The Christian Communities in the Holy Land: Studies in History, Religion, and Politics, Cardiff: University of Wales Press, 2003, pp. 57-89.

[48] Ten of thousands of Iraqi Christians since 1991 have also transited through Turkey via church and familial networks Didem Danış, "Attendre au Purgatoire: les réseaux religieux de migrants chrétiens d'Irak en transit à Istanbul", *Revue européenne des migrations internationales*, vol. 22, no. 3, 2006, pp. 109-134; Didem Danış, "A Faith That Binds: Iraqi Christian Women on the Domestic Service Ladder of Istanbul", *Journal of Ethnic and Migration Studies*, vol. 33, no. 4, 2007, pp. 601-615.

[49] Laure Guirgis, *Les coptes d'Égypte. Violences communautaires et transformations politiques (2005-2012)*, Paris: Karthala, 2012.

[50] Paolo Maggiolini, "Christian Churches and Arab Christians in the Hashemite Kingdom of Jordan", *Archives de sciences sociales des religions, vol. 171, 2015, pp. 37-58; Géraldine Chatelard, Briser la mosaïque. Les tribus chrétiennes de Madaba, Jordanie (xix-xx siècle)*, Paris: CNRS-Éditions, 2004; Géraldine Chatelard, "Les chrétiens en Jordanie, dynamiques identitaires et gestion du pluralisme", *Les Cahiers de l'Orient*, vol. 93, no. 1, 2009, pp. 41-56; Géraldine Chatelard, "The Constitution of Christian Communal Boundaries and Spheres in Jordan", Journal of Church and State, vol. 52, no. 3, 2010, pp. 476–502.

considers that it has a unique role in relation to the question of the Muslim Holy Places in Jerusalem including seeking to represent the interests and protection of Christian Holy Places and presence in Jerusalem.[51] Palestinian Christians have long suffered from the political impasse, the economic crisis, and in general from the violence in the occupied Palestinian territories.[52] Today, with the rise of political Islam and jihadism, Christians can be threatened or killed in the Middle East just because they are Christians.[53] It is increasing asserted that this recent upsurge in violence on Middle Eastern Christians is the inescapable continuation of the 1915 genocide, proof of the deadly threat which 'the crisis' in Islam and the temptation towards 'religious nationalism' represents for Christians and other religions in the region.[54]

Eastern Christianity was born in 395, with the division of the Roman Empire between the two sons of Theodosius. If this did not immediately lead to the formation of two separate Churches, it created conditions for a divergent development between the Christian communities of West and East. In effect, the destruction of political unity deepened the existing cultural divisions between the Greek and Latin territories of the Empire. The political context, despite its importance, for the divide in Christianity is often left in parenthesis in modern of theological and ecclesiological studies. The encounter between Middle Eastern Christianity with Western Christianity,[55] set against contemporary geopolitics, continues to give force to the relevance of this question.[56] John Paul II who was deeply aware of the political consequences of the divide between Eastern and Western Christianity in

---

[51] Victor Kattan writes on Jordan Monarchy and the Muslim Holy sites in Jerusalem: "The Special Role of the Hashemite Kingdom of Jordan in the Muslim Holy Shrines in Jerusalem", *Arab Law Quarterly*, vol. 35, 2021, pp. 503-548.

[52] Bernard Sabella, "Palestinian Christians: Realities and Hopes", *Studies in Church History: The Holy Land, Holy Lands, and Christian History*, vol. 36, 2000, pp. 373-397.

[53] Mayeur-Jaouen, "Les chrétiens au Moyen-Orient à l'heure de Daesh", p. 682.

[54] Reflections on the contemporary context Ahmad Fauzi Abdul Hamid, "Sociopolitical Developments in West Asia and Their Impact on Christian Minorities in the Region", in Felix Wilfred (ed.), *The Oxford Handbook of Christianity in Asia*, New York: Oxford University Press, 2014, pp. 231–256.

[55] Joseph Maïla, "De la question d'Orient à le récente géopolitique des minorités", *Proche-Orient Chrétien*, vol. 47, 1997, pp. 35-58; Joseph Maïla, "Réflexions sur les chrétiens d'Orient", *Confluences Méditerranée*, vol. 66, 2008, pp. 191-204.

[56] The reality of Eastern Christianity is often overlooked by Western, and in particular, US policy, especially in its relations with Islamic political movements, Israel and various Muslim dominant states in the Middle East. This is also noted in evaluating the Russian Orthodox Church concern for the Eastern Christian churches in the Middle East, which is seen as a state-political concern rather than a new aspect of the post-communist European context. See, Alicja Curanovic, The Religious Factor in Russia's Foreign Policy, London, Routledge, 2012. The importance of this lacuna, the lack of understanding of Eastern Christianity, is gaining a wide purchase in political circles especially with regard to the present situation in Syria and future of Christianity in the Middle East. Elizabeth H. Prodromou, "The Politics of Human Rights: Orthodox Christianity Gets the Short End", *Archons*, 5 August 2013. Available at: https://www.archons.org/el/-/the-politics-of-human-rights-orthodox-christianity-gets-the-short-end-by-dr-elizabeth-h-prodromou.

modern European history posited the central idea that today the universal Church needed to learn to breathe with two lungs.[57] Still today, beyond the divisions and reconstitution of the Christian world which history has brought through ecumenical dialogue;[58] two profoundly different sensibilities separate the Western Christianity, with its Latin tradition, from its Eastern equivalent which is itself deeply indebted to Greek and Semitic culture.[59]

The Political-Theological context for Christianity in the Middle East is one of much complexity; which is different from state to state, but also by the particular ecclesial character of the Eastern Christian culture in question. In the context of the modern 'nation-state' some churches might be understood as the 'national-church' – the Maronite Church for Lebanon; the Church of the East/Chaldean Church for Iraq and the Coptic Orthodox Church of Egypt. That said there is increasingly a desire among the Christian churches to work in common contributing from their distinct experiences and ecclesial cultures and contexts to the religious political question.[60] This is particularly important in creating political and religious space for Christianity in Middle Eastern societies thus enabling an impact on wider cultural.[61] The question of religious freedom is especially important[62] and

[57] John Paul II had the religious division in Europe primarily in his mind: Michael Sutton, "John Paul II's Idea of Europe", *Religion, State & Society*, vol. 25, no. 1, 1997, pp. 17-29; Anthony O'Mahony, "The Vatican and Europe: Political Theology and Ecclesiology in Papal Statements from Pius XII to Benedict XVI", International Journal for the Study of the Christian Church, vol. 9, no. 3, 2009, pp. 177-194.

[58] Frans Bouwen, "Unity and Christian Presence in the Middle East", in O'Mahony and Flannery (eds.), *The Catholic Church in the contemporary Middle East*, pp. 87-105 who quotes the second pastoral letter of the Catholic patriarchs of the Middle East who state "In the East, we Christians will be together or we will not be", p. 87.

[59] Joseph Yacoub, "La contribution de la Mésopotamie ancienne et syriaque au dialogue des cultures", in Joseph Yacoub (ed.), *L'Humanisme réinventé*, Paris: Cerf, 2012, pp. 165-205.

[60] Stefanie Hugh-Dovonan, "Olivier Clement. A Reflection on the 'Antiochian Paradigm' of Relations between Eastern Catholics and Eastern Orthodox in the Middle East for Today's Europe", in Jaroslav Z. Skira, Peter De Mey and Herman Teule (eds.), *The Catholic Church and its Orthodox Sister Churches Twenty-Five Years after Balamand*, Leuven: Peeters, 2022, pp. 241-260; John Whooley, "In the Shadow of Balamand: Recent Relations between the Armenian Apostolic Church and the Armenian Catholic Church", in Skira, De Mey and Teule (eds.), *The Catholic Church*, pp. 261-280; Herman Teule, "The Assyrian Church of the East, the Chaldean Church and the Roman Catholic Church: An Attempt at Understanding Their Interrelation", in Skira, De Mey and Teule (eds), *The Catholic Church*, pp. 281-294.

[61] Joseph Yacoub, "Les régimes politiques arabes et l'islam politique", in Joseph Yacoub (ed), *Fièvre démocratique et ferveur fondamentaliste Dominantes du XXIe siècle*, Paris: Cerf, 2008, pp. 121-140.

[62] See the various studies in Kail Ellis (ed.), *Secular Nationalism and Citizenship in Muslim Countries: Arab Christians in the Levant*, Basingstoke: Palgrave, 2018; Nael Georges, "La Liberté Religieuse Dans Les États de Culture Islamique", *Diplomatie*, vol. 75, 2015, 44-47; Nael Georges, "Minorités et liberté religieuse dans les Constitutions des États de l'Orient arabe", *Égypte/Monde arabe*, vol. 1. no. 10, 2013, pp. 287-305; Nael Georges, "Les chrétiens dans le monde arabe et la question de l'apostasie en islam", *Maghreb – Machrek*, vol. 3. no. 209, 2011, pp. 109-119; Nael Georges, "La Liberté Religieuse Dans Les États de Culture Islamique", *Diplomatie*, vol. 75, 2015, pp. 44-47. The model of the so-called Constitution of Medina used in both liberal – moderate and radical Islamic thought to promote notions regarding the possibility of Jews and Christians living within Dar al-Islam continues to influence Islamic political thought see, Harald

has for at least the Catholic Church in the Middle East been promoted in diplomacy and the negotiation of concordats.[63]

The Catholic Patriarchs of the East have issued a series of important letters on the religious, political, economic and culture situation and challenges of the region in the third part of the letter, 'Together for an egalitarian society', in 1992, they state:

> No one can remove religion from public life or limit it to the liturgies and devotions; because religion is dogma and life that has to do with the whole of human existence, private and public, individual and social ... To link citizenship to religious values is not an evil. On the contrary, religious values give a soul to citizenship. But in this case it is necessary that religion should orient the person totally to God, to the perfect respect of the creature of God and of every religious conviction, especially when we have to do with the religion of a minority in a given society or nation. The laws of the state must guarantee the rights of the minority religion with the same rigour as it guarantees those of the majority or of the religion of the State.[64]

Bishop Antoine Audo of Aleppo made an explicit connection between the ending of the Synod for the Middle East's final declaration (September 2012) and Benedict XVI's papal visit to Lebanon and the so-called 'Arab Spring' which articulated a need for political change in the region.[65] Audo quotes the Declaration summing up the profound desire for a re-ordering and re-orientation of religious thought towards a new understanding of the political in the context of religious freedom as a key-theme in understanding conversion and mission:

> Religious tolerance exists in a number of countries, but it does not have much effect since it remains limited in its field of action. There is a need to move beyond tolerance to religious freedom. Taking this

---

Suermann, "Die Konstitution von Medina Erinnerung an ein andreres Modell des Zusammenlebens", *Collectanea Christiana Orientalia*, vol. 2, 2005, pp. 225-244.

[63] Rafael Palomino, "The Role of Concordants Promoting Religious Freedom with Special Reference to Agreements in the Middle East", in Congregazione per le Chiese Orientali, *Ius Ecclesiarum vehiculum caritatis*, Rome, 2004, pp. 893-900.

[64] Quoted in Christian Troll, "Changing Catholic Views on Islam", in Jacques Waardenburg (ed.), *Islam and Christianity: Mutual Perceptions Since the Mid–Twentieth Century*, Leuven: Peeters, 1998, 19-77.

[65] Antoine Audo, "The Synod of Bishops: The Catholic Church in the Middle East", *One in Christ: A Catholic Ecumenical Review*, vol. 44, no. 2, 2010, pp. 196–200; Antoine Audo, "Between Christians and Muslims a Pathway of Communion, Oasis, vol. 13, 2011, Available at: https://www.oasiscenter.eu/en/middle-east-political-revolts-confessional-tensions, in which he states: "When listening to the demands of the people one cannot fail to notice a mysterious link between the final appeal of the Synod of the Catholic Church of the Middle East and everything that these societies ask for today: justice and freedom. Evidence of a historic opportunity".

step does not open the door to relativism, as some would maintain. It does not compromise belief, but rather calls for a reconsideration of the relationship between man, religion and God. It is not an attack on the 'foundational truths' of belief, since, despite human and religious divergences, a ray of truth shines on all men and women. We know very well that truth, apart from God, does not exist as an autonomous reality. If it did, it would be an idol. The truth cannot unfold except in an otherness open to God, who wishes to reveal his own otherness in and through my human brothers and sisters. Hence it is not fitting to state in an exclusive way: 'I possess the truth'. The truth is not possessed by anyone; it is always a gift which calls us to undertake a journey of ever closer assimilation to truth. Truth can only be known and experienced in freedom; for this reason we cannot impose truth on others; truth is disclosed only in an encounter of love."

Sebastian Brock has reminded us that for the Syriac tradition "Several of these Churches have existed, throughout the entire span of their history, as minority religious communities, living under governments that were often hostile. This experience has ensured that they have been free from the sort of triumphalism that has at times disfigured the Latin West and the Greek East".[66] The political-theological question is a significant issue for Eastern Christianity today especially in the Middle East[67] were this issue is marked by Christian relations with political traditions influenced by Judaism and Islam. However, the relationship between Eastern Christianity, and in particular the Eastern Orthodox churches especially in the modern history has not been straightforward historical trajectory.[68] Elizabeth Prodromou has suggested Orthodoxy's engagement with pluralism is one of discernible ambivalence.'[69] In fact Eastern Christianity relationship to the state need to

---

[66] Sebastian Brock, "The Syriac Orient: A Third "Lung" for the Church?", *Orientalia Christiana Periodica*, vol. 71, no. 1, 2005, p. 15.

[67] Frans Bouwen reflects upon many of these issues, including religious freedom, in his contribution on the Synod for the Middle East held in Rome in October 2010 by the Eastern Catholic bishops of the region: "The Synod for the Middle East: First results and Future Possibilities", in *Living Stones Yearbook 2012*, London: Melisende, 2012, pp. 18-37.

[68] On Eastern Orthodox and aspects of the politics of church-state relations in Jerusalem, see Sotiris Roussos, "The Greek Orthodox Patriarchate and Community of Jerusalem: Church, State and Identity", in Anthony O'Mahony (ed.), *The Christian Communities of Jerusalem and the Holy Land: Studies in History, Religion and Politics*, Cardiff: University of Wales Press, 2003, pp. 38-56; Sotiris Roussos, *Greece and the Middle East: The Greek Orthodox Communities in Egypt, Syria and Palestine, 1914-1940*, PhD dissertation, London: University of London, 1994; Sotiris Roussos, "Patriarchs, Notables and Diplomats: The Greek Orthodox Patriarchate of Jerusalem in the Modern Period", in Anthony O'Mahony (ed.), *Eastern Christianity*, pp. 372-387.

[69] Elizabeth H. Prodromou, "Orthodox Christianity and pluralism: Moving beyond Ambivalent?", in Emmanuel Clapsis (ed.), *The Orthodox Churches in a Pluralistic World: An Ecumenical Conversation*, Geneva: World Council of Churches Publications and Brookline, MA: Holy Cross Press, 2004, p. 24, as quoted in

take into consideration several historical experiences: (i) the Byzantine theocratic legacy, (ii) the Ottoman Legacy, (iii) the colonial-mandate régimes; (iv) the legacy of Arab, Turkish, Israeli and Iranian nationalism in relation to the identity of the `nation-state, and (iv) political Islamism. The experience of the Oriental Orthodox churches might be expression within other frameworks for example it might be noted that during the nineteenth century Armenian Church existed under the Orthodox Christian Tzars in the Russian Empire; in the Sunni Muslim dominated Ottoman Empire and in Shiite Iran.[70] The most recent phase the hoped for transformation of political governance in state and society associated with the so-called `Arab Spring' has encouraged Christian leaders, such as Cardinal Raï, Patriarch of Maronite Church to call for a `Christian Spring', that would pave the way for a "Arab spring for the Arab peoples to benefit from a climate of peace, justice and brotherhood. Raï continued that he hoped that the Arab regimes "are transformed into democratic regimes should separate religion from the state; strengthening civil liberties and human rights, the right to respect difference, and embrace diversity in unity".[71]

Even if it cannot be summed up in figures, the reality of Christianity in the modern Middle East is first of all one of numbers. The number of Christians, unfortunately, is very difficult to discern. For some decades, there have no longer been confessional censuses in the countries of the Middle East, where governments are concerned with often veiling the multi-confessional nature of their societies. The political consequences of this policy have been highlighted in the so-called 'Arab Spring' were religious and ethnic minorities, Kurds, Shiites, Christians, Druze, in the Middle Eastern region have challenged the emergence of an Islamist trend which has sought to dominate political society. However, the Middle Eastern church families represent approximately 30 million Christians of which approximately 15 million reside in the Middle East.[72]

The Middle Eastern Christian diaspora in North and South America, Australia and Europe is an important and dynamic reality for all the

---

Ina Merdjanova, "Orthodox Christianity in a Pluralistic World", *Concilium*, vol. 1, 2011, p. 39.

[70] For an ecclesial overview of Armenian Church, see Hratch Tchilingirian, "The Catholicos and the Hierarchical Sees of the Armenian Church", in Anthony O'Mahony (ed.), *Eastern Christianity*, pp. 140-159.

[71] *L'Orient-Le Jour*, 21 January 2013. The Maronite patriarchate is an important religious actor in Lebanon; see Sami E. Baroudi and Paul Tabar, "Spiritual Authority versus Secular Authority: Relations between the Maronite Church and the State in Postwar Lebanon: 1990-2005", *Middle East Critique*, vol. 18, no. 3, 2009, pp. 195-230.

[72] Statistics are very difficult to obtain in relation to the numbers of Christians in the Middle East. However, see Philippe Fargues, "The Arab Christians of the Middle East: A Demographic Perspective", in Andrea Acini (ed.), *Christian Communities in the Arab Middle East*, pp. 48-66.

churches.[73] This diaspora reality contributes to making Christian identity in the Middle East often a contested one; caught between an 'Arab' Christian identity and an 'Eastern' Christian identity.[74] The jurisdiction of each Church normally corresponds to a definite territory, but emigration of numerous faithful has also given it a personal character.[75] The churches have responded by creating numerous ecclesial structures in the West to help retain the link between the land of origin and these new Middle Eastern Christian spaces. This renewed ecclesiological link overcomes geography in this case, and the Eastern Churches, with regard to their respective Diasporas, behave as though they were independent structures, constituting distinct episcopacies on the same territory.[76] The pastoral and ecclesiology issues confronted by Middle Eastern Christians are those encountered by Eastern Catholic communities from the Carpathian regions of the Hapsburg Empire in north America during the nineteenth century.[77] Middle Eastern Christians who went to South America have often assimilated in the wider Catholic Church adopting the Latin Rite.

We might add that Middle Eastern Christianity is distinctly plural in ecclesial identity; liturgical and linguistic cultures; its orientation towards religion, politics and church-state relations in their respective societies.[78] Paolo Dall'Oglio, an Italian Jesuit who founded the new monastic

---

[73] Christian Cannuyer, "Les diasporas chrétiennes proche-orientales en Occident", in Hervé Legrand and Giuseppe Maria Croce (eds), *L'Œuvre d'Orient: Solidarités anciennes et nouveaux defies*, Paris: Cerf, 2010, pp. 319-344. The politics of Middle Eastern Christian diasporas in emerging and important reality of migration and displacement from the Middle East. Bosmat Yefet, "The Coptic Diaspora and the Status of the Coptic Minority in Egypt", *Journal of Ethnic and Migration Studies*, vol. 43, no. 7, 2017, pp. 1205-1221; Yvonne Haddad and Joshua Donovan, "Good Copt, Bad Copt: Competing Narratives on Coptic Identity in Egypt and the United States", *Studies in World Christianity*, vol. 19, no. 3, 2013, pp. 208-232.

[74] The dynamic of an increasingly global reality faced by Middle Eastern churches due, to emigration and a significant growth in a diaspora community, strongly encourages these ecclesial cultures to redefine their identity in such a way as to make it compatible with an ethnic and cultural pluralisation of its congregation this has been particularly noticeable for the Maronite Church. According to the *Annuario Pontificio* 2012 declared Maronites who relate to the Church number 3,261,797. Latin America has been a significant destination for Middle Eastern Christians, especially those from Lebanon and Syria, with some 700,00 in Argentina; 481,000 in Brazil and 153,000 in Mexico. Paul Tabor, "The Maronite Church in Lebanon: From Nation-building to a Diasporan/Transnational Institution", in Françoise De Bel-Air (ed.), *Migration et politique au moyen-orient*, Damascus: Institut français du Proche-Orient, 2006, pp. 185-201.

[75] Georges Labaki, "La juridiction territorial du patriarche maronite d'antioche: de l'orient à l'occident", Charles Chartouni (ed.), *Christianisme oriental: Kérygme et Histoire*, Paris: Geuthner, 2007, pp. 143-158.

[76] Anthony O'Mahony considers the fate of an earlier migration of a significant number of Eastern Christians from Ottoman lands into Europe in "Between Rome and Constantinople: The Italian-Albanian Church: a study in Eastern Catholic History and Ecclesiology", *International Journal for the Study of the Christian Church*, vol. 8, no. 3, 2008, pp. 232-251.

[77] Constantine Simon, "In Europe and America: The Ruthenians between Catholicism and Orthodoxy", *Orientalia Christiana Periodica*, vol. 59, 1993, pp. 169-210.

[78] Fiona McCallum, "Christian political participation in the Arab world", *Islam and Christian–Muslim Relations*, vol. 23, no. 1, 2012, pp. 3-18; Fiona McCallum, "Religious Institutions and Authoritarian States: Church-State Relations in the Middle East", *Third World Quarterly*, vol. 33, no. 1, 2012, pp. 109-124.

community of Dayr Mar Musa al-Habashi (St. Moses the Ethiopian) in Syria which is dedicated to ecumenism and relations between Christian and Muslims, considers this ecclesial plurality as an essential aspect of maintaining a religious and political plurality in the Middle East region today.[79]

The Jesuit theologian, who is from the Coptic Catholic tradition, Fadel Sidarouss, echoed the importance of this observation:

> The roots of Christianity are decidedly Eastern. Consequently, when the West adopted Christianity, it in fact adopted an 'other', something different; this Eastern alterity became constitutive of its Western identity, which enabled it to be more easily open to difference throughout its long history: we may think, for example, of what we have said about reason, but also its dialogue with modernity, admittedly difficult and onerous. There is thus a qualitative difference between the Church of the West and the Churches of the East, in the sense that they have not, throughout the centuries, experienced a different 'other', which has inevitably led them to remain within the domain of an identity without formative contacts with a constitutive alterity; and when they enter into relationship with an other – we think here of Islam – they do so in an apologetic and defensive rather than dialogical manner. Clearly, the Eastern Churches were plural from the time of their origins, and benefited from the support of Graeco-Roman culture for the first seven centuries; but with the arrival of Islam, they withdrew into a 'golden age' which imperceptibly became their 'mythical origin' on which they dwelt without further innovation, thus privileging the "pole of identity.[80]

Today it is a challenging task to undertake Christian theology in the Middle East responding to the numerous religious, political and cultural

---

[79] Paolo Dall'Oglio, "Eglises plurielles pour un Moyen-Orient pluriel", *Mélanges de sciences religieuses*, vol. 68, no. 3, 2011, pp. 31-46. Dall'Oglio is the principal founder of the contemporary monastic community Dayr Mar Musa al-Habashi in Syria, which is dedicated to ecumenism and relations between Christians and Muslims. The monastery, whilst it has its own modern rule, is in an ecclesial expression of the Syrian Catholic Church. The community should be considered as an aspect of monastic revival which has taken place across the region, but also a novel expression of Syriac Christianity, from within the Eastern Catholic tradition based upon the life and eremitical endeavour Charles de Foucauld and the religious ideas of Louis Massignon for Christian relations with Muslims and Islam. Paolo Dall'Oglio, "Massignon and jihad, through De Foucauld, al-Hallaj and Gandhi", in John J. Donahue and Christian W. Troll (eds.), *Faith, Power and Violence*, Rome: Pontificio Istituto Orientale, 1998, pp. 103-114; Paolo Dall'Oglio, "La refondation du monastère syriaque de saint Moïse l'Abyssin à Nebek, Syrie, et la Badaliya massignonienne", in Maurice Borrmans and Françoise Jacquin (eds.), *Badaliya au nom de l'autre (1947-1962) - Louis Massignon*, Paris: Cerf, 2011, pp. 372-374.

[80] Fadel Sidarouss quoted in Thom Sickin, "Théologie orientale ou théologie en orient?", *Proche-Orient Chrétien*, vol. 55, 2005, p. 320.

questions currently engaging the region.[81] Harald Suermann, a German scholar of Middle Eastern Christianity, underlining the close links between Eastern theology and Liturgy writes:

Speaking of John Damascene and Ephrem the Syrian they wrote in order to contemplate the eternal mysteries, and their theology is considered as outside time'. However, studying the hymns of Saint Ephrem leads to the conclusion that he battled against the various heresies of his region. He was aware of the currents of thought of his era and built his theology on that thought. As to John Damascene, his theology is also a dialogue with his times: should Islam be considered a religion or a heresy? What is the place of icons in churches? Should we serve the new masters? In short, "the great Eastern theological texts were written in a precise context, responding to the pressing questions of the time". This dialogue was continued later. Following the Muslim conquest, theologians began to express themselves in Arabic, thus also enabling dialogue between Christian theology and Muslim thought. Later, Muslims gained an awareness of Greek knowledge through Christian intermediaries. With the arrival of Western theologians, those in the East sought to assimilate their theologies. Finally, there was a period characterised by "the pure reception of theology and less by adaptation to the demands of time and place". However, the renewal of the Coptic Church and theological thought in the context of Palestine and Israel are striving once again to respond to the burning questions of our time.[82]

It is therefore clear for Suermann that theology must be closely connected to the questions which concern the Christians in our own time. In this connection, he enumerates a series of problems with which Eastern theology should concern itself today: the exodus of Christians. Many leave their countries for economic and social reasons. Should the Church not speak prophetically, as did the ancient prophets? Alongside renewal, there is also a form of 'conservatism' which marginalizes the churches and renders them passive and of no consequence on the political and social scene.[83] This phenomenon requires reflection on the relationship between Church and society. Many Christian thinkers today urged a new 'political-theology' which takes seriously the re-ordering of religious culture across the region. The

---

[81] Antoine Fleyfel, *La théologie contextuelle arabe, modèle libanais*, Paris: L'Harmattan, 2011.

[82] Harald Suermann quoted in Thom Sickin, "Théologie orientale ou théologie en orient?", *Proche-Orient Chrétien*, vol. 55, 2005, p. 313.

[83] Ibid, pp. 315-316.

former Melkite Archbishop of Beirut, Grégoire Haddad is often cited as an example of this type of engagement especially in arguing for an open laïcite.[84] The crisis in the relationship between religion and politics in the region was taken up by the Special Assembly of Bishops for the Middle East which was held in Rome in October 2010.[85] Mouchir Basile Aoun sees Haddad's emphasis on Liberation as the key idea:

> The word liberation does not figure prominently in the lexicon of Christian communities in today's world. Rather, the key word is survival. This is because Christian faith is seen as inflicting a heavy burden, a requirement for confinement to defending the physical existence of individuals and groups which, in Lebanon and in other countries of the Arab world, continue to depend on the message of Jesus Christ. However, there is a dividing line between liberation and survival which betrays the state of paralysis into which Christian witness delivered within societies existing in the Arab world runs the risk of falling. The theological originality of Grégoire Haddad has been to recentre this witness on the demands of a liberation which modern Arab man desires with all his heart. Since for him liberation remains the best guarantee of survival. In effect, to physically survive without engaging in the liberation of Arab man resembles more of a spiritual death, since true Christian survival in the Arab world belongs more in the register of evangelical boldness. The Christian thus finds himself invited to expend his energies in order to defend the life of others.[86]

A significant challenge for Christianity in the Middle East has been ecclesial division requires a theological and ecclesiological response one which proclaims unity in diversity, according to Antoine Fleyfel, an ecumenical theology concerned to change attitudes.[87] The challenges of diversity are especially creative for an exploration of ecclesiology. Jean Corbon, the well-known Catholic ecumenist, wrote: "The Christian Middle

---

[84] Antoine Fleyfel, *La théologie contextuelle arabe, modèle libanais*, Paris: L'Harmattan, 2011, pp. 147-175.

[85] Samir Khalil Samir, "Le synode des évêques pour le Proche-Orient", *Nouvelle Revue Théologique*, vol. 133, no. 2, 2011, pp. 191-206.

[86] Mouchir Aoun, "Pour une théologie arabe de la liberation: contribution à l'étude de la pensée de Grégoire Haddad", *Proche-Orient Chrétien*, vol. 59, no. 1-2, 2009, pp. 52-53. Liberation has been a key theme in Palestinian Christian thought, Samuel J. Kuruvilla, *Radical Christianity in Palestine and Israel: Liberation and Theology in the Middle East*, London: I.B. Tauris, 2013; Laura Robson, "Palestinian Liberation Theology, Muslim-Christian Relations and the Arab-Israeli Conflict", *Islam and Christian-Muslim Relations*, vol. 21, no. 1, 2010, pp. 39-50; Leonard Marsh, "Palestinian Christian Theology as a New and Contemporary Expression of Eastern Christian Thought", in *Living Stones Yearbook 2012*, London: Melisende, 2012, pp. 106-119.

[87] Antoine Fleyfel, "La centralité de l'œcuménisme pour l'élaboration d'une théologie arabe moderne et contextuelle", *Théologiques*, vol. 2, 2010, pp. 213-238.

East appears as the microcosm of the universal ecumenism: there where the greatest diversity had abounded in division, the grace of Communion in unity has over-abounded".[88]

The following examples demonstrate that difference is now to be seen as enriching rather than dividing. The Balamand Declaration and its rejection of `uniatism' which was considered a major obstacle in relations between Eastern Catholics and Eastern Orthodox. A renewal in the ecclesiological awareness of the Melkite Greek Catholic Church has been central to creating the environment for the Balamand declaration.[89] The ecclesiological notion of a 'return to the Catholic Church' was declared obsolete. Catholic proselytism at the expense of the Orthodox is excluded – replaced by a desire for collaboration in evangelization.[90] Vittorio Peri has remined us that the ecclesiological teaching and canonical praxis od both Catholic and Orthodox Churches expressed this conviction, this however has changed on the whole if the realization that their relation of communion was better described by the theology of Sister Churches rather than by the theology of `returning' to one Mother Church, which each identified exclusively with themselves.[91] Despite the importance of this document in the history of relations between the Catholic and the Orthodox churches the Balamand process has met with a mixed reception across Eastern Catholic and Eastern Orthodox theological communities.[92] While Balamand sought to formulate the road to reconciliation in the best way possible – and put forward a coherent programme for catholicity – the question of the relationship between the entire Church, diocesan Churches and regional Churches (patriarchates) has not been satisfactorily solved. One side clings to autocephaly, the other papal primacy – convincing neither their dialogue partner nor in fact themselves – aware that a better response is needed and possible. This must be achieved not in opposition but in collaboration.[93]

---

[88] Jean Corbon, "Ecumenism in the Middle East", in Habib Badr (ed.), *Christianity: A History in the Middle East*, Beirut: Middle East Council of Churches, 2005, p. 882.

[89] Grégorios III Laham, "The Ecumenical Commitment of the Melkite Greek Catholic Church", *The Downside Review*, vol. 135, no. 1, 2017, pp. 3-20. Melkite ecumenical outreach has by necessity been accompanied by an ecclesial renewal in the Eastern Orthodox Church of Antioch Nicolas Mrad, "The Witness of the Church in a Pluralistic World: Theological Renaissance in the Church of Antioch", in Elizabeth Theokritoff and Mary Cunningham (eds.), *The Cambridge Companion to Orthodox Christian Theology*, Cambridge: Cambridge University Press, 2008, pp. 246-260.

[90] Étienne Fouilloux, "De l'unionisme à l'oecumenisme", in *Comité mixte catholique-orthodoxe en France, Catholiques et orthodoxes. Les enjeux de l'uniatisme. Dans le sillage de Balamand*, Paris: Cerf, 2004, pp. 201-220.

[91] Vittorio Peri, "Uniatism and its origins", *Journal of Eastern Christian Studies*, vol. 49, no. 1-2, 1997, pp. 23-46.

[92] Ronald G. Roberson, "Catholic Reactions to the Balamand Document", *Eastern Churches Journal*, vol. 4, no. 1, 1997, pp. 54-73. See also Robert Taft, "The Problem of 'Uniatism' and the 'Healing of Memories': Anamnesis, not Amnesia", *Logos*, vol. 41-42, 2000-2001, pp. 155-196.

[93] Hervé Legrand, "Unité et diversité de l'Orient chrétien contemporain: un regard de théologien", in

A further example is the Melkite project for union with the Eastern Orthodox Church which demonstrates the scale of the change of attitude. Unique in the region, it nevertheless demonstrates an increasing awareness by the Churches of the Middle East of sharing in the destiny of the Arab Muslim world.[94] Since the Second Vatican Council, relations between the two Melkite Churches of Antioch have become more and more fraternal, giving rise to a deeper reflection about the reunification of the Antiochian Patriarchate. The project of ecclesial communion, presented in a statement following the meeting of the Melkite Catholic Synod of July 1996, is the fruit of a series of efforts undertaken to bring these two Melkite branches of the Antiochian Patriarchate closer and was a very bold undertaking which, however, Rome and Constantinople called for prudence uncertain how a local agreement might impact upon their relations in a wider setting.[95]

The Christological agreements with between the Catholic Church and the Oriental Orthodox churches have developed with much success. The origins of this are not just with the meeting of Paul VI with heads of the Oriental Orthodox churches after the Second Vatican Council but had been prepared by with the encyclical 'Sempiternus Rex' of Pius XII which declared that the so-called but wrongly described, 'monophysitism' of the non-Chalcedonian Christians was purely verbal.[96] Frans Bouwen, a Catholic member of the Official Dialogue Commission between the Oriental Orthodox and Catholic Church has written: "One of the most significant events in the history of the present-day ecumenical movement and one of the richest promises for the future is, beyond any doubt, the Christological consensus that has emerged, in the course of the last decades, between the churches that recognized the Council of Chalcedon and those that did not, since it was held in the year 451".[97]

The third example is the agreement for Eucharistic hospitality between the Chaldean Church and the Assyrian Church with the acceptance of the anaphora of Mar and Addai is also remarkable.[98] Relations between

---

Hervé Legrand and Giuseppe Maria Croce (eds.), *L'Œuvre d'Orient: Solidarités anciennes et nouveaux défies*, Paris: Cerf, 2010, pp. 65-87.

[94] Gaby Hachen and George Gallaro, "Between Antioch and Rome: Melkite Hierarchs on Papal Primacy and Ecumenism", *Studi Sull'Orient Cristiano*, vol. 5, no. 2, 2001, pp. 119-153.

[95] Gaby Hachen, "Un project de communion ecclésiale dans le patriarcat d'Antioche entre les Eglises grec-orthodoxe et melkite-catholique", *Irénikon*, vol. 72, 1999, pp. 453-478.

[96] See also Antonio Olmi, *Il consenso cristologica tra la chiese calcedonesi e non calcedonesi (1964-1996)*, Rome: Pontificia Univ. Gregoriana, 2003, ('Il consenso cristologico tra le chiese di tradizione siríaca', pp. 601-631), ('Il consenso cristologico tra la chiesa cattolica e la chiesa assira d'oriente', pp. 633-651).

[97] Frans Bouwen, "Consensus contemporains en christologie", *Proche-Orient Chrétien*, vol. 49, 1999, pp. 323-336.

[98] Robert Taft, "Mass Without the Consecration? The Historic Agreement on the Eucharist between the Catholic Church and the Assyrian Church of the East Promulgated 26 October 2001", *Worship*, vol. 77,

Protestant Christianity and the Eastern churches in the Middle East have not been without difficulties; especially as in recent times evangelical groups have been very successful in the East.[99] The question of relations between protestant missions and Middle Eastern Christians became an urgent question especially in Iraq in the aftermath of the end of Baathist regime after 2003.

Middle Eastern/Eastern Christian theology, political thought and ecclesiological culture is rich, complex and creative; however, it is clear that Christianity in the Middle East faces great challenges today. Mouchir Aoun, has helpfully articulated the challenge for Christian religious thought in the Middle East:

> Today, the term Eastern or Middle Eastern theology comprises a number of concepts. [...] it designates, above all, a triple task, the classic one of reviving the Patristic tradition dear to those in the East, one with a modern resonance, the inculturation of the Christ event, and finally, one of contextual significance, the updating of the kerygmatic content.[100]

To deepen our contextual understanding for theological reflection in the Middle East today, the French Jesuit and long-term resident of Lebanon, Thom Sicking, has insisted that theology in the East must confront a number of challenges:

1. A great diversity of Churches with differences and divergences, each having its own history and identity.

2. An environment marked by Islam and by Judaism and Hebrew culture in Israel.

3. The Churches of the region most often find themselves in a minority position: a situation which influences their behaviour and reflection both in their relations between themselves and in those which they have with non-Christian communities.

4. Close ties with the West and with Western Christianity in particular, considered both as an asset and a threat.

5. Significant emigration of their faithful, resulting in local Churches (the patriarchate of Antioch, Alexandria, or Jerusalem) becoming 'universal' Churches.

2003, pp. 482-509.

[99] Michael Marten, "Anglican and Presbyterian Presence and Theology in the Holy Land", *International Journal for the Study of the Christian Church*, vol. 5, 2005, pp. 182-199.

[100] Heidi Hirvonen, *Christian-Muslim Dialogue: Perspectives of Four Lebanese Thinkers*, Leiden: Brill 2013.

Recently we have witnessed the emergence of distinct theological thought among Middle Eastern Christians, for example Palestinian Liberation Theology;[101] the revival of the eremitical tradition in the Maronite Church;[102] monastic renewal in Syria[103] and Egypt.[104] The Latin Patriarch of Jerusalem, Michel Sabbah developed a unique exegetical language for reading the Bible in the Holy Land.[105]

We should also note that Eastern Christianity, though the Church of the East, opened up an engagement with Muslims which still shapes the 'canon' of Catholic thought Islam.[106] The singular figure of Timothy I, of the Church of the East in his exploration of encounter with Islam is increasingly seen as archetype in world Christianity.[107] At the Asian Synod some years ago which discussed the important relations between Christians and Muslims, the Chaldean Bishop of Aleppo, Syria and leading Eastern Catholic theologian, Antoine Audo set out his vision: "To survive and develop as living churches in the Arab and Muslim world of the Middle East, Christian Arabs or Asians need a spiritual vision of their relation with Islam, seeing themselves as sent by Christ to be witnesses of love", and that evangelization in those lands requires Christians to live "within Islam, that is, to form an integral part of society, of the Arab and Muslim culture without complexes, but at the same

---

[101] Harald Suermann, "Palestinian Contextual Theology", *Al-Liqa*, vol. 5, 1995, pp. 7-26; Samuel J. Kuruvilla, "Theologies of Liberation in Latin America and Palestine-Israel in Comparative Perspective: Contextual Differences and Practical Similarities", *Holy Land Studies: A Multidisciplinary Journal*, vol. 9, no. 1, 2010, pp. 51-69.

[102] Guita Hourani and Antoine B. Habachi, "The Eremitical Tradition in the Maronite Church", in Anthony O'Mahony (ed.), *Christianity in the Middle East: Studies in Modern History, Theology and Politics*, London: Melisende, 2010, pp. 500-538.

[103] Anna Poujeau, "Renouveau monastique et historiographie chrétienne en Syrie", *Archives de sciences sociales des religions*, vol. 151, 2010, pp. 129-147; Anna Poujeau, "A National Monasticism? Monastic Politics of the Syriac Orthodox Church in Syria", in Enzo Pace, Luigi Berzano and Giuseppe Giordan (eds.), *Sociology and Monasticism. Annual Review of the Sociology of Religion,* Leiden: Brill, 2014, pp, 169–184; Anna Poujeau, "Monasteries, Politics, and Social Memory: The Revival of the Greek Orthodox Church in Syria during the Twentieth Century", in Chris Hann and Hermann Goltz (eds.), *Eastern Christians in Anthropological Perspective*, California: University of California Press, 2010, pp. 171-192.

[104] Anthony O'Mahony, "Tradition at the heart of Renewal: the Coptic Orthodox Church and monasticism in Modern Egypt", *International Journal for the Study of the Christian Church*, vol. 7, no. 3, 2007, pp. 164-178.

[105] Leonard Marsh, "The Theological Thought of Michel Sabbah in the Context of the Challenges to the Christian Presence in the Holy Land", in O'Mahony and Flannery (eds.), *The Catholic Church in the Contemporary Middle East*, pp. 253-262. Apart from the important pastoral letters of the Patriarch, Michel Sabbah, see his "Reading the Bible Today in the Land of the Bible" (November 1993) which is an important text in the context of scripture articulated in support of political theologies of exclusive claim to the land. See Alain Marchadour and David Neuhaus, *The Land, the Bible and History*, New York: Fordham University Press, 2007.

[106] Sidney H. Griffith, "Arabic Christian Relations with Islam: Retrieving from History, Expanding the Canon", in O'Mahony and Flannery (eds.), *The Catholic Church in the Contemporary Middle East*, pp. 263-290.

[107] Frederick W. Norris, "Timothy I of Baghdad, Catholicos of the East Syrian Church, 780-823: Still a Valuable Model", *International Bulletin of Missionary Research*, vol. 30, no. 3, 2006, pp. 133-136.

time to be witnesses of the evangelical liberty in ways that go beyond this culture, seeking to read the language of the Qu'ran as a language of human relations".[108]

The role of the patriarch as a representative of the Christian church in the public sphere in the Middle East has grown in significance, especially in the context of religious leadership in the Middle East. The patriarch has often acted as an intermediary between the Christian community and the state; however, this role has not been universally welcomed among Christians.[109] That said between 2011 and early 2013 patriarchal leadership in the Middle East has been renewed with the head of the Maronite Church Patriarch Boutros Raï; Tawadros II of the Coptic Orthodox Church; Orthodox Patriarch of Antioch, John X; and Patriarch Louis Sako I Raphael of the Chaldean Church being newly elected.[110]

There are other shared characteristics among the Christians in the Middle East: anxieties in the face of the re-awakening of a militant Islamism; a deep awareness that in Islam the marker is between Muslim and non-Muslim not between different types of Christian; growing marginalization of erratic identities in modern states; especially in the context were religious identity reinforces nationalist ideology, for example in Turkey between Sunni Islam and Turkish nationalism;[111] Shiite Islam and Iranian nationalism;[112] Judaism and Israeli identity; growing exodus to destinations outside of the region. For example, it is now estimated up some 600,000 Iraqi Christians have left since 2003.[113]

---

[108] Declaration at the Asian Synod, February 2003, quoted in Anthony O'Mahony, "The Chaldean Catholic Church: The Politics of Church-State Relations in Modern Iraq", *The Heythrop Journal*, vol. XLV, 2004, p. 450. See also the studies of Antoine Audo as background to the encounter between Eastern Christian thought and Catholic *ressourcement* in the Middle East today: "Eastern Christian Identity: A Catholic Perspective", in O'Mahony and Flannery (eds), *The Catholic Church in the Contemporary Middle East*, pp. 19-38.

[109] Fiona McCallum, Christian Religious Leadership in the Middle East: The Political Role of the Patriarch London: Mellon, 2010; Fiona McCallum, "The Political Role of the Patriarch in the Contemporary Middle East", Middle Eastern Studies, vol. 43, no. 6, 2007, pp. 923-940; Fiona McCallum, "Walking the Tightrope: Patriarchal Politics in Lebanon", in Franck Mermier and Sabrina Mervin (eds.), Leaders et partisans au Liban, Paris: Karthala, 2012, pp. 315-337.

[110] Elizabeth Monier, "The Chaldean Patriarch and the Discourse of 'Inclusive Citizenship': Restructuring the Political Representation of Christians in Iraq since 2003", *Religion, State & Society*, vol. 48, no. 5, 2020, pp. 361-377.

[111] Elizabeth H. Prodromou, "Turkey between Secularism and Fundamentalism? The 'Muslimhood Model' and the Greek Orthodox Minority", *The Review of Faith & International Affairs*, vol. 3, no. 1, 2005, pp. 11-22.

[112] Anthony O'Mahony, "The Christian Churches, Shi'a Islam and Muslim-Christian Relations in Modern Iran", in Anthony O'Mahony and Emma Loosely (eds.), *Christian Responses to Islam*, Manchester: Manchester University Press, 2008, pp. 175-188.

[113] Herman Teule, "La situation des chrétiens d'Irak à la lumière des résolutions du Synode romain pour le Moyen-Orient", *Mélanges de Science Religieuse*, vo. 68, no. 3, 2011, pp. 47-60.

On the other hand, one can point to the significant renewal of the Coptic church despite many challenging societal, political and religious challenges;[114] the increasing participation of the laity; new ecumenical perspectives; monastic renewal; and fervent piety. For Christians in the East, the twentieth century, which began with the Armenian genocide, ended with the rapid losses due to the migrations by Christians from the East to the West. The prophets of the 'death' of the Christians of the East had no lack of arguments to condemn the millions of Eastern faithful who remained behind to an end which was nigh. Paul Rowe has however reminded us that, the 'widespread concern today that Christians are in declining numbers in the Middle East easily falls prey to the enervating assertion that they are victims of persecution or mere relics of a fading past and runs the risk of once again robbing Christians of agency as powerful actors in their own societies".[115]

Catherine Jaoun-Mayeur reflects: "The meaning of the presence of native Christians in the Middle East and their question of their remaining or not raises that of a real citizenship (*muwatana*), based in a state under the rule of law, still wishful thinking in the Middle East: an identity which would not, for all that, reject communities and confessions - which would lead to a further weakening of the Christians -, but would refuse to employ protected (*dhimmi*) status under the umbrella of a protector state - whether or not such a status might appear favourable. Vital for the Christian communities of the region, this question is also one for the Muslims of the region, harshly confronted by events with the need for an *aggiornamento*. A state under the rule of law (or civil state: *dawla madaniyya*) or sectarian conflict: pluralism or forced homogenisation: these are challenges common to all, and on which depend the fate of the Christians of the East".[116]

The Catholic Patriarchs of the East have issued a series of important letters on the religious, political, economic and cultural situation and challenges of the region. In the third part of the letter, "Together for an egalitarian society", written in 1992, they state: "No one can remove religion from public life or limit it to the liturgies and devotions; because religion is dogma and life that has to do with the whole of human existence, private and public, individual and social ... To link citizenship to religious values is not an evil. On the contrary, religious values give a soul to citizenship. But in this case it is necessary that religion should orient the person totally to

---

[114] Fiona McCallum, "Desert Roots and Global Branches: The Journey of the Coptic Orthodox Church", *Bulletin of the Royal Institute for Inter-Faith Studies*, vol. 7, 2005, pp. 69-97.

[115] Paul Rowe, "The Middle East Christian as Agent", *International Journal of Middle Eastern* Studies, vol. 42, no. 3, 2010, p. 473.

[116] Catherine Mayeur-Jaouen, "Les chrétiens au Moyen-Orient à l'heure de Daesh", *Annuaire Français des Relations Internationals*, vol. XVII, 2016, p. 695.

God, to the perfect respect of the creature of God and of every religious conviction, especially when we have to do with the religion of a minority in a given society or nation. The laws of the state must guarantee the rights of the minority religion with the same rigour as it guarantees those of the majority or of the religion of the State".[117]

Antoine Audo made an explicit connection between the conclusion of the final declaration of the Synod for the Middle East (September 2012), Benedict XVI's papal visit to Lebanon and the so-called Arab Spring. Audo quotes the declaration, summing up the profound desire for a reordering and reorientation of religious thought towards a new understanding of the political in the context of religious freedom as a key theme to understanding conversion and mission: "Religious tolerance exists in a number of countries, but it does not have much effect since it remains limited in its field of action. There is a need to move beyond tolerance to religious freedom. Taking this step does not open the door to relativism, as some would maintain. It does not compromise belief, but rather calls for a reconsideration of the relationship between man, religion and God. It is not an attack on the 'foundational truths' of belief, since, despite human and religious divergences, a ray of truth shines on all men and women. We know very well that truth, apart from God, does not exist as an autonomous reality. If it did, it would be an idol. The truth cannot unfold except in an otherness open to God, who wishes to reveal his own otherness in and through my human brothers and sisters. Hence it is not fitting to state in an exclusive way: 'I possess the truth'. The truth is not possessed by anyone; it is always a gift which calls us to undertake a journey of ever closer assimilation to truth. Truth can only be known and experienced in freedom; for this reason we cannot impose truth on others; truth is disclosed only in an encounter of love". [118]

To sum up, Christianity originated in the Middle East. The Christian presence there today bears witness to the global Church of the unity of its origins and the diversity of its expression. Christians also help maintain and sustain the diversity in the Middle East. However, there has been large-scale flight from the Middle East, Christianity in the Middle East has a witness beyond itself: let us hope that the churches of East and West rise rapidly rise to this challenge for the key to the future of this important region may lie with the few.

---

[117] Quoted in Christian Troll, "Changing Catholic Views on Islam", in Jacques Waardenburg (ed.), *Islam and Christianity: Mutual Perceptions Since the Mid–Twentieth Century*, Leuven: Peeters, 1998, pp. 19–77.

[118] Antoine Audo, "The Synod of Bishops: The Catholic Church in the Middle East"; Antoine Audo, "Between Christians and Muslims a Pathway of Communion", *Oasis*, vol. 13, 2011, Available at: https://www.oasiscenter.eu/en/middle-east-political-revolts-confessional-tensions.

Bibliography

Agenzia Fides, "The alarm of Chaldean Patriarch Sako: world crisis and war in Ukraine aggravate the "alarming" exodus of Christians from the Middle East", 23 August 2022. Available at: http://www.fides.org/en/news/72688.

Anagnostopoulos, Nikodemos, *Orthodoxy and Islam: Theology and Muslim-Christian Relations in Modern Greece and Turkey*, London: Routledge, 2017.

Anderson, Kjartan, "Pilgrims, Property and Polities: The Russian Orthodox Church in Jerusalem", in Anthony O'Mahony (ed.), *Eastern Christianity: Studies in Modern History, Religion and Politics*, London: Melisende, 2004, pp. 388-430.

Aoun, Mouchir, "Pour une théologie arabe de la liberation: contribution à l'étude de la pensée de Grégoire Haddad", *Proche-Orient Chrétien*, vol. 59, no. 1-2, 2009, pp. 52-76.

Ashdown, Andrew, "Eastern Christian Mystical Traditions and the Development of Ecumenical and Interreligious Dialogue: Louis Massignon, Olivier Clement, Georges Khodr and Paolo Dall'Oglio, with a Protestant Contribution", in *Living Stones Yearbook 2020*, London: Melisende, 2020, pp. 86-118.

Ashdown, Andrew, *Christian–Muslim Relations in Syria: Historic and Contemporary Religious Dynamics in a Changing Context,* London: Routledge, 2020.

Asia News, "Pope and Ecumenical Patriarch: May the martyrdom of the Middle East nourish the journey of Christian unity", 30 November 2014. Available at: https://www.asia news.it/news-en/Pope-and-Ecumenical-Patriarch:-May-the-martyrdom-of-the-Middle-East-nourish-the-journey-of-Christian-unity-32836.html.

Audo, Antoine, "Between Christians and Muslims a Pathway of Communion, Oasis, vol. 13, 2011, Available at: https://www.oasiscenter.eu/en/middle-east-political-revolts-confessional-tensions.

Audo, Antoine, "Christianity in the Middle East: Current Challenges and Opportunities for the Future, through the Experience of Syria", in *Living Stones Yearbook 2022*, London: Melisende, 2022, pp. 136-141.

Audo, Antoine, "Eastern Christian Identity: A Catholic Perspective", in Anthony O'Mahony and John Flannery (eds.), *The Catholic Church in the Contemporary Middle East*, London: Melisende, 2010, pp. 19-38.

Audo, Antoine, "Reflections on the Apostolic Exhortation of Benedict XVI and the Papal Visit to Lebanon", in Dietmar Winkler (ed.), *Towards a Culture of Co-Existence in Pluralistic Societies: The Middle East and India*, Piscataway, NJ: Gorgias Press, 2021, pp. 135-148.

Audo, Antoine, "The Church in the Middle East. The Future of Christians in the Region", in Harald Suermann and Michael Altripp (eds.), *Orientalisches Christentum. Perspektiven aus der Vergangenheit für die Zukunft*, Leiden: Brill/Schöningh, 2021, pp. 52–65.

Audo, Antoine, "The Current situation of Christianity in the Middle East, especially Syria, after the Synod of the Middle East's Final Declaration (September 2012) and the Papal Visit to Lebanon", in *Living Stones Yearbook 2012*, London: Melisende, 2012, pp. 1-17.

Audo, Antoine, "The Synod of Bishops: The Catholic Church in the Middle East", *One in Christ: A Catholic Ecumenical Review*, vol. 44, no. 2, 2010, pp. 196–200.

Austen, Elie, "L'émigration massive des chrétiens d'Orient", *Etudes*, vol. 373, no. 1-2, 1990, pp. 101-106.

Azeez, Dahlia Khay, "The Schism of the Eastern Syriac Church (the 'Nestorian Church') in the Twentieth Century", *Orientalia Christiana Periodica*, vol. 87, no. 2, 2021, pp. 453-493.

Balanche, Fabrice, "Un scénario à l'irakienne pour les chrétiens de Syrie", in Marie-Hélène Robert and Michel Younès (eds.), *La vocation des chrétiens d'Orient. Défis actuels et enjeux d'avenir dans leurs rapports à l'islam*, Paris: Karthala, 2015, pp. 27-44.

Baroudi, Sami E. and Tabar, Paul, "Spiritual Authority versus Secular Authority: Relations between the Maronite Church and the State in Postwar Lebanon: 1990-2005", *Middle East*

Critique, vol. 18, no. 3, 2009, pp. 195-230.

Bouwen, Frans, "Consensus contemporains en christologie", *Proche-Orient Chrétien*, vol. 49, 1999, pp. 323-336.

Bouwen, Frans, "For the future of Christian presence in the Middle East", *One in Christ: A Catholic Ecumenical Review*, vol. 50, no. 2, 2016, pp. 173-186.

Bouwen, Frans, "The Churches in the Middle East", in Lawrence S. Cunningham (ed.), *Ecumenism. Present Realities and Future Prospects*, Indiana: University of Notre Dame Press, 1998, pp. 25-36.

Bouwen, Frans, "The Synod for the Middle East: First results and Future Possibilities", in *Living Stones Yearbook 2012*, London: Melisende, 2012, pp. 18-37.

Bouwen, Frans, "Unity and Christian Presence in the Middle East", in Anthony O'Mahony and John Flannery (eds.), *The Catholic Church in the Contemporary Middle East: Studies for The Synod of the Middle East*, London: Melisende, 2010, pp. 87-105.

Brock, Sebastian, "The Syriac Orient: a third "lung" for the church?", *Orientalia Christiana Periodica*, vol. 71, no. 1, 2005, pp. 5-20.

Cannuyer, Christian, "Les diasporas chrétiennes proche-orientales en Occident", in Hervé Legrand and Giuseppe Maria Croce (eds.), *L'Œuvre d'Orient: Solidarités anciennes et nouveaux défies*, Paris: Cerf, 2010, pp. 319-344.

Chatelard, Géraldine, "Les chrétiens en Jordanie, dynamiques identitaires et gestion du pluralisme", *Les Cahiers de l'Orient*, vol. 93, no. 1, 2009, pp. 41-56.

Chatelard, Géraldine, "The Constitution of Christian Communal Boundaries and Spheres in Jordan", *Journal of Church and State*, vol. 52, no. 3, 2010, pp. 476–502.

Chatelard, Géraldine, *Briser la mosaïque. Les tribus chrétiennes de Madaba, Jordanie (xix-xx siècle)*, Paris: CNRS-Éditions, 2004.

Corbon, Jean, "Ecumenism in the Middle East", in Habib Badr (ed.), *Christianity: A History in the Middle East*, Beirut: Middle East Council of Churches, 2005, pp. 871-883.

Costet-Tardieu, Francine, *Les minorités chrétiennes dans la construction de l'Égypte modern 1922-1952*, Paris: Karthala, 2016.

Dall'Oglio, Paolo, "Eglises plurielles pour un Moyen-Orient pluriel", *Mélanges de Sciences Religieuses*, vol. 68, no. 3, 2011, pp. 31-46.

Dall'Oglio, Paolo, "La refondation du monastère syriaque de saint Moïse l'Abyssin à Nebek, Syrie, et la Badaliya massignonienne", in Maurice Borrmans and Françoise Jacquin (eds.), *Badaliya au nom de l'autre (1947-1962) - Louis Massignon*, Paris: Cerf, 2011, pp. 372-374.

Dall'Oglio, Paolo, "Massignon and jihad, through De Foucauld, al-Hallaj and Gandhi", in John J. Donahue and Christian W. Troll (eds.), *Faith, Power and Violence*, Rome: Pontificio Istituto Orientale, 1998, pp. 103-114.

Danış, Didem, "A Faith That Binds: Iraqi Christian Women on the Domestic Service Ladder of Istanbul", *Journal of Ethnic and Migration Studies*, vol. 33, no. 4, 2007, pp. 601-615.

Danış, Didem, "Attendre au Purgatoire: les réseaux religieux de migrants chrétiens d'Irak en transit à Istanbul", *Revue Européenne des Migrations Internationales*, vol. 22, no. 3, 2006, pp. 109-134.

Daughrity, Dyron B., "Christianity Is Moving from North to South – So What About the East?", *International Bulletin of Missionary Research*, vol. 35, no. 1, 2011, pp. 18-22.

Dimanopoulou-Cohen, Pandora, *Rendez à César ce qui est à César et à Dieu ce qui est à Dieu?: le rapprochement des Églises anglicanes avec l'Église orthodoxe grecque, 1903-1930*, Paris: Cerf, 2016.

Ellis, Kail (ed), *Secular Nationalism and Citizenship in Muslim Countries: Arab Christians in the Levant*, Basingstoke: Palgrave, 2018.

Fargues, Philippe, "The Arab Christians of the Middle East: A Demographic Perspective", in Andrea Acini (ed.), *Christian Communities in the Arab Middle East: The Challenge of the Future*, Oxford: Clarendon Press, 1998, pp. 48-66.

Fleyfel, Antoine, "La centralité de l'œcuménisme pour l'élaboration d'une théologie arabe moderne et contextuelle", *Théologiques*, vol. 2, 2010, pp. 213-238.

Fleyfel, Antoine, *La théologie contextuelle arabe, modèle libanais*, Paris: L'Harmattan, 2011.

Fouilloux, Étienne, "De l'unionisme à l'oecumenisme", in *Comité mixte catholique-orthodoxe en*

France, Catholiques et orthodoxes. Les enjeux de l'uniatisme. Dans le sillage de Balamand, Paris: Cerf, 2004, pp. 201-220.

Gaunt, David, Atto, Naures & Barthoma, Soner O. (eds.), *LET THEM NOT RETURN: Sayfo – The Genocide Against the Assyrian, Syriac, and Chaldean Christians in the Ottoman Empire*, Oxford: Berghahn, 2017.

Georges, Nael, "La Liberté Religieuse Dans Les États de Culture Islamique", *Diplomatie*, no. 75, 2015, 44-47.

Georges, Nael, "Les chrétiens dans le monde arabe et la question de l'apostasie en islam", *Maghreb – Machrek*, vol. 3. no. 209, 2011, pp. 109-119.

Georges, Nael, "Minorités et liberté religieuse dans les Constitutions des États de l'Orient arabe", *Égypte/Monde Arabe*, vol. 1. no. 10, 2013, pp. 287-305.

Girling, Kristian, "Displaced Populations", in Kenneth R. Ross, Mariz Tadros, and Todd M. Johnson (eds.), *Christianity in North Africa and West Asia*, Edinburgh: Edinburgh University Press, 2018, pp. 427-438.

Girling, Kristian, "Engaging 'the Martyred Church' - The Chaldean Catholic Church, Assyrian Church of the East and the Holy See in Ecumenical Dialogue 1994-2012 and the Influence of the Second Vatican Council", in *Living Stones Yearbook 2012*, London: Melisende, 2012, pp. 38-64.

Girling, Kristian, "Patriarch Louis Raphael I Sako and Ecumenical Engagements between the Church of the East and the Chaldean Catholic Church", *One in Christ*, vol. 50, 2016, pp. 100-121.

Girling, Kristian, "To Live within Islam: The Chaldean Catholic Church in modern Iraq, 1958–2003", *Studies in Church History*, vol. 51, 2015, pp. 366-384.

Girling, Kristian, *The Chaldean Catholic Church: Modern History, Ecclesiology and Church-State Relations*, London: Routledge, 2017.

Griffith, Sidney H., "Arabic Christian Relations with Islam: Retrieving from History, Expanding the Canon", in Anthony O'Mahony and John Flannery (eds.), *The Catholic Church in the Contemporary Middle East: Studies for the Synod for the Middle East*, London: Melisende, 2010, pp. 263-290.

Griffith, Sidney H., *The Church in the Shadow of the Mosque: Christians and Muslims in the World of Islam*, New Jersey: Princeton University Press, 2008.

Guirgis, Laure, *Les coptes d'Égypte. Violences communautaires et transformations politiques (2005-2012)*, Paris: Karthala, 2012.

Hachen, Gaby and Gallaro, George, "Between Antioch and Rome: Melkite Hierarchs on Papal Primacy and Ecumenism", *Studi Sull'Orient Cristiano*, vol. 5, no. 2, 2001, pp. 119-153.

Hachen, Gaby, "Un project de communion ecclésiale dans le patriarcat d'Antioche entre les Eglises grec-orthodoxe et melkite-catholique", *Irénikon*, vol. 72, 1999, pp. 453-478.

Haddad, Yvonne and Donovan, Joshua, "Good Copt, Bad Copt: Competing Narratives on Coptic Identity in Egypt and the United States", *Studies in World Christianity*, vol. 19, no. 3, 2013, pp. 208-232.

Hamid, Ahmad Fauzi Abdul, "Sociopolitical Developments in West Asia and Their Impact on Christian Minorities in the Region", in Felix Wilfred (ed.), *The Oxford Handbook of Christianity in Asia*, New York: Oxford University Press, 2014, pp. 231–256.

Heyberger, Bernard and Girard, Aurélien, "Chrétiens Au Proche-Orient", *Archives De Sciences Sociales Des Religions*, vol. 171, no. 3, 2015, pp. 11-35.

Heyberger, Bernard and Vergeron, Nathalie, "Les Minorités Chrétiennes d'Orient Au Cœur Des Tensions Liées à La Question Nationale", *Diplomatie*, no. 93, 2018, pp. 58–61.

Heyberger, Bernard, "La France et la protection des chrétiens maronites. Généalogie d'une representation", *Relations Internationales*, vol. 173, no. 1, 2018, pp. 13-30.

Heyberger, Bernard, "Le christianisme oriental à l'époque ottomane: du postcolonial au global (1960-2020)", *Annales. Histoire, Sciences Sociales*, vol. 76, no. 2, 2021, pp. 301-337.

Heyberger, Bernard, "Migration of the Middle Eastern Christian and European Protection: A Long History", in Andreas Schmoller (ed.), *Middle Eastern Christians and Europe Historical*

Legacies and Present Challenges, Vienna: Lit Verlag, 2018, pp. 23-42.

Heyberger, Bernard, *Les chrétiens au Proche-Orient. De la compassion à la compréhension*, Paris: Payot, 2013.

Hirvonen, Heidi, *Christian-Muslim Dialogue: Perspectives of Four Lebanese Thinkers*, Leiden: Brill 2013.

Hourani, Guita and Habachi, Antoine B., "The eremitical tradition in the Maronite Church", in Anthony O'Mahony (ed.), *Christianity in the Middle East: Studies in Modern History, Theology and Politics*, London: Melisende, 2010, pp. 500-538.

Hugh-Dovonan, Stefanie, "Olivier Clement: A Reflection on the 'Antiochian Paradigm' of Relations between Eastern Catholics and Eastern Orthodox in the Middle East for Today's Europe", in Jaroslav Z. Skira, Peter De Mey and Herman Teule (eds.), *The Catholic Church and its Orthodox Sister Churches Twenty-Five Years after Balamand*, Leuven: Peeters, 2022, pp. 241-260.

Jenkins, Philip, *God's Continent: Christianity, Islam and Europe's Religious Crisis*, Oxford: Oxford University Press, 2007.

Jenkins, Philip, *The New Faces of Christianity: Believing the Bible in the Global South*, Oxford: Oxford University Press, 2006.

Jenkins, Philip, *The Next Christendom: The Coming of Global Christianity*, Oxford: Oxford University Press, 2002.

Johnson, Todd M. and Zurlo, Gina A., "Ongoing Exodus: Tracking the Emigration of Christians from the Middle East", *Harvard Journal of Middle Eastern Politics and Politics*, vol. 3, 2013-2014, pp. 39-45.

Kalkandjieva, Daniel, *The Russian Orthodox Church, 1917-1948: From Decline to Resurrection*, London: Routledge, 2015.

Kattan, Victor, "The Special Role of the Hashemite Kingdom of Jordan in the Muslim Holy Shrines in Jerusalem", *Arab Law Quarterly*, vol. 35, 2021, pp. 503-548.

Kenworthy, Scott. M., "Beyond Schism: restoring Eastern Orthodoxy to the History of Christianity", *Reviews in Religion and Theology*, vol. 15, no. 2, 2008, pp. 171-178.

Kévorkian, Raymond, *The Armenian Genocide: A Complete History*, London: Taurus, 2011.

Kim, Sebastian and Kim, Kirsteen, *Christianity as a World Religion*, London: Bloomsbury, 2016.

Kuruvilla, Samuel J., "Theologies of Liberation in Latin America and Palestine-Israel in Comparative Perspective: Contextual Differences and Practical Similarities", *Holy Land Studies: A Multidisciplinary Journal*, vol. 9, 2010, pp. 51-69.

Kuruvilla, Samuel J., *Radical Christianity in Palestine and Israel: Liberation and Theology in the Middle East*, London: I.B. Tauris, 2013.

Labaki, Boutros, "Les chrétiens du Liban (1943-2008). Prépondérance, marginalisation et renouveau", *Confluences Mediterranée*, vol. 66, 2008, pp. 99-116.

Labaki, Boutros, "The Christian communities and the Economic and Social situation in Lebanon", in Andrea Pacini (ed.), *Christian Communities in the Arab Middle East: the Challenge of the Future*, Oxford: Clarendon Press, 1998, pp. 222-258.

Laham, Grégorios III, "The Ecumenical Commitment of the Melkite Greek Catholic Church", *The Downside Review*, vol. 135, no. 1, 2017, pp. 3-20.

Legrand, Hervé, "Unité et diversité de l'Orient chrétien contemporain: un regard de théologien", in Hervé Legrand and Giuseppe Maria Croce (eds.), *L'Œuvre d'Orient: Solidarités anciennes et nouveaux defies*, Paris: Cerf, 2010, pp. 65-87.

Leustean, Lucian N. (ed.), *Eastern Christianity and Politics in the Twenty-First Century*, London: Routledge, 2014.

Leustean, Lucian N. (ed.), *Eastern Christianity and the Cold War, 1945-91*, London: Routledge, 2010.

Lia, Brynjar and Aarseth, Mathilde Becker, "Crusader Hirelings or Loyal Subjects? Evolving Jihadist Perspectives on Christian Minorities in the Middle East", *Islam and Christian–Muslim Relations*, vol. 33, no. 3, 2022, pp. 255-280.

Maggiolini, Paolo, "Christian Churches and Arab Christians in the Hashemite Kingdom of Jordan", *Archives de Sciences Sociales des Religions*, vol. 171, 2015, pp. 37-58.

Maïla, Joseph, "De la question d'Orient à le récente géopolitique des minorités", *Proche-Orient Chrétien*, vol. 47, 1997, pp. 35-58.

Maïla, Joseph, "Réflexions sur les chrétiens d'Orient", *Confluences Mediterranée*, vol. 66, 2008, pp. 191-204.

Marchadour Alain and Neuhaus, David, *The Land, the Bible and History*, New York: Fordham University Press, 2007.

Marsh, Leonard, "Palestinian Christian Theology as a new and contemporary expression of Eastern Christian Thought", in *Living Stones Yearbook 2012*, London: Melisende, 2012, pp. 106-119.

Marsh, Leonard, "The Theological Thought of Michel Sabbah in the Context of the Challenges to the Christian Presence in the Holy Land", in Anthony O'Mahony and John Flannery (eds.), *The Catholic Church in the Contemporary Middle East*, London: Melisende, 2010, pp. 253-262.

Marten, Michael, "Anglican and Presbyterian Presence and Theology in the Holy Land", *International Journal for the Study of the Christian Church*, vol. 5, 2005, pp. 182-199.

Mayeur-Jaouen, Catherine, "Les chrétiens au Moyen-Orient à l'heure de Daesh", *Annuaire Français des Relations Internationales*, vol. XVII, 2016, pp. 681-695.

McCallum, Fiona, "Christian political participation in the Arab world", *Islam and Christian–Muslim Relations*, vol. 23, no. 1, 2012, pp. 3-18.

McCallum, Fiona, "Desert Roots and Global Branches: The Journey of the Coptic Orthodox Church", *Bulletin of the Royal Institute for Inter-Faith Studies*, vol. 7, 2005, pp. 69-97.

McCallum, Fiona, "Religious Institutions and Authoritarian States: Church-State Relations in the Middle East", Third World Quarterly, vol. 33, no. 1, 2012, pp. 109-124.

Merdjanova, Ina, "Orthodox Christianity in a Pluralistic World", *Concilium*, vol. 1, 2011, pp. 39-50.

Merlo, Francesca, "Pope: 'Never forget plight of Syria and Christians in Middle East'", *Vatican News*, 20 June 2022. Available at: https://www.vaticannews.va/en/pope/news/2022-06/pope-francis-discourse-greek-melkite-synod.html.

Migliorino, Nicola and Sanjian, Ara, "Les communautes armeniennes du Proche-Orient arabe", *Confluences Mediterranée*, vol. 66, 2008, pp. 73-82.

Miller, Charles and O'Mahony, Anthony (eds.), "The Orthodox churches in contemporary contexts", *International Journal for the Study of the Christian Church*, vol. 10, no. 2-3, 2010, pp. 82-89.

Monier, Elizabeth, "The Chaldean Patriarch and the Discourse of 'Inclusive Citizenship': Restructuring the Political Representation of Christians in Iraq since 2003", *Religion, State & Society*. vol. 48, no. 5, 2020, pp. 361-377.

Morris, Benny and Ze'evi, Dror, *The Thirty-Year Genocide: Turkey's Destruction of Its Christian Minorities, 1894–1924*, Harvard: Harvard University Press, 2019.

Mrad, Nicolas, "The Witness of the Church in a Pluralistic World: Theological Renaissance in the Church of Antioch", in Elizabeth Theokritoff and Mary Cunningham (eds.), *The Cambridge Companion to Orthodox Christian Theology*, Cambridge: Cambridge University Press, 2008, pp. 246-260.

Nasry, Wakif (ed), *Samir Khalil Samir, S.J. on Islam and the West*, San Francisco: Ignatius Press, 2008.

Norman, Jeremias, "Eastern Christianity in China", in Ken Parry (ed.), The Blackwell Companion to Eastern Christianity, Oxford: Oxford University Press, 2007, pp. 280-290.

Norris, Frederick W., "Timothy I of Baghdad, Catholicos of the East Syrian Church, 780-823: Still a Valuable Model", *International Bulletin of Missionary Research*, vol. 30, no. 3, 2006, pp. 133-136.

O'Mahoney, Anthony and Loosley, Emma (eds.), *Eastern Christians in the Modern Middle East*, London: Routledge, 2010.

O'Mahony, Anthony and Flannery, John (eds.), "Eastern Orthodoxy: Modern History and Contemporary Theology", *Journal of Eastern Christian studies*, vol. 63, no. 1-2, 2011, pp. 125-126.

O'Mahony, Anthony and Flannery, John (eds.), *The Catholic Church in the Contemporary Middle East*, London: Melisende, 2010.

O'Mahony, Anthony, "Between Rome and Constantinople: the Italian-Albanian Church: A Study in Eastern Catholic History and Ecclesiology", *International Journal for the Study of the Christian Church*, vol. 8, no.3, 2008, pp. 232-251.

O'Mahony, Anthony, "Christianity in the Middle East: Modern History and Contemporary Theology and Ecclesiology: An Introduction and Overview", *Journal of Eastern Christian Studies*, vol. 63, no. 3-4, 2013, pp. 231-260.

O'Mahony, Anthony, "Christianity in the Middle East: The Challenge of Coexistence", in Edward G. Farrugia and Gianpaolo Rigotti (eds.), *A Common Mission: The Oriental Congregation and the Oriental Institute (1917-2017)*, Rome: Orientalia Christiana Analecta, 2020, pp. 425-468.

O'Mahony, Anthony, "Christianity in the Wider Levant Region: Modern History and Contemporary Context", in Kail Ellis (ed.), *Secular Nationalism and Citizenship in Muslim Countries: Arab Christians in the Levant*, Basingstoke: Palgrave, 2018, pp. 61-88.

O'Mahony, Anthony, "The Chaldean Catholic Church: The Politics of Church-State Relations in Modern Iraq", *The Heythrop Journal*, vol. XLV, 2004, pp. 435-450.

O'Mahony, Anthony, "The Christian Churches, Shi'a Islam and Muslim-Christian Relations in Modern Iran", in Anthony O'Mahony and Emma Loosely (eds.), *Christian Responses to Islam*, Manchester: Manchester University Press, 2008, pp. 175-188.

O'Mahony, Anthony, "The Greek Orthodox Patriarchates in the Middle East", in Anthony O'Mahony (ed.), *Eastern Christianity and the Cold War, 1945-91*, London: Routledge, 2010, pp. 240-252.

O'Mahony, Anthony, "The Vatican and Europe: Political Theology and Ecclesiology in Papal Statements from Pius XII to Benedict XVI", International Journal for the Study of the Christian Church, vol. 9, no. 3, 2009, pp. 177-194.

O'Mahony, Anthony, "Tradition at the heart of Renewal: the Coptic Orthodox Church and monasticism in Modern Egypt", *International Journal for the Study of the Christian Church*, vol. 7, no. 3, 2007, pp. 164-178.

Olmi, Antonio, *Il consenso cristologica tra la chiese calcedonesi e non calcedonesi (1964-1996)*, Rome: Pontificia Univ. Gregoriana, 2003.

Palomino, Rafael, "The Role of Concordants Promoting Religious Freedom with Special Reference to Agreements in the Middle East", in Congregazione per le Chiese Orientali, *Ius Ecclesiarum vehiculum caritatis*, Rome, 2004, pp. 893-900.

Pasa, Zeljko (ed.), *Between the Cross and Crescent: Studies in Honor of Samir Khalil Samir, S.J. on the Occasion of His Eightieth Birthday*, Rome Orientalia Christiana Analecta, 2018.

Peri, Vittorio, "Uniatism and its origins", *Journal of Eastern Christian Studies*, vol. 49, no. 1-2, 1997, pp. 23-46.

Pew Foundation, "Global Christianity: A Report on the Size and Distribution of the World's Christian Population", 19 December 2011. Available at: https://assets.pewresearch.org/wp-content/uploads/sites/11/2011/12/Christianity-fullreport-web.pdf.

Poujeau, Anna, "A National Monasticism? Monastic Politics of the Syriac Orthodox Church in Syria", in Enzo Pace, Luigi Berzano, Giuseppe Giordan (eds.), *Sociology and Monasticism. Annual Review of the Sociology of Religion*, Leiden: Brill, 2014, pp, 169–184.

Poujeau, Anna, "Monasteries, Politics, and Social Memory: The Revival of the Greek Orthodox Church in Syria during the Twentieth Century", in Chris Hann and Hermann Goltz (eds.), *Eastern Christians in Anthropological Perspective*, California: University of California Press, 2010, pp. 171-192.

Poujeau, Anna, "Renouveau monastique et historiographie chrétienne en Syrie", *Archives de Sciences Sociales des Religions*, vol. 151, 2010, pp. 129-147.

Prodromou, Elizabeth H., "Orthodox Christianity and pluralism: Moving beyond Ambivalent?", in Emmanuel Clapsis (ed.), *The Orthodox Churches in a Pluralistic World: An Ecumenical Conversation*, Geneva: World Council of Churches Publications/Brookline, MA: Holy Cross Press, 2004, pp. 22-46.

Prodromou, Elizabeth H., "The Politics of Human Rights: Orthodox Christianity Gets the Short End", *Archons*, 5 August 2013. Available at: https://www.archons.org/el/-/the-politics-of-human-rights-orthodox-christianity-gets-the-short-end-by-dr-elizabeth-h-prodromou.

Prodromou, Elizabeth H., "Turkey between Secularism and Fundamentalism? The 'Muslimhood Model' and the Greek Orthodox Minority", *The Review of Faith & International Affairs*, vol. 3, no. 1, 2005, pp. 11-22.

Rabo, Annika, "We Are Christians, and We Are Equal Citizens: Perspectives on Particularity and Pluralism in Contemporary Syria", *Islam and Christian–Muslim Relations*, vol. 23, no. 1, 2012, pp. 79-93.

Roberson, Ronald G., "Catholic Reactions to the Balamand Document", *Eastern Churches Journal*, vol. 4, no. 1, 1997, pp. 54-73.

Robson, Laura, "Palestinian Liberation Theology, Muslim-Christian Relations and the Arab-Israeli Conflict", *Islam and Christian-Muslim Relations*, vol. 21, no. 1, 2010, pp. 39-50.

Roussos, Sotiris, "Patriarchs, Notables and Diplomats: The Greek Orthodox Patriarchate of Jerusalem in the Modern Period", in Anthony O'Mahony (ed.), *Eastern Christianity: Studies in Modern History, Religion and Politics*, London: Melisende, 2004, pp. 372-387.

Roussos, Sotiris, "The Greek Orthodox Patriarchate and Community of Jerusalem: Church, State and Identity", in Anthony O'Mahony (ed.), *The Christian Communities of Jerusalem and the Holy Land: Studies in History, Religion and Politics*, Cardiff: University of Wales Press, 2003, pp. 38-56.

Roussos, Sotiris, *Greece and the Middle East: The Greek Orthodox Communities in Egypt, Syria and Palestine, 1914-1940*, PhD dissertation, London: University of London, 1994.

Rowe, Paul, "The Middle East Christian as Agent", *International Journal of Middle Eastern Studies*, vol. 42, no. 3, 2010, pp. 472-474.

Royel, Mar Awa, "The Pearl of Great Price: The Anaphora of the Apostles Mar Addai & Mar Mari as an Ecclesial and Cultural Identifier of the Assyrian Church of the East", *Orientalia Christiana Periodica*, vol. 80, 2014, pp. 5-22.

Sabella, Bernard, "L'émigration des arabes chrétiens: dimensions et causes de l'exode", *Proche-Orient Chrétien*, vol. 47, 1997, pp. 141-169.

Sabella, Bernard, "Palestinian Christian Emigration from the Holy Land", *Proche-Orient Chrétien*, vol. 41, 1991, pp. 74-85.

Sabella, Bernard, "Palestinian Christians: Realities and Hopes", *Studies in Church History: The Holy Land, Holy Lands, and Christian History*, vol. 36, 2000, pp. 373-397.

Sabella, Bernard, "Socio-Economic Characteristics and Challenges to Palestinian Christians in the Holy Land", in Anthony O'Mahony (ed), *Palestinian Christians: Religion, Politics and Society in the Holy Land*, London: Melisende, 1999, pp. 222-251.

Samir, Samir Khalil, "Le synode des évêques pour le Proche-Orient", *Nouvelle Revue Théologique*, vol. 133, no. 2, 2011, pp. 191-206.

Samir, Samir Khalil, *Rôle culturel des chrétiens dans le monde arabe*, Beirut: Cahiers de l'Orient Chrétien, 2003.

Sanjian, Ara, "The Armenian Church and Community in Jerusalem and the Holy Land (From their origins until the modern era)", in Anthony O'Mahony (ed.), The Christian Communities in the Holy Land: Studies in History, Religion, and Politics, Cardiff: University of Wales Press, 2003, pp. 57-89.

Sanjian, Ara, "The Armenian Minority Experience in the Modern Arab World", *Bulletin of the Royal Institute for Inter-Faith Studies*, vol. 3, no. 1, 2001, pp. 149-179.

Schmoller, Andreas, "Anti-Islamic Narratives of Middle Eastern Diaspora Christians: An Interdisciplinary Analytical Framework", in Herman Teule and Joseph Verheyden (eds.), *Eastern and Oriental Christianity in the Diaspora*, Leuven: Peeters, 2020, pp. 189-214.

Schmoller, Andreas, "Now My Life in Syria Is Finished: Case Studies on Religious Identity and Sectarianism in Narratives of Syrian Christian Refugees in Austria", *Islam And Christian–Muslim Relations*, vol. 27, no. 4, 2016, pp. 419-437.

Sickin, Thom, "Théologie orientale ou théologie en orient?", *Proche-Orient Chrétien*, vol. 55,

2005, pp. 309-333.

Simon, Constantine, "In Europe and America: the Ruthenians between Catholicism and Orthodoxy", *Orientalia Christiana Periodica*, vol. 59, 1993, pp. 169-210.

Suermann, Harald, "Die Konstitution von Medina Erinnerung an ein andreres Modell des Zusammenlebens", *Collectanea Christiana Orientalia*, vol. 2, 2005, pp. 225-244.

Suermann, Harald, "Palestinian Contextual Theology", *Al-Liqa*, vol. 5, 1995, pp. 7-26.

Sutton, Michael, "John Paul II's Idea of Europe", *Religion, State & Society*, vol. 25, no. 1, 1997, pp. 17-29.

Tabor, Paul, "The Maronite Church in Lebanon: From Nation-building to a Diasporan/Transnational Institution", in Françoise De Bel-Air (ed.), *Migration et politique au moyen-orient*, Damascus: Institut françai du Proche-Orient, 2006, pp. 185-201.

Taft, Robert, "Mass Without the Consecration? The Historic Agreement on the Eucharist between the Catholic Church and the Assyrian Church of the East Promulgated 26 October 2001", *Worship*, vol. 77. 2003, pp. 482-509.

Taft, Robert, "The Problem of 'Uniatism' and the 'Healing of Memories': Anamnesis, not Amnesia", *Logos*, vol. 41-42, 2000-2001, pp. 155-196.

Tchilingirian, Hratch, "The Catholicos and the Hierarchical Sees of the Armenian Church", in Anthony O'Mahony (ed.), *Eastern Christianity: Studies in Modern History, Religion and Politics*, London: Melisende, 2004, pp. 140-159.

Teule, Herman, "Christianity in Iraq and its Contribution to Society", in Dietmar W. Winkler (ed.), *Syriac Christianity in the Middle East and India: Contributions and Challenges*, Piscataway, NJ: Gorgias Press, 2013, pp. 23-42.

Teule, Herman, "Christianity in West Asia", in Felix Wilfred (ed.), *The Oxford Handbook of Christianity in Asia*, New York: Oxford University Press, 2014, pp. 17-29.

Teule, Herman, "Christians in Iraq an Analysis of Some Recent Political Developments", *Der Islam*, vol. 88, no. 1, 2012, pp. 179-98.

Teule, Herman, "La situation des chrétiens d'Irak à la lumière des résolutions du Synode romain pour le Moyen-Orient", *Mélanges de Science Religieuse*, vo. 68, no. 3, 2011, pp. 47-60.

Teule, Herman, "Middle Eastern Christians and Migration: Some Reflections", *The Journal of Eastern Christian Studies*, vol. 54, 2002, pp. 1-23.

Teule, Herman, "The Assyrian Church of the East, the Chaldean Church and the Roman Catholic Church: An Attempt at Understanding Their Interrelation", in Jaroslav Z. Skira, Peter De Mey and Herman Teule (eds.), *The Catholic Church and its Orthodox Sister Churches Twenty-Five Years after Balamand*, Leuven: Peeters, 2022, pp. 281-294.

Troll, Christian, "Changing Catholic Views on Islam", in Jacques Waardenburg (ed.), *Islam and Christianity: Mutual Perceptions Since the Mid–Twentieth Century*, Leuven: Peeters, 1998, pp. 19-77.

Valognes, Jean-Pierre, *Vie et mort des chrétiens d'Orient des origines à nos jours*, Paris: Fayard, 1994.

Vatican News, "Continental Synodal Assembly for the Middle East opens in Lebanon", 14 February 2023. Available at: https://www.vaticannews.va/en/church/news/2023-02/continental-synodal-assembly-for-the-middle-east-opens.html.

Vermander, Benoît, "The Impact of Nestorianism on Contemporary Chinese Theology", in Roman Malek and Peter Hofrichter (eds.), *Jingjiao: The Church of the East in China and Central Asia*, London: Routledge, 2006, pp. 181-194.

Whooley, John, "In the Shadow of Balamand: Recent Relations between the Armenian Apostolic Church and the Armenian Catholic Church, in Jaroslav Z. Skira, Peter De Mey and Herman Teule (eds.), *The Catholic Church and its Orthodox Sister Churches Twenty-Five Years after Balamand*, Leuven: Peeters, 2022, pp. 261-280.

Winkler, Dietmar W. and Baum, Wilhelm, *The Church of the East. A Concise History*, London: Routledge, 2003.

Winkler, Dietmar W., "Christianity in the Middle East: some historical remarks and preliminary demographic figures", in Dietmar Winkler (ed.), *Syriac Christianity in the Middle East and India*, Piscataway, NJ: Gorgias Press, 2013, pp. 107-125.

Yacoub, Joseph, "La contribution de la Mésopotamie ancienne et syriaque au dialogue des cultures", in Joseph Yacoub (ed), *L'Humanisme réinventé*, Paris: Cerf, 2012, pp. 165-205.

Yacoub, Joseph, "Les régimes politiques arabes et l'islam politique", in Joseph Yacoub (ed.), *Fièvre démocratique et ferveur fondamentaliste Dominantes du XXIe siècle,* Paris: Cerf, 2008, pp. 121-140.

Yacoub, Joseph, *Babylone chrétienne. Géopolitique de l'Église de Mésoptamie*, Paris: Desclée de Brouwer, 1996.

Yacoub, Joseph, *Une diversité menacée. Les chrétiens d'Orient face au nationalisme arabe et à l'islamisme*, Paris: Salvator, 2018.

Yefet, Bosmat, "The Coptic Diaspora and the Status of the Coptic Minority in Egypt", *Journal of Ethnic and Migration Studies*, vol. 43, 2017, 1205-1221.

Yégavian, Tigrane, "Les chrétiens d'Orient ont-ils encore un avenir?", *Études*, vol. 6, 2022, pp. 67-78.

www.ingramcontent.com/pod-product-compliance
Lightning Source LLC
Chambersburg PA
CBHW071742270326
41928CB00013B/2773